# DISEASE IN THE CIVIL WAR

# DISEASE IN THE CIVIL WAR

## Natural Biological Warfare in 1861-1865

*By*

**PAUL E. STEINER, Ph.D., M.D.**

*Professor of Pathology*
*School of Medicine*
*University of Pennsylvania*
*Philadelphia, Pennsylvania*

**CHARLES C THOMAS · PUBLISHER**
*Springfield · Illinois · U.S.A.*

*Published and Distributed Throughout the World by*
CHARLES C THOMAS · PUBLISHER
Bannerstone House
301-327 East Lawrence Avenue, Springfield, Illinois, U.S.A.
Natchez Plantation House
735 North Atlantic Boulevard, Fort Lauderdale, Florida, U.S.A.

*With* THOMAS BOOKS *careful attention is given to all details of
manufacturing and design. It is the Publisher's desire to present books
that are satisfactory as to their physical qualities and artistic possibilities
and appropriate for their particular use.* THOMAS BOOKS *will be true
to those laws of quality that assure a good name and good will.*

*Printed in the United States of America*
H-19

Those who forget history, may have to repeat it.

—Santayana

# Preface

THE HISTORY OF the American Civil War has been interpreted from nearly all aspects except that of disease. The term *disease* is here used in a restricted sense to encompass only sickness, omitting wounds and injuries. This gap in history is major because disease is known to have produced far more casualties than did firearms. The point admitted, it is then usually ignored. Nevertheless, disease was a tremendous force in some military problems and their outcome. It eroded troops from the day of enlistment to discharge, interfering with efficiency at nearly every step of the way. From the military viewpoint the infectious diseases, the chief culprits, were unpredictable, mysterious in origin, uncontrollable and hence feared but often disregarded. From the viewpoint of the pathogenic microorganisms, this was an opportunity to show their capabilities almost undeterred. The result was rampant disease—natural biological warfare—on a large scale.

Today these communicable diseases are nearly all under control. The public has forgotten their names, physicians rarely or never see a case, and medical students only read about them in textbooks or sometimes see them in a museum jar or under the microscope. In wartime, some of them again become important in remote places such as North Africa, the South Pacific, Korea, and Viet Nam. Guadalcanal with its malaria, dysentery, and tsutsu-gamushi fever will long remain a sensitive memory in marine corps and army medicine. Pappataci fever in Africa, filariasis on Samoa, scrub typhus on Guadalcanal, schistosomiasis on Leyte, and Japanese B encephalitis on Okinawa identify a few of the medical lessons that had belatedly and painfully to be learned. But, except for a short time, none of them seriously retarded military operations and none was a crucial factor in the outcome, differing in both respects from some diseases in the Civil War.

The germs of these exotic diseases, as of those common in the nineteenth century, have not been eradicated. They persist in obscure places ready to spring if our guard drops. Some, probably, also exist as captives in munitions ready to be released by human hands in biological warfare. Unlike atomic weapons, every country has the capability for using microorganisms. The usage and results might not resemble those in our Civil War, but it seemed worthwhile to study what the natural diseases did.

The military and medical minds have different viewpoints toward casualties. To the former the lesions represent a hierarchy of honorability. To the latter this is nonsense as any list bears little relation to the degree of military harm and none to the degree of human suffering or of scientific interest. The military evaluation grades them approximately, in descending order: Combat death, wound, injury, burn, capture, noninfectious disease, infectious disease and mental disorder. The physician sees, in a soldier doing his duty, no greater valor in a shrapnel than in an appendectomy scar, in a bomb flash than in a napalm burn, in a gas pneumonitis than in a viral pneumonia, or in a camp diarrhea than in one contracted at "Sloppy Joe's place."

This volume presents an evaluation of the military effects of the pathogenic microorganisms native here a hundred years ago under natural conditions, *i.e.* without enhancement, effective deterrence, interference, or deliberate usage. In documenting these effects, the types and levels of disease will be described. This will establish a crude base line for the pathogenic capabilities of the microorganisms under the conditions that existed.

In one sense this book represents the reverse of what Brigade Surgeon John H. Brinton had planned in 1862. When he was ordered to begin the surgical history of the war, he hoped to include a historical semi-military account of the military movements that influenced the medical and surgical conditions. This plan could not be carried out, and the history omitted nearly all military information so that the medical matters were presented out of context. Fortunately, many additional medical data have become available during the century to help the present study on what the diseases did to some military events.

A study based on so many different sources and touching several professions over a period of many years obviously owes much to others. The *Medical and Surgical History of the War of the Rebellion* and the *Official Records* have been major sources, but neither interprets the data very far nor bridges the medical: military gap, both essential to the present thesis. The wartime medical literature has also been a productive lode. The helpful persons and institutions cannot all be named, but chief among them are the Library of the Military Order of the Loyal Legion, the Library of the College of Physicians of Philadelphia, and the Virginia State Library. My special thanks go to, among others, Mrs. Stephanie Benko of the Loyal Legion, Mr. Elliott H. Morse and the members of the library staff at the College, and to Mr. Milton C. Russell and staff at the State Library, who have greatly facilitated the work. Mrs. Delphine O. Richardson of the University of Pennsylvania libraries has cheerfully and ably obtained material from obscure sources.

P.E.S.

# Contents

# Contents

# Tables

# DISEASE IN THE CIVIL WAR

By the Same Author

Cancer: Race and Geography, 1954
Physician-Generals in the Civil War, 1966
Medical-Military Portraits, 1967

# I

## Natural Biological Warfare

## The Nature of the Disease Problem in 1861

THIS IS A STUDY of the influence of infectious diseases on some selected military affairs in the American Civil War. At the same time it is a historical account of natural biological warfare, inasmuch as the diseases were not intentionally produced. In some instances the harmful effects were just as great as if they had been planned. In such examples this becomes a study in the military potential of natural biological warfare. "Natural" is here used in contrast to "deliberate," and it refers to the expression of the inherent disease-producing capabilities of microbes or their products in warfare in the absence of effective restraints on one hand or of artificial enhancements on the other.

The casualty-producing capability of disease was very great through 1865. Many military decisions were won on the battlefield, but what reached the field was determined in large part by what had happened medically during the preceding months. Military history usually concentrates its attention on the clash of arms, although at the time of the Civil War this might represent less than half the paper strength of one or both sides. The rest was beneath the sod, in hospitals, on medical leave, or sick in camp. The manpower loss in internecine warfare by microorganisms within an army was far greater than that lost in battle between enemy armies.

The casualties produced in battle often determined the outcome of that clash of arms because they all came within a brief period of time. The losses from disease were usually more scattered and hence less important, but a number of sharp epidemics occurred that had the military effectiveness of a battle.

It is widely recognized that disease was far more common than wounds as a cause of disability and death in that war, but the military consequences of this fact have not been systematically assessed. To the degree that wars are won or lost because of casualties, the ability to make war and the will to continue ignoring the role played by disease results in a distorted view of history.

The offensive military weapons available in 1861 were few. They included chiefly field artillery of small caliber and short range, the musket, bayonet, and saber. The lurking bio-military armamentarium, in contrast, was potentially far greater. Moreover, it had the advantages of invisibility, secrecy, versatility, surprise, small bulk, and speed. Microbes could also multiply, reduplicating themselves at the point of impact so as greatly to increase the original dose, whereas arms and munitions had laboriously to be brought up from factories and arsenals, sometimes overseas.

This war provides the last opportunity in the pre-microbiological era to study natural biological warfare on a large scale. The Franco-Prussian war that followed was quickly over. The Spanish-American and Boer wars had much disease, but they were fought on a far smaller scale. Although some of the new bacteriological knowledge was used in them, more that might have been useful was, unfortunately, ignored. By World War I, casualties from the enteric infections were greatly reduced and by World War II some of the respiratory infections also were controllable. The admission rate for the specific fevers and diseases of the intestine (including dysentery and diarrhea) was twenty-nine times as high in 1861-62 as in 1917-18 and the death rate was 258 times as high (1). Today they are even lower. It is understandable that dysentery could be a formidable enemy to the men in Blue and Gray. And, dysentery had virulent allies to supplement its effects.

In 1861, the existence and importance of the pathogenic microbes was still unknown. The concept of living, subvisible, self-multiplying, invasive organisms, some of them widely disseminated and even ubiquitous, as the cause (*i.e. conditio sine qua non*) of disease had not yet been accepted. Hypotheses had suggested an important role for animalcules and vegetable spores but substantial evidence was lacking. Most of the common infectious diseases were clinically recognized, but their causation, transmission, and control were not.

The only exception was smallpox; the available vaccines were not invariably effective and were not always used, but they were administered to enough of the soldiers so as greatly to modify the epidemiology of the disease and to prevent the variola virus from exhibiting its full capabilities. In therapy, the only really effective drug was quinine in the treatment of malaria. When administered almost to full tolerance it was nearly a specific, otherwise a palliative. Attempts to use it as a suppressant usually failed, possibly because of under-dosage. At the end of the war many had abandoned it for prophylaxis, and malaria was essentially uncontrolled. All communicable diseases except smallpox proliferated relatively unrestrained. Quarantine was sometimes used to break transmission, but it often failed because its rationale was not understood, so it was misused and its full capabilities remained unknown.

The chief reliance for protection was on field sanitation and hygiene. They were ineffective because they were based on physical and chemical concepts of cleanliness rather than on microbiological ones. Contamination could occur under subvisible conditions, and dilution did not eliminate infection. The literature records many expressions of dismay at having much camp disease despite superior gross sanitation, and at less disease appearing in some filthy camp. The medical officers suffered from infectious disease like every one else, and 285 died (contrasted with forty-two killed and mortally wounded); hundreds more received medical discharges. They shared the hazards of disease common to all officers but, in addition, they were heavily exposed in their work as no adequate precautions were taken. The commanders of the regiments and larger units, who bore the ultimate responsibility for the camp sanitation, themselves contracted much infectious disease. Nearly one hundred commanders of regiments, brigades, divisions, or army corps were physicians. Insofar as the health records of their commands have been traced, they were no better than those of other units (2). A comparison of the health of some regiments recruited in 1861 and 1864 shows that the late units melted away from disease as fast as the early volunteers.

Control of the infectious disease as measured by these various criteria was impossible, and it did not improve during the war, undocumented claims to the contrary notwithstanding. Assistant Secretary of War Thomas A. Scott, from Cairo, Illinois, in March, 1862 requested

Secretary Stanton to send troops to the West from the Army of the Potomac (idle for eight months) because the regiments were constantly dwindling in numbers from death and sickness (3). This statement would have been equally true of conditions three years later. No medical or camp lore available in 1861-1865 could have kept the soldiers free of any communicable disease except smallpox. The microbes had nearly all the advantages.

Moreover, army life in wartime sometimes greatly enhanced the pathogenic potential of microorganisms over civilian conditions in a number of ways. Most of the amenities of civil life were lacking, including many that unknowingly protected against disease. The military service brought together large numbers of disease-susceptibles, often under conditions of overcrowding and bad ventilation. Some of the common insect vectors of disease (then regarded merely as pests), notably flies of various types, mosquitoes, lice, fleas, and others, might multiply greatly because of poor personal hygiene and camp sanitation. Food, milk, and water supplies became contaminated for the same reasons. Lack of refrigeration for foods and inadequate culinary, galley, and scullery practices all contributed to the spread of disease. Healthy or chronic carriers of the agents of dysentery, malaria, typhoid fever, tuberculosis, and other diseases were present in every sizeable group of Americans, and glanders found a reservoir in their horses. Widespread malnutrition when the army ration failed reduced any natural or acquired resistance.

Moreover, army traffic and military activities commonly created mosquito breeding sites by disrupting drainage systems; they also caused the accumulation of animal offal, garbage, and human excreta, attracted diseased camp followers, and often required of the soldier exposure to the elements — heat, cold, dust, mud, rain. Many soldiers had contacts with diseased horses, mules, cattle, swine, poultry, rabbits, sheep, rats and other animals, so the zoonoses could spread when present. The paratyphoids and salmonelloses, brucellosis, trichinosis, encephalitis, tularemia, relapsing fever, infectious jaundice, infectious hepatitis, and other diseases were unknown or not recognized, although there is evidence that some of them existed (*e.g.* paratyphoid, infectious hepatitis). Staphylotoxin food poisoning almost surely existed (4). Conditions were favorable at times for the dispersion of all of these diseases.

The soldier usually had to drink any water available, but if he, his surgeon, or his colonel could choose, the criterion was the inadequate one of potability rather than the absence of pathogens. Often, water supplies were shared by drinkers, bathers, launderers, cooks, horses, mules, the commissary's cattle, flies, mosquitoes, and other fauna as well as, unwittingly, some protozoa and bacteria coming from skins, nearby latrines, and other obvious sources. Pediculosis was said to have been universal whenever conditions prevented bathing or the boiling of clothes. The civilian use of window and door screens, mosquito bars, covered water supplies, protected toilets and other amenities unwittingly reduced disease, although they were being used merely to circumvent supposed pests and nuisances. In contrast, camp and field life in many respects microbiologically required or represented a reversion nearly to the cave-life stage of sanitation.

Even before the rise of microbiology, certain disease epidemics had died out for reasons that are not apparent except that some leave no carrier state or reservoir of infection. Thus, four epidemics of cholera had disappeared in the United States and Western Europe in the nineteenth century, and several plague epidemics died out in Europe over the centuries. Certain common sense and aesthetic general measures in public health and sanitation had also been initiated, and claims have been made that they had slightly reduced some mortality rates even before the microbial causes were known. The principal effective measures were the construction of closed underground sewers and the provision of abundant piped water. The spread of agriculture with tillage of the soil after drainage, and the avoidance of "miasmatic" locations (*i.e.* foul-smelling) for dwellings had incidentally reduced malaria in some places. None of these measures pertained to military populations, and most of the proposals in military sanitation were defective microbiologically according to information learned later.

Because of little or no inhibition of their capabilities—and sometimes even enhancement—the microorganisms in wartime had an opportunity to display their greatest innate natural potential. The infective conditions were natural inasmuch as artificially exaggerated doses, unnatural portals of entry, adjuvants, immunization, and other factors used in experimental laboratories did not ordinarily enter the picture. Even so, the result was infectious disease on a large scale. The noncommunicable diseases were not proportionally increased except for scurvy and rheumatism, both old military pests and the latter sometimes a sequel of infection.

Consequently, in the Union forces, 6,454,834 medical diagnoses were reported. In all, 223,535 soldiers were discharged for physical disability, some of them to die later. The Confederate morbidity rate was probably similar and the actual numbers proportional to the smaller size of their military population. Some widely used figures admit to 359,528 Union deaths from all causes; these include 199,720 deaths from disease and 110,070 killed and mortally wounded. Corresponding Confederate figures show 74,524 killed and mortally wounded and 59,297 dead of disease. The latter figure must be an underestimation because all available data show the incidence, prevalence, and mortality rates (*i.e.* per unit population) to have been in the same range as the Union figures, in which the mortality from disease was nearly double that from wounds.

Under these conditions the half-life of a regiment depended somewhat on its location and combat experience, but even without action it was only about a year. Unless recruits were added, regiments tended to disappear by being discontinued or consolidated after about three years. A regimental organization was hard to maintain when the enrollment, originally about 1,000, fell below 200. The stage immediately preceding this fate was vividly described by a regimental historian when the governor of Iowa inspected all regiments from that state at the siege of Atlanta in 1864 (5). An experienced soldier, he had been elected to office the previous year while serving in the field as a colonel. The commander of the Sixth Iowa, a regiment in service since Shiloh, withdrew it into a ravine safe from sharpshooters for the review. The governor noticed the formation and commented that the site seemed safe for that company. Visibly moved, its colonel replied: "Sir, that is the regiment."

By their attrition intercurrent diseases stopped some campaigns, prevented others even from starting, and influenced the result in a third group. These effects occurred despite all caution, knowledge, and forewarning used in the prior military planning by senior commanders. The potential hazards of epidemics were known to able military strategists, but their occurrence was not predictable and commanders were often tempted or required to take chances. General

Scott's original anaconda constrictor plan for winning the war specified that a strong column should pass down the Mississippi, but in November after ". . . the return of frosts to kill the virus of malignant fevers below Memphis" (6). His qualification was ignored, and the first attempt to take Vicksburg, in the summer of 1862, met the disaster from malaria described in Chapter 7.

In this monograph the influence of disease on eight battles or campaigns will be described. Some of these campaigns had a great military potential but they were aborted by disease, some without a battle. To the extent that they were primarily not blood-letting and militarily spectacular in the usual sense, they have been largely ignored by historians. Even a little hemoglobin shed from wounds in battle would have rescued these campaigns from near oblivion. Now this must be accomplished by a study of the havoc produced by their attendant microbes. The specific problems to be studied are: What were the most important diseases; under what conditions did they occur; what levels did they reach; and what were their military effects?

## Diseases of Military Importance

The total Federal medical casualties recorded from May 1, 1861 to June 30, 1866 were 6,454,834, of which at least 195,627 died (7). These casualties fell into about 171 accepted diagnostic categories. If the 425,274 (38,115 deaths) traumatic cases (*i.e.* wounds, accidents, and injuries) are subtracted, the remainder, constituting essentially the diseases, numbered 6,029,560 cases (157,512 deaths.* This group encompasses our present interests. This morbidity occurred in a military population of less than 2,772,408 because this widely cited enrollment figure includes unknown thousands of multiple enlistments occurring chiefly among the short-term (*i.e.* 90-day, 100-day, 6-month, 9-month, and 1-year) soldiers and the bounty-jumpers. The loyal civilian population relevant to these various figures numbered about 21,000,000, according to the census of 1860, the uncertainty arising from the correct allocation of the people in the border states, who

---

*The mortality figures given here are smaller than those mentioned earlier because not all the deaths and wounds came under the cognizance of the medical department, whose figures are here used.

were divided in their loyalty. Corresponding comprehensive Confederate figures are not available.

The diseases that had military importance in 1861 were nearly all infectious. They vary in many ways, including the method of transmission, the amount of natural and acquired resistance, the type and size of the reservoir of infection, the degree of infectivity and contagion, the length of the incubation period, the degree and duration of incapacity, the mortality, the complications and sequels, the amount and duration of the immunity after recovery, the types and numbers of carriers after recovery, and in other respects.

Most of the diseases of military importance in 1861 are listed in Table I by number of cases and deaths. The chief exceptions, rheumatism and scurvy, are listed in Table II with some other noninfectious but common diseases. In most of the latter group the mortality was low and, in general, the impairment of military efficiency was slight

TABLE I

Infectious Diseases of Military Importance
in the Federal Army, 1861-1866*

| | Diagnosis | Number cases | Number deaths |
|---|---|---|---|
| 1 | Diarrhea and dysentery, acute and chronic | 1,739,135 | 44,558 |
| 1a | Cholera morbus | 26,366 | 305 |
| 2 | Intermittent and remittent fevers (malaria) | 1,315,955 | 10,063 |
| 3 | Epidemic catarrh, catarrh, and bronchitis | 283,075 | 585 |
| 4 | Typhoid, typho-malarial, and continued fevers | 148,631 | 34,833 |
| 5 | Gonorrhea (excludes epididymis and urethral stricture) | 102,893 | 7 |
| 6 | Purulent ophthalmia and inflammation of conjunctiva | 84,986 | 4 |
| 7 | Boils | 83,170 | 0 |
| 8 | Syphilis (primary and secondary) | 79,589 | 151 |
| 9 | Inflammation of lungs (pneumonia) | 77,335 | 19,971 |
| 10 | Jaundice, endemic and epidemic | 77,236 | 414 |
| 11 | Measles | 76,318 | 5,177 |
| 12 | Inflammation of tonsils | 66,665 | 109 |
| 13 | Mumps | 60,314 | 84 |
| 14 | Abscess | 49,622 | 201 |
| 15 | Tuberculosis (consumption, scrofula, lung hemorrhage) | 29,510 | 6,946 |
| 16 | Erysipelas | 24,812 | 2,107 |
| 17 | Smallpox and varioloid | 18,952 | 7,058 |
| 18 | Acute inflammation of liver (chiefly abscesses) | 12,395 | 327 |
| 19 | Diphtheria | 8,053 | 777 |
| 20 | Inflammation of brain, meninges and spinal cord | 3,999 | 2,660 |
| 21 | Typhus fever | 2,624 | 958 |
| 22 | Yellow fever | 1,371 | 436 |
| 23 | Scarlet fever | 696 | 72 |
| 24 | "Other miasmatic diseases," not classified | 94,997 | 2,363 |
| 25 | Debility in miasmatic diseases | 18,782 | 153 |

*Data from *Medical and Surgical History of the War of the Rebellion*, Vol. I, Part I.

## TABLE II

Some Noninfectious Diseases in the Federal Army, 1861-1866*

| Diagnosis | Number cases | Number deaths |
|---|---|---|
| Rheumatism, acute and chronic | 286,863 | 710 |
| Scurvy | 46,931 | 771 |
| Night-blindness | 8,087 | 0 |
| Nostalgia | 5,547 | 74 |
| Insanity | 2,603 | 90 |
| Neuralgia | 58,774 | 18 |
| Sunstroke | 6,617 | 261 |
| Itch ("army itch") | 32,080 | 0 |
| Hernia | 24,353 | 39 |
| Piles | 57,745 | 30 |
| Varicocele | 7,060 | 1 |
| Varicose veins | 8,258 | 2 |
| Headache | 66,862 | 1 |
| Asthma | 9,365 | 75 |
| Colic | 75,098 | 77 |
| Constipation | 145,960 | 23 |
| Dyspepsia | 37,514 | 31 |

*Data from *Medical and Surgical History of the War of the Rebellion,* Vol. I, Part I.

because the diseases were sporadic and mild. Soldiers were lost not only by death but also by disability, which led to a medical discharge for 223,535 Union soldiers. Among the diagnoses listed in Table II, the largest number of discharges were given for rheumatism (12,635) and hernia (9,360). Natural bacteriological warfare concerned essentially the microbial diseases—those in which the causative agent was capable of dissemination, multiplication, invasion, and the production of sickness, especially in epidemics. The most important examples were diarrhea and dysentery, malaria, typhoid fever, and the acute respiratory tract infections, all at the top of the list in Table I.

In the Civil War, wounds also represented a type of natural bacterial warfare because nearly every wound was infected regardless of its cause by bullet, shrapnel, bayonet, or saber. Attempts to control wound infection by surgical methods were only partly successful. The amputation of an extremity for shot fracture to remove infection, for example, in the preantiseptic days invariably resulted in reinfection of the fresh stump. The recently introduced general anesthetics, chloroform and ether, eliminated operative pain, but by permitting the surgeon to linger they may have increased infection by allowing more contacts between the contaminated hands and instruments and the exposed tissues. The total adverse effects of infection in wounds were far greater than those of the shock, hemorrhage, or loss of function. The mortality, period of convalescence, and amount of permanent disability were all increased by infection. In addition, toxemia, septicemia, pyemia, tetanus, and hospital gangrene were some of the serious direct effects. Amyloidosis, metastatic arthritis, and other late sequels must have existed although they were not recognized. Important as it is, wound infection deserves great attention but it must be omitted from this study.

## The Pattern of Disease

Disease soon appeared in nearly all troops, and its pattern was fairly uniform. It came in two waves, as the acute infections of childhood and the camp diseases.

Most new regiments had outbreaks of the contagious diseases of childhood in the camp of assembly or soon thereafter. It was found that about half the volunteers, especially those from rural areas, were susceptible (8, 9). The chief offenders were measles and mumps (Table I). To these were often added the acute respiratory tract infections and diarrhea. It was said that new troops could be distinguished from old at night by the amount of coughing (10). Whooping cough also was around, but it was not separately reported in the official records. For some unknown reason, scarlet fever was rarely diagnosed. From the large amount of pharyngitis, tonsillitis, otitis media, and rheumatism recorded, it was probably far more common than the figures indicate, and it may have been confused with measles, putrid sore throat, and other diseases. Diphtheria made an irregular appearance: The reason for its erratic behavior is not apparent. One of the worst outbreaks occurred on Ship Island in four Maine regiments going to Louisiana in 1862 (11). Terms sometimes used as synonyms were membranous croup and putrid sore throat. German measles and chicken pox were not diagnosed as such. Probably the rubella passed as rubeola and the varicella as variola.

Some of the medical officers of the old regular army expressed surprise at the epidemics that swept the camps of recruits because they had not occurred in the prewar army. The explanation was simple: The old army had been small and its units widely dispersed;

recruitment had been continual but on a small scale, and large numbers of susceptibles had not been brought together as in 1861. These airborne contagious diseases flared up again in 1862 and 1864 when many new regiments entered the service. Because of the solid immunity conferred by an attack of most of these diseases, the interims were relatively quiet.

All knowledgeable military commanders recognized this early conditioning period. For General Lee it caused disaster from underestimation in western Virginia in 1861 as told in Chapter 2. However, when the Confederate army was burdened with about 4,500 sick at Winchester less than three weeks after the Battle of Antietam, Lee realistically wrote to the secretary of war that (12)

> . . . they are principally, if not altogether, the conscripts and recruits that have joined since we have been stationary. They are afflicted with measles, camp fever, etc. The medical director thinks that all the conscripts we have received are thus afflicted, so that, instead of being an advantage to us, they are an element of weakness, a burden. I think, therefore, that it would be better that the conscripts be assembled in camps of instruction, so that they may pass through these inevitable diseases, and become a little inured to camp life.

This advice was not followed.

"Well-seasoned troops" were soldiers who had survived the epidemics that struck nearly all recent enlistees and had become immune to some. These airborne early diseases were regarded as a kind of chrysalis state through which men had to pass to become fitted for the military life (13). Typical was the reply of General Mansfield Lovell to a request from Richmond that he forward new troops from New Orleans in January, 1862. He would send them ". . . as soon as I can have them put through the measles; a process which they are now undergoing one-half of them now being sick" (14).

Of the early contagious diseases, measles was the most important from the viewpoints of numbers, serious complications, and easy communicability. It was regarded as more severe in adults than in children. Black measles could be fatal. Measly boys developed acute and chronic bronchitis and pneumonia, and they were predisposed to consumption. The 76,318 cases, with 5,177 deaths, in Table I fail to depict the great importance of this disease. Many additional cases occurred while the new troops were still in the state services, and many deaths were reported under other diagnoses, usually those of the complications and sequels. A Confederate surgeon who saw about 10,000 soldiers pass through a camp of instruction at Raleigh in five months in early 1862 wrote that about 4,000 contracted measles (15). The disease interfered with training in the South when entire companies and regiments had to be disbanded for a time and the men sent home (16). Of the approximately 2,000 Federal and 800 Confederate regiments, probably none escaped measles.

The "camp diseases," common to all armies prior to the twentieth century, also inevitably appeared in every unit in endemic or epidemic form. They were diarrhea and dysentery, malaria, and typhoid fever. Healthy, latent, or mildly ill carriers of the causative agents existed in every sizeable group of Americans. The simple but efficient transmission chain of the enteric infections through the fecal contamination of things later ingested and of malaria by the bite of the widely prevalent infected anophelene mosquito made them major opponents. In addition, the dysenteries and malaria were formidable because of the many types and the lack of cross immunity. A soldier could serially or simultaneously have several infections. Moreover, the low degree of protection conferred by an attack insured that many susceptibles would always exist. Dysentery and malaria maintained high prevalence rates to the end of the war, but that of typhoid declined slightly, probably because of a reduction in the pool of susceptibles.

These camp diseases greatly reduced military efficiency by their high morbidity, considerable mortality, and protracted course. Even more important was their ability to occur in epidemics. The sick burdened the military machine, and the sudden unexpected reduction of soldiers behind guns could be serious. The agents of these three diseases were the principal natural pathogens influencing the outcome of some campaigns and battles, to be described.

Two other mosquito-disseminated diseases were serious threats. Yellow fever was dreaded because of its mysterious origins and high virulence. Its aggressiveness was blunted by the absence of healthy carriers, by the restricted range of the *Aedes* mosquito, and because frost terminated the outbreaks. Yellow fever attained military importance in South Carolina in 1862 (Chapter 3) and a few other times elsewhere. At New Berne in 1864, about 280 soldiers died of the 600 infected (17). Dengue fever does not appear in the official lists, but it existed at the time and was sometimes diagnosed. An influenza-like disease causing quick prostration ("broken-bone fever"), its course was brief, complications few and mortality virtually nil. It disappeared with the fall frosts, and did not reappear unless reintroduced, so it did not prosper. Both yellow and dengue fevers entered the country by sea, generally from the Caribbean area. Yellow fever could be controlled by a strict quarantine but, the incubation period not being understood, it broke out at Port Royal despite quarantine. It was kept from New Orleans for several years from 1862 by this method. This demonstration should have ended the old debate over its endogenous versus its imported origin but it did not and the disease reappeared in New Orleans after the war. Dengue was harder to control by the quarantine of overt cases because a viremia was present for several days before the clinical appearance of the disease, so the transmission chain was not broken by isolating only the sick.

Some other communicable diseases were common enough to have military importance (Table I) without, however, greatly influencing the outcome of campaigns or battles because they were not epidemic. Thus, tuberculosis killed many soldiers, filled hospitals, and led to many medical discharges, but the prolonged incubation period, insidious onset, protracted course, and gradual incapacitation prevented crucial damage to military operations. Typhus fever ("ship fever," "jail fever") broke out in several regiments crowded aboard ships infested with infected lice but the disease did not spread. The largest epidemic occurred in 1865, at Wilmington, where the infection was brought by soldiers released from Salisbury prison. About 300 soldiers died, including nine medical officers (18). Another type of "spotted fever", cerebrospinal meningitis, was also seen occasionally but it soon died out (15).

Smallpox made its appearance in every month from May, 1861 to June, 1866 to a total of 18,952 cases (Table I), but it caused no large epidemics because most of the soldiers had been vaccinated. However, it was said that about 5,000 Confederate soldiers were sick at the time of the Battle of Chancellorsville from spurious vaccination reactions (19). In the Army of Northern Virginia, the disease had flared up after the Antietam campaign in 1862 (20). Epidemic and sporadic jaundice was widespread but mild so that it received little attention. It was probably principally infectious (viral) hepatitis rather than Weil's infectious jaundice. The venereal diseases, gonorrhea and syphilis, found many victims but were not epidemic; the late serious complications of gonorrhea were largely ignored and the delayed tertiary stage cardiovascular and central nervous system manifestations of syphilis were either unknown or not related to that disease. Prostitutes collected wherever soldiers were numerous. Although many had been expelled from Nashville by boat and train (21), the city had 460 licensed prostitutes and a hospital for prostitutes and another for syphilitic soldiers in October, 1864 (22).

Pneumonia was an important cause of morbidity and mortality, but chiefly as a secondary complication in other diseases and not as a primary epidemic disease. It is probable that the paratyphoid fevers, relapsing fever, and brucellosis occurred in sizeable numbers but they were not recognized and separated from the large pool of miasmatic diseases shown in Table I. Tularemia of the tick-borne type may also have existed in the south although it was not diagnosed. Many horses had to be destroyed for glanders (23, 24, 25), but the disease rarely spread to man.

*Dysentery* and *diarrhea* were the most important military diseases from the viewpoints of number of victims, mortality, chronicity, sequels, relapses, and repeated attacks. These diagnostic terms included all illnesses in which frequent loose stools were the predominant symptom. They were separated only on the basis of gross blood. Either disease might be fatal in the acute or chronic stages, and postmortem examination usually revealed the lesion to be distinctive and identical; it was ulceration of the large intestine. The lesions in the mild cases were unknown. In severity it ranged from a benign, mild, "walking" purging to protracted, painful, febrile, half-hourly, blood and pus evacuations. The resulting picture varied from an acute self-limited attack lasting a few days to a chronic emaciating disease extending over many years. These diagnostic terms must have included examples of most, if not all, of the numerous diarrheic diseases recognized today: Their various bacterial, protozoal, viral, helminthic, chemical, and metabolic causes were unknown. The toxin and fever-producing *Shigellas* probably accounted for many cases, and others were amebic, as is indicated by the many complicating abscesses of the liver. The hypotheses on causation numbered many dozens (26). The factor most commonly named was "exposure," but this broad term included most of the vicissitudes of camp life among which the ultimate agents were never correctly pinpointed.

Cavalryman Charles Francis Adams, Jr. vividly but incorrectly interpreted the camp conditions for enteritis in a letter to his father, the U. S. Minister to London, in September, 1863 (23):

> Still an army, any army, does poison the air. It is a city without sewerage, and policing only makes piles of offal to be buried or burned. Animals die as they do not die in cities and, if buried, they are apt to be insufficiently so. Then animals are slaughtered for beef and so, what with fragments of food and scraps of decaying substances, all festering under a mid-summer sun, an army soon breeds a malaria which engenders the most fatal of fevers . . .

The bulldozer and diesel fuel, so important in camp and battlefield sanitation in World War II, had not been developed. One regimental surgeon thought that the fecal odor that developed around every camp might be dangerous and proposed to get rid of it. His colonel claimed this was impossible as the odor was inseparable from an army and that it was a "patriotic odor." However, by adding an inch of soil to the latrine trenches every night, the odor was abolished (27).

These cosmopolitan dysenteries often began in the recruiting camps and they increased in number throughout the four years. Some recruits must have been carriers and others were soon added. The simple transmission chains in the bacterial types, *i.e.* from feces by fingers or flies to food or water, were not recognized. There were no diagnostic aides of any type. Since there were diverse causes and many relapses, diarrhea occurred at all seasons, in all climates, and in all geographical areas. Although some men were prostrated, others were up and about, so this was a disease both of static and moving armies. Much of the straggling on the march resulted not from cowardice but from the weakness, frequent bowel movements, fever, and anemia of dysentery. Photographs of Pennsylvania Avenue made during the two day victory parade in 1865 disclose no emergency street toilets, so it is certain that many soldiers with uncontrollable bowels dared not risk the march of eight hours and stayed behind in camp. Many men with the disease continued on duty and were mustered out at the end of the war. The medical records of the pension bureau contain thousands of cases, many of them fatal.

From the second year of the war, much of the chronic and recurrent diarrhea was inextricable from the common "scorbutic taint" in the records. This was a condition of malnutrition containing scorbutic and other components. It predisposed to infections of many types, retarded recovery, delayed wound healing, and produced lassitude, weakness, and depression. It was benefitted miraculously by fresh fruit and vegetables, which often stopped even the diarrhea.

The treatments for enteritis were numerous but none were specific and, probably, none were effective. The ipecac and its alkaloids, emetine and ipecacuanha, often administered as nauseant expectorants and emetics, were probably not beneficial even in the amebic type because of low dosage. Because many cases were self-limited, many remedies seemed good for acute diarrhea. One surgeon thought the sulphate of magnesia effective in the Corinth campaign of 1862, and it was said that 150 barrels of it were ordered by the medical director of Grant's command (28). The chronic cases, cadaverous skeletons, later filled the regimental, divisional, and general hospitals far back into the interior. One unhappy captain wrote from a tent hospital near Atlanta, in 1864, that "The hundreds of thin disgusting sick patriots that creep around these grounds form a sight that I loathe with every power in me" (29). They resembled the emaciated victims in Hitler's camps.

The burden and effects of diarrhea and dysentery on the Federal military machine are shown not only by the cases, which totalled 1,739,135, but also by the number of deaths, chronic cases, and medical discharges. These were, respectively, 44,558, 211,037, and 19,748. Even these figures fall far short of actuality because many cases were reported as enteritis, peritonitis, hemorrhage from the bowels, anemia, pneumonia, debility, "unstated causes," and in other diagnostic categories. The disease became more severe during the four years. The death rate per 1,000 mean strength increased from 4.2 in the first year to 21.3 in the last year (30). Despite greater emphasis on military sanitation, this disease failed to be controlled. Chronic dysentery cases even in large numbers could be tolerated by an army, the acute epidemics hurt military operations far more.

The cases diagnosed cholera morbus numbered 26,366 in the Union army; 305 of them died. These were probably examples of acute gastroenteritis from various causes, and a differentiation from the acute diarrhea category was not sharp. Surgeon C. Macfarland saw about 2,000 men in two regiments become suddenly sick one night after eating a delicious pudding (4). This may be an early example of food poisoning by staphylotoxin or metal (zinc, cadmium).

Every army was heavily involved with enteritis and only the fortitude of the soldiers kept some units in the field. For example, an inspection report of Grant's army for June, 1863, when it was besieging Vicksburg, claimed that half or more were suffering from diarrhea (31). Most soldiers realized early that good guts were more important than good brains, and many resented any suggestion that they lacked the guts for soldiering.

Comprehensive data on diarrhea and dysentery in the Confederate army are not available, but such information as exists shows that it was at least as common. For example, in the nine-month period from July, 1861 to March, 1862 the prevalence rates in the opposing Confederate and Union Armies of the Potomac were, respectively, 740 and 407 per 1,000 soldiers (16). A prominent Confederate surgeon writing in 1866 (16), described these diseases as very prevalent and difficult to manage, ". . . few soldiers ever had a natural or moulded evacuation." Another experienced Confederate surgeon wrote that nine-tenths of all recruits had diarrhea, and that it led to much invalidism (15). Although most of the victims were never sent to a hospital, this was the most common disease in the large Chimborazo Hospital at Richmond (33). During the period from October 10, 1861 to November 1, 1863, there were 6,329 admissions for acute and chronic diarrhea.

The experience of the Third Wisconsin was typical of many regiments (34). It rendezvoused at Fond du Lac on June 20, 1861 and went east and encamped at Harper's Ferry about a month later:

> Soon there was much sickness in camp . . . that worst foe with which the soldiers had to contend, the camp diarrhoea. Under its debilitating

effects the vigor and strength soon vanished; men wasted to skeletons; and while most of its victims still clung to duty, did their drilling and guard duty, it was in weakness and languor. When it became chronic, as in many instances it did, the poor victims, with a face like shriveled parchment, lips bloodless, and nearly paralyzed with sheer muscular weakness, was an object pitiful to see.

The compiled statistics fail to describe the full numbers and effects of these enteritides. Suspecting that the problem was serious, the surgeon general of Massachusetts had all training camps inspected late in 1862. The inspector found that practically every Massachusetts recruit in every regiment had been affected (35). Camps of assembly at Worcester, Groton, Cambridge, Lynnfield, Boxford, Wenham, Readville, Long Island, West Roxbury, and Lakeville had all been involved. He was puzzled because the disease had occurred in all places, conditions, and habits, leaving no clue to causation. Similar conditions existed in the other states. Probably many of these early cases were not included in the Federal statistics.

The big central training and distribution camps exposed every regiment that passed through. About fifty regiments from Missouri, Iowa, Illinois, Wisconsin, and Minnesota were so exposed at Benton Barracks in St. Louis in 1861-1862. The numbers infected at Camp Curtin, Harrisburg, at Camp Dennison near Cincinnati and Camp Chase at Columbus, and elsewhere were only slightly fewer. In the large fields on Meridian Hill and Kalorama Heights in present-day Washington, used for temporary campsites in 1861-1862, many of the regiments that made up the original Army of the Potomac were infected with dysentery and typhoid fever, apparently through the water supplies. An open stream passed near their uncovered latrines.

*Malaria* was the second most common camp disease and in some respects the most important. Its distribution was more regional and seasonal than that of dysentery. It killed many soldiers and disabled many thousands more, some many times. Because the disease conferred no solid, permanent protection, it increased throughout the four years. It was present in all military districts, but prevailed more in those that were warm and wet. Overall, it built up from a low incidence in the spring to peaks in September and October, but sharp epidemics occurred earlier a number of times. The cold winter months were not free of the disease because of chronic cases, relapses, and the first clinical appearance of some infections previously suppressed by quinine used prophylactically. At that time, malaria occurred throughout the lower and upper South and far north of the Mason-Dixon line, especially in the low country along streams. Parts of New Jersey, Pennsylvania, and New York had frequent visitations. Many people in southern Ohio, Indiana, Illinois, and Iowa expected an attack of the ague every autumn. The sallow complexion, emaciation, and fatigue of chronic malaria had not been limited to the south, so that many Northern regiments also carried the seeds of the disease to war with them. However, the most severe outbreaks occurred in the South where there was a combination of a long warm season, much water, many mosquitoes, and many persons chronically infected with the plasmodium. The Union regiments from the New England states, Michigan, Wisconsin and Minnesota were struck the hardest. At Baton Rouge, First and Second Vicksburg, on the Gulf coast, in Arkansas, and in the departments of North and South Carolina, they paid a heavy price.

The combined cases of intermittent and remittent fevers recorded by the Union forces numbered 1,315,955, and the deaths 10,063 (7). The most common type was the quotidian intermittent with 511,250 examples (510 deaths). The other types in descending frequency were tertian, 426,215 (435 deaths); remittent, 317,135 (4,855 deaths); quartan, 45,146 (99 deaths); and congestive, 16,209 (4,164 deaths). The mortality rate was high only in the congestive and remittent forms. Congestive intermittent fever seems to have been chiefly cerebral malaria. The term remittent fever appears to have been used either to characterize the type of fever or for an intermittent fever that had relapsed after a remission induced by therapy. It may also have included some examples of falciparum malaria.

Malaria, like dysentery, could damage or destroy the effectiveness of a military unit but the epidemics usually had a less explosive onset. Many soldiers went through the war having periodic bouts of chills and fever, which continued after the war. The disease was not often the cause for a medical discharge. Assistant Surgeon Junius N. Bragg of the Eleventh Arkansas regiment, who had chills and fever periodically for three years, was afraid of the criticism he would arouse by taking even a medical leave for this common disease (36).

Antiperiodic drugs, chiefly quinine, were used in large quantities.

In the Union army alone 595,544 ounces of quinine sulphate and 518,957 ounces of a fluid cinchona extract were issued (37). When administered as a prophylactic, the quinine was dissolved in whiskey, but many soldiers preferred the vehicle alone. Some surgeons even argued that any prophylactic benefit was derived from the ethanol.

The wholesale effects of malaria were described when eight, nine-month New England regiments passed through Cleveland in August, 1863. Here they were washed, fed, and given medical care by the volunteers of the Soldier's Aid Society (38). They were going home for discharge from the trenches at Port Hudson, where several diseases were epidemic, but principally malaria. The Twenty-eighth Maine had five cars full of their sick. Regarding the Forty-seventh Massachusetts, ". . . our hearts have been sorely tried by the dreadful state in which the men were found." Their surgeon, Doctor John Blackmer, had to be removed and carried to a hospital. The Twenty-eighth Connecticut, down to about 500 and ". . . so worn and weary the men looked, and they straggled so painfully into the depot that it touched every heart." Their colonel had gone home sick, the lieutenant colonel, two surgeons, and many company officers were dead, and "The sick had been brought up in the care of the 2d assistant surgeon, Mr. Henry Rockwell, a mere boy in appearance, but a miracle in faithfulness, kindness and energy." The colonel and lieutenant colonel of the Forty-ninth Massachusetts were absent wounded and Surgeon Frederick Winsor ". . . was exceedingly careful of his men." Malaria could have finished the ruin of these regiments in a few weeks more.

*Typhoid fever* had a great potential for harm because of its relatively high mortality, protracted course, high infectivity, numerous sources of infection, easy communicability, and high rate of attack in new troops. Nevertheless, its cumulative damage in the military population proved to be distinctly limited and less than that of dysentery and malaria. A few regiments, however, suffered so severely that they were called "typhoid" regiments. Some recruits were immune because of a pre-war infection, and all who recovered carried a solid protection. Although its complications were serious (peritonitis, massive melena), sequels were few. The importance of this disease in the armies decreased each year because of a reduction in the susceptibles. Because it was spread chiefly from silent carriers or active clinical cases by way of the fecal contamination of food and water supplies, it was a disease predominantly of static troops although some cases first appeared during movements because of the long incubation period.

The frequency of typhoid carriers in this country in 1861 is unknown. However, in 1908 Park reported that in New York two per cent of convalescents passed typhoid bacilli in their feces or urine, some of them for long periods of time. Moreover, among adults who had never had the disease two in each thousand were carriers (39). Typhoid Mary fell into this group. There is no reason to believe the carrier state was less common in 1861, and it was probably even more prevalent.

The distinctive pathological lesion was known to be greatly hyperplastic, ulcerated Peyer's patches. Despite the large experience of most physicians, the diagnosis was not always reliable, even in epidemics, especially in army practice because of the concurrence of other diseases. This uncertainty is revealed by the common terms, sometimes used in the same outbreak, such as typhomalaria, typhoid pneumonia, low typhoid, common continued fever, typhus, remittent bilious fever and others. Surgeon John F. Ely recognized long after the war that an epidemic diagnosed as atypical typhoid fever had in reality been trichinosis (40), and other mistakes must have been common. Typhoid fever was classified among the "continued" fevers rather than with the "intermittent" fevers, but in practice this separation depended on clinical impressions as the clinical thermometer was rarely used.

The paratyphoid fevers were not separately recognized and diagnosed, although they must have been common. In some outbreaks the "low typhoids" predominated. Many medical officers insisted that the "common continued fever" prevalent in the camps during the first winter was not like the typhoid fever of their previous civilian experience. At least two medical boards appointed to investigate the problem reached no clear decision (41, 42). In the second year, the term typhomalarial fever was introduced to the diagnostic list to accommodate these debatable cases. This became a popular category —something of a dumping ground at times. Postmortem examinations in some instances disclosed the characteristic typhoid ulcers.

The number of cases and deaths reported in the various members of the typhoid fever group is shown in Table III. In the typical typhoids the mortality rate was high—over one-third. Its severity ranked with smallpox, yellow fever, typhus fever, and pneumonia but below meningitis. The typhomalarial group might have included many of the mild or modified typhoid cases, but the very low mortality in the common continued fever group casts doubt on its identity with typhoid fever. This group might have included some of the paratyphoid cases. The same statement applies to the large number reported as "Other diseases of this order." The treatments were legion and probably ineffective. Some of them, such as bleeding, turpentine, emetics, and mercurialization to the point of severe salivation, might have been harmful.

TABLE III

Typhoid Fever and Related Diseases in the
Union Army, 1861-1866*

| Diagnosis | Number cases | Number deaths | Percentage fatal |
|---|---|---|---|
| Typhoid fever | 79,462 | 29,336 | 37.0 |
| Typho-malarial fever | 57,400 | 5,350 | 9.3 |
| Common continued fever | 11,769 | 147 | 1.3 |
| Total typhoid group | 148,631 | 34,833 | —— |
| Other diseases of this order (*i.e.* miasmatic) | 94,997 | 2,363 | 2.5 |

*Data from *Medical and Surgical History of the War of the Rebellion*, Vol. I, Part I.

The alleged causes were numerous, most of them related to environmental factors of the "miasmatic" type. The relation to previous cases was not recognized, probably because of the relatively long incubation period, the existence of the healthy carrier state, and the indirect transmission by water, milk, and food of many types. Moreover, the bacillus could probably multiply to a limited extent in nature, under appropriate conditions, increasing the available pathogens without disclosing their ultimate origin. Like the dysenteries, typhoid fever resulted from the ingestion of specific bacteria whose ultimate source was excremental.

The occurrence of typhoid fever was often thought to be related to the prolonged occupation of campsites and to the accumulation of garbage and sewage, but troops in motion in clean country sometimes became sick to confuse the picture. One textbook writer thought that a few weeks in camp sufficed to develop the typh poison (43). The commander of the post at Columbia, Kentucky pleaded for marching orders in December, 1861 (44):

> Typhoid fever is striking our men a heavy blow; 233 of my regiment are down, and dying daily. . . . Unless we are moved the regiment will soon be greatly weakened. While marching we never have any sick; when we stop the men sicken and fall like leaves. . . . We would rather die in battle than on a bed of fever.

The Meridian Hill campsite in Washington, so unhealthy for many regiments, was described by an inspector in January, 1862, because of complaints from the Seventy-seventh New York (45):

> . . . the atmosphere is impregnated with a malarial odor, arising from the decomposition of animal matter just below in an open field, where a large number of dead horses are deposited upon the surface and allowed to remain and decompose. This, with the rather poor policing of the camp, has given rise to typhoid fever, from which, I regret to say, we have lost some ten or twelve men already.

The exact source of the infection is unknown but it was probably the drinking water. The nearby Twenty-third Pennsylvania had fifty-three deaths from typhoid fever (46), and many other regiments were infected. The Sixtieth New York, possibly infected here, was among those known as a "typhoid regiment." It eventually had over 700 cases.

The pattern of army disease was so consistent that it was recognized by many lay writers. One regimental historian described it succinctly (47):

> Measles and mumps began to prevail; Rheumatism made the men lame, Chronic Diarrhea weakened them, Typhoid fever fired their blood, and Jaundice painted their skins and eyeballs yellower than saffron. Two hospital tents were soon filled to overflowing . . .

The reaction to the large amount of camp disease was strong in the medical profession at home but their concern was usually misdirected, just as it was in the army medical department. Numerous critical articles appeared in the medical periodicals. Representative of these was an editorial in the *American Medical Times* (48). It was published in August, 1862 after the failure of McClellan's Grand Army on the Yorktown Peninsula to take Richmond. It attributed the failure to sickness. Fifty thousand soldiers had been sent to the rear and a hundred regiments invalided. The causes were four: (a) the mustering of unfit persons; (b) the unhealthy location and inadequate provision of camps; (c) the disregard of camp police, and (d) improper and badly cooked food. A critical study of this campaign follows in Chapter 5.

A part of the problem of managing the epidemics in camp, illustrated by the Peninsular campaign and its preparatory period, arose from the attitude of many commanders, and some medical officers, to ignore them, as if they would go away. A part of this silence may have represented a desire to suppress alarm there or at the seat of government or at home. The silence was bad, however, when it led to the deception of self or the civil superiors in the government. Within the army, knowledge of the epidemics could not be entirely suppressed, because of the nature of army life and the medical service. The majority of the hundreds of postwar histories and memoirs comment on the epidemics, often quite candidly but always bravely though sadly.

The large losses involved nearly every family, more by disease than by battle. Well into the present century the great names were common household words. Chickahominy long evoked a picture of camp disease more than wounds. Corinth was remembered for its dysentery almost as well as Shiloh and Kenesaw Mountain for their bloodshed. The fall of Vicksburg to arms only partly assuaged the memory of the four-month-long horror of typhoid and dysentery on the levees and in nearly swamps with hardly enough solid ground to accommodate the dead. "Potomac flats" and "Potomac fever" have lost their original connotations only in recent decades; the original Potomac fever was an unavoidable typhoid whereas the modern usage refers only to an unseemly neurosis.

## Adverse Military Effects of Disease

The harmful military effects of disease assumed many forms. Units of all sizes from individuals to armies were affected, and the severity varied from slight to extinction. Disease also took the lives of important civilian leaders as well as of soldiers. It interfered with training. Some severely affected troops had to be held in camp or with-drawn from the field for recovery, and a few regiments had even to be disbanded or discontinued. Organizations in size from batteries and companies to army corps and even departments were rendered ineffective. Intercurrent disease aborted some campaigns in the planning stage, arrested others before they could come to battle, and actually stopped attacks that were under way. Disease was a factor in the failure to renew several important campaigns that had been stopped by military force. Its influence was generally greater on campaigns than on battles because of their longer duration and static periods. Sickness almost constantly burdened the military organization, and its harmful effects were commonly additive to other adverse conditions. The threat of disease according to season, geography, seasoning of the troops and other factors had always to be considered in military planning. Examples will be given of each type of effect.

There can be little doubt that the premature deaths of civilians such as the Hon. Stephen A. Douglas, from typhoid, and others, greatly influenced the war. Also the death of a number of promising military leaders had a noticeable effect: The illness of Major General C. F. Smith left Grant and Sherman the only trained general officers in a sizeable army on the field at Shiloh, and his early death opened rare opportunities to them. As will be seen, General O. M. Mitchel succumbed to yellow fever in 1862 at a time when he was badly needed. Major General David B. Birney was probably the ablest commander in the Army of the James when typhoid fever and/or dysentery ended his life in 1864 (49). General John Buford, who opened the Battle of Gettysburg, died of typhoid fever at a time when aggressive Union cavalry leaders were badly needed. The subsequent history of the Department of the Missouri might have been better if General E. V. Sumner had lived to take over in 1863. General Ewell's osteomyelitis and diarrhea terminated his corps leadership at a time when it could not well be spared, and the loss of Stonewall Jackson from a postoperative acute lung infection was not compensable.

Disease interfered with training as well as with the performance of assigned duty many times. In May, 1861, on taking charge of the defenses at Harper's Ferry, General Joseph E. Johnston found nearly forty per cent of the troops sick in the hospitals or elsewhere with measles and mumps (50). By July 15, just before going to First Bull Run, his regiments had been reduced to half strength. The Third Tennessee, a regiment of 1,100 men, had 650 cases of measles in the first two months of training (51). Drills had to be discontinued because of measles in a brigade composed of four Indiana and Ohio regiments in October, 1861 (52). Confederate units in size up to regiments had to be disbanded for a time and the men sent home on account of measles (16).

Many regiments were rendered ineffective by medical casualties so that they had to be withdrawn from field service until they recovered or were discontinued. A morbidity of one-hundred per cent was not rare, but a few of the mildest cases usually remained on duty to keep the regimental organization in existence. The Twenty-third Wisconsin had hardly a well man because of miasmatic diseases at Young's Point in January, 1863 (53). At Fernandina, Florida in 1863, nearly every soldier in the Eleventh Maine was suffering from the "shakes," and their surgeon died from a four-day attack of congestive fever, despite which the regimental health was regarded as fairly good (54). The Twelfth Connecticut was quickly reduced by swamp fever (probably malaria) within a few weeks in 1863 near Brashear City, Louisiana to 225 men for duty, although actually most of these also were sick. Their historian considered that ". . . if they were at home they would be in bed and asking the prayers of the congregation" (55). In one period of forty-two days they lost forty-two men by death. In 1862, the Sixtieth New York was made ineffective with about 767 cases of typhoid fever (called endemic!) and had to be withdrawn, missing Second Bull Run (56, 57). Two Mississippi regiments were reduced by measles to a battalion hardly able to guard their area in Kentucky in 1861 (58).

Other examples of the incapacitation of small units included a Confederate regiment in Texas, in 1864, which had to be relieved because of reactions to spurious vaccine matter and measles (59). Because of typhoid and other fevers contracted at Gloucester Point, Virginia, in 1863, the One-hundred-eighteenth New York had to be sent to a healthier site (Norfolk) to recover. Congressional influence was brought to bear when the departmental commander at first disapproved their request for the transfer (60). Governor O. P. Morton, in 1862, requested that the Forty-ninth Indiana be moved from Cumberland Ford, Kentucky to a healthier site. In an enrollment of 900, its effectives had dropped to 220 and the sick list was still increasing daily. Food was scarce and not enough straw or hay was available within eighty miles to fill the bed-ticks of their sick (61). The Seventh New Hampshire was declared unfit for duty in August, 1862, at Beaufort, South Carolina because of typhoid fever, typhus, diarrhea, malaria, and scurvy contracted chiefly since June. They were shipped to St. Augustine, as the healthiest place on the south Atlantic coast, to recover (62). They departed only a few days before yellow fever broke out at Beaufort. Earlier that year they had forty-eight cases of smallpox. The Twenty-seven Massachusetts was sent to St. Augustine in 1863 because of incapacitation by dysentery; it soon improved (63).

Ordered by Jefferson Davis in October, 1861 to send forward his brigade of two Mississippi regiments, General J. W. O'Ferrald protested that they were not fit to move to a cold climate, where half would be lost, because two-thirds of them were just recovering from measles. He recommended that they first be sent to the southern coast for a few months (64). The Fourth Ohio disembarked at Harrison's Landing on July 2, 1862, with over 800 men. On the 10th they were struck by a prostrating diarrhea which, within six weeks, laid low over 600 of them. On November 10th, the regiment was militarily ineffective, having only 120 for duty. Yet, they had lost only one man in battle, and eight or ten wounded (65). The reduction of the Sixth Minnesota from 937 strong to seventy-nine in a few weeks by malaria, at Helena, Arkansas in 1864, is described elsewhere (Chapter 9). In 1864, General W. N. Pendleton found that a battery on James River was unable to man its guns; with a nominal aggregate of 253 men, it had only forty for duty because of malaria; their surgeon thought he could control the chills if he could get quinine (66).

To these examples of regiments made ineffective by disease many more could be added. One historian, a physician, vividly wrote for many (67): His newly recruited Ninety-sixth Ohio arrived on the levee near Vicksburg, on December 27, 1862, and camped in a flooded cotton field. Scurvy, erysipelas, pneumonia, dysentery, and typhoid fever rapidly filled the hospital but the medical supplies were exhausted and vegetables were not obtainable. Twenty-three days after the sickest had been shipped to St. Louis, 234 more were unable to march. As for the rest . . .

> No abatement of the rain, no abatement of the diseases that did their fearful work; our hearts sank within us as we saw our feeble comrades bearing the uncoffined dead to their graves. The row of little mounds on the levee day by day became longer; our members, day by day, less; eyes more sunken, steps more feeble, souls more spiritless.

When the regiment struck camp on March 12th to march south with Grant, despite the large number of sick previously sent North to hospitals, they left 196 graves on the levee.

Healthy regiments were the exception and they attracted unwelcome attention. The Thirteenth Iowa was twice inspected on suspicion of falsifying the sick report (68). When the Ninety-seventh Pennsylvania arrived in Washington in November, 1861 it was met by ambulances and expressions of surprise that they had no hospital cases. Most regiments had ten or twelve after a two-day trip (69).

Not only regiments and brigades but entire divisions and army corps were sometimes made ineffective by sickness, even though it was unlikely that all their component units would be severely struck simultaneously. The Ninth corps, loaned to Grant by Burnside for about six or seven weeks in 1863, was described as pitiable when it returned to Cincinnati in August (8). At Vicksburg it had not been in the trenches but on guard by the bayous and marshes near the Big Black River:

> Malarial fever ate out their vitality, and even those who reported for duty dragged themselves about, the mere shadows of what they had been. General Parke reported their arrival and was then obliged to go upon sick-leave himself. General Welsh . . . reported that his division must recuperate for a few weeks before it could take the field. He made a heroic effort to remain on duty, but died suddenly . . .

The two divisions were scattered in healthy camps in the Kentucky hills, each camp, at first, a hospital. Improvement was gradual but recovery was only partial.

In another example, the Nineteenth corps was shipped to the Army of the James in the summer of 1864 from the Department of the

Gulf, where many of its component units had suffered greatly in Louisiana swamps for two years. Their troubles were not over, as they arrived on the James during wet, hot weather, and went at once into the Petersburg trenches. The commander, General E. O. C. Ord, reported 2,103 men sick in ten days, during which period the sick list increased from seven to twenty per cent and was still growing (70). The rains had filled the pits. Unless they were relieved from their present duty, the corps would be reduced by half in a month.

Disease also seriously affected armies and military departments. In addition to the examples described in the chapters that follow, a few are here depicted briefly: Thus, General A. S. Johnston was severely criticised in 1862 for his failure to send more support to Fort Donelson. One of his confidential couriers is responsible for the statement that prior heavy losses from disease around his base at Bowling Green prevented such aid (71). General L. P. Walker could not forward troops to Johnston at the end of October because his four regiments had been "much thrown back by measles and other camp diseases" (72). General Lloyd Tilghman wrote that health conditions in his camps were very bad (73). General Alcorn's camp at Hopkinsville was one vast hospital, hardly able to guard itself, because sixty-seven per cent of the command was sick. A few days later, on November 6, 1861, Tilghman had 750 sick and not a well officer who could handle a hundred men. At about the same time, General T. C. Hindman's brigade at Rocky Hill Station was greatly weakened, had less than half its quota of surgeons, and was without medicines (74). General Johnston conceded to the war department in November that his condition was weakened by disease (75). He had even been forced to draw 5,000 men from General Polk on the Mississippi, weakening that line; he was planning to evacuate his sick to Nashville hospitals at the rate of 250 a day. Although his subordinates continued to report much disease, Johnston's Western Department, on December 31, 1861, numbered 91,988 aggregate present and absent (exclusive of three brigades) but the number present for duty was only 54,004 (76). There can be little doubt that disease was greatly interfering with army strength and training badly needed a few weeks later at Fort Donelson.

At about the same time, General Zollicoffer, serving under Johnston, was holding the eastern anchor of the Confederate main defense line across southern Kentucky. He was defeated and killed in battle by General George Thomas at Mill Springs, in January, 1862, in the first substantial Federal victory of the war. Zollicoffer's force was always small and it had a large burden of disease, which it could not tolerate. When he advanced from Cumberland Ford in Kentucky just before the battle, 1,000 sick had to be left behind at the Ford (77).

Another example of sickness rendering a military department ineffective is provided by the Confederate Department of East Tennessee at Knoxville in the spring of 1862. Major General E. Kirby Smith, who had been criticized for inactivity, wrote an explanation to Richmond on May 28, 1862 (78): He was threatened by 12,000 Union troops at Cumberland Gap and 9,000 in northern Alabama, whereas his effectives were only 8,000:

> This command, composed of new levies from Tennessee, Northern Alabama, and Georgia troops, has been afflicted with almost every disease incident to camp life. With a paper force of 17,000, scarcely 8,000 are effective; regiments 800 and 900 strong report only 200 or 300 for duty. . . . This unexampled sickness, while it has in a great measure prevented drills and discipline, has tended much to dishearten and demoralize; so that it has required every exertion on my part to keep up the spirits of the men.

These were new troops but in a country usually regarded as healthy. Typhoid fever had accounted for a part of this sickness (78). Disease had prevented the indicated military countermeasures. This example is inconspicuous in history because it resulted in the loss of no battle or department. This command was inefficient until late that summer, when it won the Battle of Richmond (Kentucky) and supported Bragg at Perryville.

At Island No. 10 a Confederate inspection, on March 26, 1862, disclosed about 2,000 effective but 1,557 on the sick report, scattered in private houses and elsewhere (79). The principal diseases were "bowel complaint and fever," probably a shigellosis. At nearby New Madrid and Tiptonville conditions were similar, and Pope's advance found success easier because of this sickness, his troops being healthier at that time.

The campaign for Atlanta between Sherman and J. E. Johnston, in the summer of 1864, is usually thought of as having been healthy on both sides. The word "healthy" in this context requires definition. Actually, disease was common. The prevailing infections in the Union force were dysentery, diarrhea, malarial, typho-malarial and typhoid fevers, respiratory infections during the rainy season, "land" scurvy, and a sprinkling of the exanthemata (80). When the field corn became edible, the scurvy rapidly decreased, and the troops entered Atlanta in better condition than at Chattanooga. The largest of Sherman's three armies was the Army of the Cumberland, and to its divisional hospitals alone 43,153 sick had been admitted during the four months. Of these patients, 26,184 were transferred back to the general hospitals. These figures do not include the sick admitted to the regimental hospitals or treated without hospitalization. This army contained over half the soldiers in the army group. Such figures would today not be interpreted as showing a healthy army. There was much sickness even though the armies were moving. Disease of this amount must have influenced the military operations even if it did not reverse the end result.

In the Savannah campaign that followed, much less sickness was experienced. The reasons are of interest. The medical director of Sherman's army had ordered in advance that a 5,000-bed hospital be held on the South Atlantic coast ready to be shipped to the point of emergence (81). The hospital was not needed even though few sick soldiers had been abandoned along the route. Compared with the Atlanta campaign the favorable factors were: The duration was shorter (one month compared with four) although the distance was nearly three times longer; the season was healthier (November-December); the diet was better, as they benefitted from the harvest in good agricultural country; they were not following behind another infected army; their faster motion permitted them to walk away from their own pollutants. However, by the standards of today, this army was not healthy and the ambulances were usually full.

In the military effects of other classes, disease sometimes greatly influenced battles and campaigns without, however, being a crucial factor in their outcome. This was because both sides were affected in proportion to their numbers and the prior ratio of strength was not materially changed. The battle of Gettysburg would have been on a far larger scale if there had been little sickness in either army during the preceding six months, but the result would probably have been no different. The armies that met at Antietam, at Stone's River, at Chancellorsville, at Chickamauga, and at many other places had been reduced by disease but their relative strength had not been substantially changed.

In still other instances, disease struck one side far harder than the other, yet it played no part in the military result. This was because the stronger force, although it was disproportionately more affected, was able to absorb the damage and yet retain a superiority. An example was General Banks' campaign on Port Hudson in 1863. It appears that the position held by the Confederates was less unhealthy than the nearby areas inhabited by the Union troops who, however, remained more numerous even after heavy losses. Many of these besieging troops were nine-month regiments from New England states that went home shadows of their original strength (38). The Vicksburg campaign from November, 1862 to July, 1863 illustrates this point even better. The enormous morbidity from disease in the Union force, both prior to and after the investment, was tolerable only because the army was larger and a rather high proportion recovered and kept returning to duty. If the Confederate medical department could have found a miraculous cure for dysentery, the outcome might have been different.

In other situations, disease seriously reduced the capability of armies, yet this effect cannot be measured because the army was inactive at the time. Such disease influenced planning and subsequent operations in ways that cannot be expressed. The large attrition in the Army of the Potomac during seven weeks at Harrison's Landing, in the summer of 1862, is an example discussed in Chapter 5. After the Battle of Shiloh, the three Union armies encamped on the field were eroded by sickness, whose magnitude and effects are hidden by the reinforcements that poured in. At the same time, the damage from a large amount of illness in Beauregard's opposing force around Corinth was a factor in his decision not to defend that important railroad center (Chapter 6).

One of the best examples of an effect of this type occurred after the capitulation of Vicksburg. The Confederate force was dispersed, except for the 6,000 to 7,000 sick and wounded left in hospitals (82). From July to October, Grant's army of over 60,000, comprising the major parts of five army corps, gradually broke off small garrison and combat units for various chores in Arkansas, Mississippi, and Tennessee, but the major part camped for a time in the unhealthy triangle between Vicksburg, the bluffs on the Yazoo, and the Big Black River. An increase in disease was expected by the authorities to come in August and September, and they were not disappointed (83). To the dysentery and typhoid fever present before the surrender was added afterward much malaria and a disease (not yellow fever) that caused much jaundice (84). The two divisions of the Ninth corps on loan from Kentucky were reduced to a condition from which, it is said, they never fully recovered (8, 85). Even General Sherman's nine-year-old son died of typhoid fever contracted in his camp (86), although an inspector had graded it a model in sanitation (83). Orders were issued to dispense with music at funerals because it was depressing and with the firing of salutes over the graves because they became so frequent as to sound like an engagement (5). As in many other regiments, in the Thirty-sixth Massachusetts not a man could call himself well (87). Except for a garrison force, the troops departed the area that autumn.

The effects of disease were often added to other adverse factors. In western Virginia in 1861, disease was additive to difficult terrain, poor roads and transportation, unseasonable weather, and insufficient food and clothing to produce military ineffectiveness (Chapter 2). In turn, the bad food and supply situation worsened the serious disease problem. It was impossible to haul the sick to the rear where others could provide care, and their continued presence further embarrassed military operations. A higher infection rate could be tolerated by a military unit if it was able to shed its sick.

Although the effects of losses from disease were additive to other losses, in some respects they were worse. Like the wounded, the sick burdened and weakened the military machine because they required care. This tied up manpower for nursing and other hospital attention, and for the transportation of equipment, supplies, food, and the sick. For each soldier disabled by disease, approximately two more were made militarily ineffective. In contrast, the soldier who was taken prisoner or killed was no longer a drain on the military machine, which had been weakened by only one man.

For these various reasons, it is impossible to name an infection rate that would invariably render a military command ineffective. The diseases and circumstances varied in their ability to handicap military efficiency.

## Some General Consequences of the Disease

When the sick-burdened Confederate army withdrew from Corinth, Mississippi on May 30, 1862, a "Battle of Corinth," potentially of a magnitude of Chickamauga or Gettysburg, failed to materialize, and the campaign went into the history books in a single sentence, if at all. Gory battles provide the headlines, the subject of songs, the boasts of veterans, and the curriculum of war colleges. The prospective battle that is aborted wins little acclaim, few promotions, and scanty laurels. Only the casualty attended with hemorrhage through the skin broken by a weapon is worthy of a medal; the same amount of blood shed from a typhoid ulcer contracted under similar conditions of service is ignored or hidden in shame. Actually, the prolonged disabling disease that is not fatal may be militarily more effective than the fatal wound, by disarming a greater number of military personnel for its care. There was a Battle of Corinth later in 1862. It was fought on October 3rd between Generals Rosecrans and Van Dorn and Price with fewer than one-third of the troops assembled there in May. It is well known to history, although it accomplished only a small fraction of what the bacilli had achieved here in casualties and military results a few months earlier.

To document how severe the effects of disease could be as measured by the number of deaths alone, the twenty Union regiments having the most deaths from disease were collected in Table IV. All had more than 360 deaths, five had more than 500, and two had over 700. Many of these regiments were among the largest; they appear in the table for that reason and not because their percentage of death was the highest. Thus, heavy artillery and cavalry regiments are unduly represented because they were large originally and they

## TABLE IV

Union Regiments Having the Most Deaths from Disease*

| Rank | Regiment | Died of disease, accidents and in prison | Killed or mortality wounded | Total deaths | Date of organiza-tion |
|------|----------|------|------|------|------|
| 1 | 65th U.S. Colored Infantry | 755 | 0 | 755 | Jan. 1864 |
| 2 | 5th U.S. Col. Heavy Arty. | 701 | 128 | 829 | Aug. 1863 |
| 3 | 2nd Tennessee Infantry | 613 | 27 | 640 | Sept. 1861 |
| 4 | 3rd Tennessee Cavalry | 536 | 10 | 546 | Jan. 1863 |
| 5 | 6th Michigan Infantry** | 502 | 78 | 580 | Aug. 1861 |
| 6 | 49th U.S. Colored Infantry | 465 | 62 | 527 | May 1863 |
| 7 | 5th Illinois Cavalry | 419 | 29 | 447 | Sept. 1861 |
| 8 | 32nd Missouri Infantry | 414 | 20 | 434 | Oct. 1862 |
| 9 | 1st Vermont Heavy Arty. | 412 | 164 | 576 | Sept. 1862 |
| 10 | 25th Wisconsin Infantry | 409 | 51 | 460 | Sept. 1862 |
| 11 | 7th Vermont Infantry | 407 | 13 | 420 | Feb. 1862 |
| 12 | 2nd Penn. Heavy Arty.*** | 390 | 226 | 616 | Feb. 1862 |
| 13 | 3rd Michigan Cavalry | 384 | 30 | 414 | Oct. 1861 |
| 14 | 7th New York Heavy Arty. | 378 | 291 | 669 | Aug. 1862 |
| 15 | 12th Michigan Infantry | 375 | 53 | 428 | Feb. 1863 |
| 16 | 2nd Mass. Heavy Arty. | 367 | 15 | 382 | July, 1863 |
| 17 | 3rd U.S. Colored Cavalry | 367 | 37 | 404 | Dec. 1862 |
| 18 | 13th Illinois Cavalry | 364 | 21 | 385 | Feb. 1862 |
| 19 | 56th Illinois Infantry | 362 | 27 | 389 | Feb. 1862 |
| 20 | 6th Tennessee Cavalry | 361 | 35 | 396 | Aug. 1862 |

*Data compiled from Fox's *Regimental Losses* and the *Official Records*.
**Became the First Michigan Heavy Artillery.
***Formed from two regiments consolidated; data are incomplete.

were kept nearly full by constant recruitment, which was easy for them because these services were regarded as offering the most desirable military duty.

The regiment with the most deaths from disease (755) had no combat death, and most of the nineteen others had never been in a major action. Only four had more than a hundred combat deaths, a small figure for such oversize units. Confederate prisons accounted for many of the deaths from disease in some regiments and for unknown numbers in others. It is also noteworthy that the rank of a regiment in this table bears little relation to the date of its organization: Four began their service in 1861, ten in 1862, five in 1863, and one in 1864. The latter, with just over a year of wartime duty, ranked highest. The control of disease did not improve during the war years. The toll from disease in a regiment was sometimes enormous.

What was the soldier's attitude toward disease? In general, conditioned by experiences since infancy, it was one of helpless, stolid, quiet acquiescence which sometimes reflected sorrow, fear, sullenness, or indifference. All home communities also had much sickness, some of it in periodic epidemics. The reaction of the soldier to sickness was, however, different than to wounds. In part this was due to their lack of understanding of disease, to its known inevitability, and to its mysterious, unpredictable origins, advent, and departure. Moreover, disease was not a clean fighter or valorous opponent. One volunteer officer expressed the views of many when he wrote from Harper's Ferry, in November, 1861, where his regiment was beset by sickness (92):

> I hope we shall steadily improve. There is a hopeless desperation chilling one when engaged in a contest with disease. The unseen malaria has such an advantage in the fight. I had rather meet anything for the regiment than the enemy who surprised us in our former camping-ground and who seems hardly yet to have given up beat. . . . A week on a high piece of ground *three miles* from the river would put us all on our feet again. But as long as the morning sun rises only to quicken the fatal exhalations from this pestilential Potomac, and the evening dews fall only to rise again with fever in their breath, the contest is unequal and the victory uncertain.

The rate of attrition from disease was often greater than in a bomber command in World War II, and stress effects sometimes made an appearance. The breaking point was high, however, as these men had been accustomed to seeing much disease since childhood.

From the medical viewpoint it is clear, in retrospect, that a golden opportunity for important discoveries and dramatic advances was missed. The time was not quite ripe. All attention was concentrated on the fierce social and political upheaval rather than on commonplace disease. Medical education was still authoritarian and dogmatic, and it did not stimulate skepticism and inquiry. Military medicine did not welcome criticism and challenge. Therefore the accumulated tremendous epidemiological information was hardly used. Viewed retrospectively, some of the small sharp epidemics seem to point quite clearly to answers if the questions had been asked.

No major discovery emerged on the classification, diagnosis, or treatment of disease, just as no new surgical operation made an appearance. Contagion and infection in disease were recognized but not the role of living microorganisms. Some microbes had been seen under the microscope by Leeuwenhoek and his successors in the seventeenth, eighteenth, and nineteenth centuries. Delafond, in 1853, had transferred anthrax from animal to animal by blood in which the microorganisms were seen. Semmelweis and Holmes had recognized perpetual sepsis as transmitted. Doctor Daniel Leasure, who became an infantry general during the war (2), had written about the relationship of childbed fever and erysipelas and their interchangeable transmission in the same epidemic (93). Only the important third technic—culture methods—was lacking in 1861. At this time, the mind of Pasteur was already generating the chain of ideas that would revolutionize medical power over disease within a few decades.

Today, the accounts of the morbidity and mortality from wounds and, especially, from the diseases are shocking. There is at first a tendency to blame them on incompetence and inefficiency. This view is abetted by some claims to the same effect during and after the war.

If these charges of medical incompetence are correct, the occurrence of about 2,500,000 cases of diarrhea and dysentery in the Union and Confederate armies, and of the other communicable diseases in corresponding relative numbers, would constitute a terrible indictment of the medical officers; also, of their responsible military superiors and commanders in the line, of the two medical departments, of the civilian physicians and the medical organizations scrutinizing the scene but not protesting, of the Federal, Confederate, and State governments, of the civilian populations at home who knew from oral and written communications much about conditions but made no popular outcry, and of the newspapers and weekly periodicals. In fact, if there was blame the culpability would be great and widespread.

The basic and blunt fact, however, is that the knowledge with which to prevent these diseases or effectively to treat them if they occurred was almost completely nonexistent. Nearly all of these infectious diseases and the wound infection developed because of the ignorance of the times and not from incompetence and carelessness. The war literature, official and nonofficial, often attributes camp disease to a failure to enforce the existing sanitary regulations. There was much failure to apply the current information on personal hygiene and camp sanitation, but this failure was not a major factor in causing the diseases that occurred.

The diseases responsible for the bad record are all controllable to-day. The origins of the knowledge making this possible can be traced. Virtually all of it dates after 1865, and most of it came in the present century. With regard to the control of the three major camp diseases, only typhoid vaccination, the purification of all water, milk and other beverages, the elimination of all food handling by persons bearing enteric pathogens, and the destruction of all flies and mosquitoes or their exclusion by screens would have appreciably reduced them in 1865. None of these essential measures were effectively covered by the sanitary regulations of that time. For diseases in which there were "healthy" and only mildly ill, mobile carriers, a general cleaning up and tidying was not very effective in prevention.

For example, the sanitary measures ordered by Surgeon Jonathan Letterman, in July, 1862, to stop a mixed epidemic at Harrison's Landing are discussed in Chapter 5. The situation was serious, as many thousands had been shipped to Northern hospitals and about twenty per cent of those still on the rolls of the Army of the Potomac were sick. He ordered that wells be dug where possible, that fresh vegetables be issued, that food be prepared by companies rather than by squads, that tents be raised daily and struck or moved to new ground weekly, that camps be near but not in woods, that the men have breakfast before marching, that the men bathe once a week, that sinks should be used and six inches of earth be added to them daily, that similar holes be dug for kitchen refuse, and that refuse from stables and dead animals be burned or deeply buried.

The order regarding the tents might be helpful against some of the air-borne diseases but these were not now a problem. It might dislodge a few hidden mosquitoes, but not enough to stop the malaria. It was found impossible to dig deep wells in most regiments, and no arrangements were made bacteriologically to protect them or to sterilize the canteens or other water containers, previously contaminated, before re-using them. Soil added daily to the latrine trenches would reduce fly breeding but there were many other breeding places. Moreover, the addition of soil once a day would still leave diarrheic feces exposed to the flies for many hours every day with resulting contamination of food, water, open wells, mess gear, water containers, etc. Malaria, typhoid fever, and dysentery infections would not be materially influenced by these rules. They would not effectively check the vectors or eliminate the supply of infectious agents. The order did not meet the microbiological problems, either in theory or, as the results showed, in practice, although they were as good as any set of rules issued during that war.

At the same time it must be conceded that even the available correct knowledge was not always fully used. This usually concerned a failure in the humane care of the sick and wounded men even though the deficiency did not influence the outcome. There were failures in personnel, supply, communications, organization, foresight, and improvisation. These factors improved during the war, resulting in more humane if not medically better care. The improvements, however, concerned chiefly the organization and administration of medical supply and patient care rather than in the discovery and application of new medical knowledge. It was merely the old medical knowledge better used. Even this was a great gain. No new drug or combination of drugs was introduced to improve the chances of the patient having dysentery, typhoid fever, malaria, or any other disease.

Although the military medicine practiced was usually as good as the individual doctors were able to give, it sometimes fell below the medical knowledge of the times in a number of respects. For example, better physical examinations at enlistment could have eliminated some of those unfit for soldiering. This screening was often prevented by the various political pressures to fill a regiment regardless of the physical disqualifications. The efficacy of smallpox vaccination was known, but its use was not routine because of short supplies, carelessness, or the fear of spurious reactions. Inadequate isolation and nursing care were often given in the initial epidemics of measles, whooping cough and mumps or in the communicable diseases that struck later. The nursing care in the hospitals was often inadequate, but all nursing at the time was relatively unskilled. An improved field hospital system was not developed until late 1862, and it sometimes broke down under the demands of large battles. No adequate system of first aid on the battlefields to stop hemorrhage promptly and transfer the wounded was ever developed, although great improvements were made. Water is essential for life but little responsibility for providing it, healthy or contaminated, was assumed by commanders; one battle with about 7,000 casualties (Battle of Perryville) developed in part from the competition for the water in the green scummed holes in a drying Kentucky creek. Scurvy was known to result from inadequate diets, but armies developed the disease and a "scorbutic taint" a number of times as well as other accompanying forms of malnutrition then not yet named. As far as the record goes, no colonel or medical or commissary officer was ever punished for the violation of the regulations.

Also, commanders who were physically or mentally medically incompetent even by the standards of that time remained on duty; there was no medical authority to cover the situation. Because the mechanism for returning convalescents from the general hospitals or their homes forward to their units was poor, many sick were retained at the front who would have done better in the rear. Shortages going all the way back to the manufacturer or importer were sometimes felt at the front. Surgeon General Hammond worked hard to relieve obstructions to better service but himself met an immovable object in the secretary of war that ended his good work. This firm obstacle was to him not greater than were many colonels and other officers who controlled, loosely or rigidly and wisely or badly, the medical resources of the regimental surgeons. This regimental surgeon, a major, was the only person in the entire regiment who could not hope ever to receive a promotion as a reward for good service, exceptional valor, unusual competence, or anything else.

## Allegations on the Use of Biological Warfare

Bacterial warfare, active and passive and direct and indirect, was mentioned a number of times during the Civil War. General J. E. Johnston, in rebuttal to criticism of inactivity, claimed that McClellan's army was daily losing a regiment by being kept like frogs in the swamps of the Chickahominy region rather than by being forced back by battle. General John E. Wool, the oldest (78 years in 1861) general officer in the war and a field campaigner since 1812, predicted in July, 1862 that the rebels would try to hold McClellan's army on the Peninsula, where it would be reduced one-half by disease (88). The Twentieth Maine was in isolation for smallpox at the beginning of the Chancellorsville campaign when its commander requested active duty, saying that if they "... couldn't do anything else we could give the rebels the small pox" (89). The proffer of this service was ignored. To Confederate Surgeon General Samuel P. Moore is attributed the allegation that the Yankees drove a Negro with smallpox across the Rappahannock River to spread the infection (90). After an exchange of prisoners at Fort Pillow on the Mississippi in May, 1862, it was found that several of the Confederates were suffering from smallpox. The ensuing correspondence produced no evidence that the act had been deliberate (91). Because of the general availability of vaccine, it is unlikely that smallpox would have been selected as the weapon of choice, or that it would have been very effective in any of these situations. In summary, no evidence is found for the deliberate use of disease as an offensive weapon by either side.

## Introduction to Chapters that Follow

The eight studies that follow were selected because of the documentation available on both the amount and type of disease and on its military effects. They illustrate the effects of various pathogens, usually in combinations, and environments on military units of different sizes and types in diverse seasons and geographical locations.

The first example, the failure of Lee's Army of the Northwest to recover western Virginia in 1861, illustrates the termination without battle of a campaign made ineffective by disease. The principal diseases were measles, diarrhea and dysentery, typhoid fever, and the respiratory infections including pneumonia. Although other adverse factors were present, the *conditio sine qua non* seems to have been uncontrolled infectious disease. If it had not existed, the other deterrents could have been tolerated or overcome.

The second example, the first Union campaign on the South Atlantic coast, illustrates the use of knowledge on disease by the commanders on both sides in their planning, the stoppage of two campaigns by the combined effects of existing disease and the threat of even more, and the death of a needed, aggressive departmental and army commander from yellow fever. Although yellow fever was a specter, dysentery and malaria were the principal aggressors. Disease won this campaign, and its threat subsequently helped to neutralize for nearly three years forces up to a small army in strength.

The winter campaign of 1861-1862 in Eastern Kentucky illustrates the crucial effects of the acute childhood, respiratory, and camp diseases combined. To these were added exceptionally large amounts of the enteric infections after a flood. Of the major pathogens in natural biological warfare, only malaria was absent. Both sides became greatly weakened, but the Union force achieved its objective because of greater tenacity and higher morale from better leadership. Future President James A. Garfield persisted in adversity and won the campaign long after a sensible professional soldier would have given up.

Disease was a decisive factor in three major decisions in the fourth example, the Peninsular campaign. It deprived McClellan of the number of troops he claimed on June 28th he needed to drive into Richmond; at Harrison's Landing in July and August it deprived him of the number he thought necessary to resume his operations against Richmond; and in August the threat of high autumnal disease rates was a factor in his orders to depart the Peninsula, ending the campaign. The diseases were dysentery, typhoid fever, and, later, malaria. This was the most important victory for disease except, possibly, for the aftermath at Corinth.

The attrition of disease was an important factor in the withdrawal of Beauregard from Corinth without giving battle in May, 1862. The large sick list in Halleck's army group and the threat of even more disease was given by him as a reason for not continuing the campaign deeper into Mississippi in July. Consequently one of the finest and largest armies assembled was fragmented into inefficient units, and the course of the war was greatly changed. It is uncertain whether Halleck feared Beauregard, but it is certain that he feared Disease.

The sixth example concerns the first campaign for Vicksburg in 1862. It resulted in a Union repulse without any attack by the army because the regiments had been made ineffective by malaria. Disease won this campaign for the Confederates even though they also suffered much from sickness.

The Confederate attempt to recapture Baton Rouge, in 1862, failed because the assigned troops had been reduced by half within a few days by epidemic disease, chiefly malaria. The military leaders of both sides were especially obtuse with respect to disease in this campaign. Here Disease won for the National force, aided by new breech loading rifles in one regiment.

In the last example, the Department of Arkansas during the last two years of the war, large Union and Confederate forces confronted each other but neither gained any important military advantage. The troops were steadily eroded away despite sizeable reinforcements. One-half to two-thirds of the soldiers were usually absent, chiefly from sickness. This was one of the few departments in which malaria predominated. With a monthly strength of only about 15,000 present for duty, the total medical diagnoses in twenty-four months totalled 178,194. The reduction of one regiment in a few weeks from 937 strong men to 79 illustrates natural disease at its most impressive form in warfare a century ago.

## References*

1. ASHBURN, P. M.: *A History of the Medical Department of the United States Army.* Boston and New York, Houghton Mifflin Co., 1929, 448 p.
2. STEINER, P. E.: *Physician-Generals in the Civil War: A Study in Nineteenth Mid-Century American Medicine.* Springfield, Charles C Thomas, 1966, 194 p.
3. KAMM, S. R.: *The Civil War Career of Thomas A. Scott.* Philadelphia, Univ. of Penn. Press, 1940, 208 p.
4. MACFARLANE, C.: *Reminiscences of an Army Surgeon, 1861-1865.* Oswego, Lake City Print Shop, 1912, 82 p.
5. WRIGHT, H. H.: *A History of the Sixth Iowa Infantry.* Iowa City, State Historical Society of Iowa, 1923, 539 p.
6. SCOTT, W.: *O.R., 51*: Part 1, 369-370.
7. *Med. and Surg. Hist.,* Vol. 1, Part 1.
8. COX, J. D.: *Military Reminiscences of the Civil War.* New York, Charles Scribner's Sons, 2 vols., 1900.
9. GORDON, J. B.: *Reminiscences of the Civil War.* New York, Charles Scribner's Sons, 1904.

---

*Throughout all references in this book, *O.R.* refers to the *War of the Rebellion: A Compilation of the Official Records of the Union and Confederate Armies,* Washington, Government Printing Office, 1880-1902, published in four series with 69 volumes composed of 128 parts (*i.e.* separate books). Unless otherwise specified, the reference is to Series I.

*Med. and Surg. Hist.* refers to *Medical and Surgical History of the War of the Rebellion* (1861-1865), prepared under the direction of the surgeon general, U. S. Army. Washington, Government Printing Office, 1875-1888, published in three volumes each of two parts (*i. e.* six books).

10. BLAKE, H. N.: *Three Years in the Army of the Potomac.* Boston, Lee & Shepard, 1865, 319 p.

11. GORDON, S. C.: *War Papers, Vol. 1.* Commandery of the State of Maine, Military Order of the Loyal Legion, Portland, Thurston Print, 1898, 352 p.

12. LEE, R. E.: *O.R., 19*: Part 2, 657.

13. STEVENSON, T, M.: *History of the 78th Regiment O.V.V.I.* Zanesville, Hugh Dunne, 1865, 349 p.

14. LOVELL, M.: *O.R., 6*:817.

15. BROWN, B.: Personal experiences in observing the results of good and bad sanitation in the Confederate States Army. *Va. Med. Monthly, 20*:589, 1893-4.

16. EVE, P. F.: Answers to certain questions . . *Nashville Med. and Surg. Jour.* (N.S.), *1*:12-32; 162-179, 1866.

17. HAND, D. W.: *Med. and Surg. Hist.,* Vol. I, Part I, Appendix p. 238.

18. HAND, D. W.: *Glimpses of the Nation's Struggle,* Vol. 1. Minnesota Commandery of the Military Order of the Loyal Legion, St. Paul, St. Paul Book and Stationery Co., 1887, p. 305.

19. *Med. and Surg. Hist.,* Vol. I, Part III, 638.

20. *O.R., 19*: Part 2, 679, 686, and *51*: Part 2, 636.

21. WILSON, E. A.: *Memoirs of the War.* Cleveland, W.M. Bayne Printing Co., 1893, 435 p.

22. WALLACE, R.: United States Hospitals at Nashville. *Cincinnati Lancet and Observer, 7*:587, 1864.

23. FORD, W. C.: *A Cycle of Adams Letters, 1861-1865.* Boston and New York, Houghton, Mifflin & Co., 1920, Vol. 1, 171, 247 and Vol. 2, 78-79.

24. CROWNINSHIELD, B. W.: *A History of the First Regiment of Massachusetts Cavalry Volunteers.* Boston and New York, Houghton, Mifflin Co., 1891, 61, 101.

25. THOMAS, G.: *O.R., 45*: part 2, 71.

26. *Med. and Surg. Hist.,* Vol. I, Part I, Appendix.

27. BOWEN, J. R.: *Regimental History of the First New York Dragoons.* Published by the author, 1900, 464 p.

28. WALKER, T. H.: *Chicago Med. Jour., 5*:478, 1862.

29. MERRILL, S.: Letters from a Civil War Officer. *Miss. Valley Hist. Rev., 14*:510, 1927-8.

30. *Med. and Surg. Hist.,* Vol. I, Part II, 2, 6.

31. SUMMERS, J. E.: *Med. and Surg. Hist.,* Vol. I, Part II, 95.

32. *Med. and Surg. Hist.,* Vol. I, Part II, 26-31.

33. HABERSHAM, S. E.: *Observations upon the Statistics of Chimborazo Hospital.* Nashville, University Book & Job Office, 1866, 15 p.

34. BRYANT, E. E.: *History of the Third Regiment of Wisconsin Veteran Volunteer Infantry.* Madison, Veteran Assoc., 1891, 445 p.

35. JARVIS, E.: *Boston Med. and Surg. Jour., 67*:381, 1862.

36. GAUGHAN, T. J.: *Letters of a Confederate Surgeon, 1861-1865.* Camden, Ark., Hurley Co., Inc., 1960, 276 p.

37. *Med. and Surg. Hist.,* Vol. I, Part III, 966.

38. M.C.B. Special Relief in the Home Field. *Sanitary Reporter, 1*:57-58, Sept. 1, 1863.

39. PARK, W. H.: Typhoid Bacilla Carriers. *J.A.M.A., 51*:981, 1908.

40. ELY, J. F.: *War Sketches and Incidents.* Iowa Commandery of the Military Order of the Loyal Legion, Des Moines, P. C. Kenyon, Vol. 1, 1893, 44.

41. *Med. and Surg. Hist.,* Vol. I, Part III, 365.

42. NEWELL, J. K.: *"Ours." Annals of the 10th Regiment, Massachusetts Volunteers, in the Rebellion.* Springfield, C. A. Nichols & Co., 1875, 609 p.

43. FLINT, A. (Ed.): *Contributions Relating to the Causation and Prevention of Disease.* New York, U. S. Sanitary Commission, 1867, 667 p.

44. BRAMLETT, T. E.: *O.R., 7*:513.

45. WARREN, J. H.: *Med. and Surg. Hist.,* Vol. I, Part III, 486.

46. WRAY, W. J.: *History of the Twenty Third Pennsylvania Volunteer Infantry.* (No city: No publisher, no date), 432 p.

47. VAILL, T. F.: *History of the Second Connecticut Heavy Artillery.* Winsted, Conn., Winsted Printing Co., 1868, 366 p.

48. Editorial. *Amer. Med. Times, 5*:65, 1862.

49. STEINER, P. E.: Medical-Military Studies on the Civil War. III. Major General David Bell Birney, U.S.V. *Military Medicine, 130*:606, 1965.

50. JOHNSTON, J. E.: *Narrative of Military Operations.* New York, D. Appleton & Co., 1874, 16, 33.

51. STOUT, S. H.: *Confederate Military History.* Atlanta, Confed. Publ. Co., Vol. 8, 1899, 256.

52. JOHNSON, R. W.: *A Soldier's Reminiscences in Peace and War.* Philadelphia, J. B. Lippincott Co., 1886, 428 p.

53. ANGELL, J. W.: *Med. and Surg. Hist.,* Vol. I, Part II, 97.

54. HILL, J. A.: *The Story of One Regiment.* New York, J. J. Little & Co., 1896, 435 p.

55. DEFOREST, J. W.: *A Volunteer's Adventures.* New Haven, Yale. Univ. Press, 1946, 237 p.

56. EDDY, R.: History of the Sixtieth Regiment New York State Volunteers, Philadelphia, By the author, 1864, 360 p.

57. MCPARLIN, T. A.: *Med. and Surg. Hist.,* Vol. I, Part I, Appendix, 112, 119.

58. ALCORN, J. L.: *O.R., 4*:463.

59. DUFF, J.: *O.R., 34*: Part 2, 917.

60. CUNNINGHAM, J. L.: *Three Years with the Adirondack Regiment.* Norwood, Mass. For private circulation, 1920, 286 p.

61. MORTON, O. P.: *O.R., 10*: Part 2, 630.

62. LITTLE, H. F. W.: *The Seventh Regiment New Hampshire Volunteers in the War of the Rebellion.* Concord, I. C. Evans, 1896, 567 p.

63. BRIGGS, W. D. B.: *Civil War Surgeon in a Colored Regiment.* Berkeley, No Publisher, 1960, 166 p.
64. O'FERRALD, J. W.: *O.R.,* 4:454.
65. LESTER, C. E.: *The Light and Dark of the Rebellion.* Philadelphia, Geo. W. Childs, 1863, 303 p.
66. PENDLETON, W. N.: *O.R.,* 42: Part 2, 1222.
67. WOODS, J. T.: *Services of the Ninety-Sixth Ohio Volunteers.* Toledo, Blade Printing & Paper Co., 1874, 247 p.
68. THRALL, S. B.: An Iowa doctor in blue. *Iowa Jour. Hist.,* 58:97-188, 1960.
69. PRICE, I.: *History of the Ninety-Seventh Regiment Pennsylvania Volunteer Infantry.* Philadelphia, By the author, 1875, 608 p.
70. BUTLER, B. F.: *Private and Official Correspondence of Gen. Benjamin F. Butler.* (No city), Privately issued, 1917, Vol. V, 89.
71. LIDDELL, S. J. R.: *Southern Bivouac,* 4:415, 1885.
72. WALKER, L.P.: *O.R.,* 4:475.
73. TILGMAN, L.: *O.R.,* 4:485, 523.
74. HINDMAN, T. C.: *O.R.,* 4:505.
75. JOHNSTON, A. S.: *O.R.,* 4:528.
76. JOHNSTON, A.S.: *O.R.,* 7:813.
77. CHURCHWELL, W. M.: *O.R.,* 4:462.
78. SMITH, E. K.: *O.R.,* 10: Part 2, 308, 556.
79. BLAKE, E. D.: *O.R.,* 8:136.
80. COOPER, G. E.: *Med. and Surg. Hist.,* Vol. I, Part I, Appendix p. 301 *et seq.*
81. MOORE, J.: *Med. and Surg. Hist.,* Vol. I, Part I, Appendix, 320.
82. KITTOE, E. J.: The Rebel sick and wounded at Vicksburg. *Sanitary Reporter,* 1:52, 1863.
83. FITHIAN, W.: Dr. Fithian's Report. *Sanitary Reporter,* 1:59, 75, 1863.
84. HOWARD, R. L.: *History of the 124th Regiment Illinois Infantry Volunteers.* Springfield, H. W. Rokker, 1880, 519 p.
85. WOODBURY, A.: *Major General Ambrose E. Burnside and the Ninth Army Corps.* Providence, Sidney S. Rider & Bro., 1867, 554 p.
86. SHERMAN, W. T.: *Memoirs of Gen. W. T. Sherman.* Chicago, Charles L. Webster & Co., 4th ed., two volumes in one, 1891.
87. SWORDS, H. L.: My campaigning with the Army of the Tennessee. *War Sketches and Incidents,* Iowa Commandery of the Military Order of the Loyal Legion, Des Moines, P. C. Kenyon, Vol. 1, 1893, 400 p.
88. WOOL, J. E.: *O.R.,* 11: Part 3, 330.
89. CHAMBERLAIN, J. L.: *In Memoriam.* Commandery of the State of Maine, Military Order of the Loyal Legion, Circular No. 5, Series of 1914, 14 p.
90. KEAN, R. G. H.: *Inside the Confederate Government.* New York, Oxford Univ. Press, 1957, 241 p.
91. *O.R.,* Series II, 3:556, 572, 575.

92. DWIGHT, W.: *Life and Letters of Wilder Dwight.* Boston, Ticknor & Fields, 1868, 349 p.

93. LEASURE, D.: The erysipelatous disease of lying-in women. *Amer. Jour. Med. Sci., 31*:45, 1856.

# II

## The Confederate Campaign for Western Virginia in 1861

IN THE POLITICAL DIVISION of 1861, the western counties of Virginia refused to secede. A military struggle for the area ensued in which epidemic diseases played an important role by checking the attempt of General Robert E. Lee to recover jurisdiction over the area. His campaign was aborted without a battle, giving the North a sizeable political, military, and psychological victory. A combination of four unchecked, natural contagious diseases, summating their effects to other factors, produced this result. This campaign, then, represents an example in which disease substantially influenced the outcome of an important military effort and, thus, the course of history.

### Military and Political Problems

The contested area extended from the main Appalachian chain in Virginia to the Ohio River. Here wooded mountains and hills alternated with valleys inhabited by a substantial agricultural population. The area had been economically unsuited for slavery, growing no cotton or sugar cane and little tobacco. Most of the valleys, unfortunately, ran across the direction of the main communications. Their streams flowed either south to the Kanawha or north to the Potomac or the Monongahela. For military operations the unfavorable terrain, the unpredictable weather, the unreliable information, the poor roads and communications, the necessity of importing all supplies and much of the food, and the political division of the population, some of it hostile to each side, were factors recognized in advance so that at least some appropriate measures could be taken. The constant threat of epidemic disease was known to all experienced campaigners, but its potential magnitude in raw troops having green commanders in an area with few medical facilities but unusual problems in field sanitation was either underestimated or ignored. The result was disaster. Both sides suffered severely, but the disability peaked in the Confederate force during its main offensive—a most inopportune time—so that the harmful consequences were greater for them than for the National army.

At stake in or near the area were some thousands of potential army recruits, some minerals including salt in southern Virginia, control of the important railroad line along its northern border, and two railroads, the Virginia Central and the Virginia and Tennessee, both in the southern part of the state. Also to be considered were the political prestige and the morale-building effects of a great victory early in the war. The objectives, therefore, were both political and military on each side. The campaigns here and for Missouri were the first to begin in April and May, and they were similar in being contests to prevent secession.

In this area three main lines of military activity quickly developed (1). The Baltimore and Ohio railroad, an important link between Washington and the west, was quickly occupied by Union troops and subsequently held during most of the war, although it was temporarily severed a number of times, usually at points farther east. In a second theater, Federal and Confederate troops collided on the Kanawha River about fifty miles above Charleston. This was on the line to Staunton. The river was navigable during high water by sizeable boats nearly to this point. Here the Confederate generals John B. Floyd and Henry A. Wise sparred for some months from July, 1861 with a force under Generals William S. Rosecrans and Jacob D. Cox. The principal named military engagements took place at Carnifex Ferry on September 10th and at Cheat Mountain on September 12 and 13, 1861. They resulted in a Confederate repulse caused, in part, by the inability of the two chieftains to cooperate with each other or with General Lee, their superior, and in part by disease. Military activity continued on the Kanawha, however, intermittently as late as 1864.

## The Collapse of the Crucial Campaign

The third and crucial combat theater developed between the

railroad and the river along the general line of the highway from Staunton to Parkersburg. On this difficult front of operations, General McClellan moved quickly from the railroad at Grafton with three-month Ohio and Indiana regiments. Equally promptly Virginian and a few Confederate troops moved forward from the east under General Robert S. Garnett. After small actions in May and June, they met again at Rich Mountain on July 11th, at Beverly on the 12th, and at Carrick's Ford on the 13th. Here Garnett was killed and his nearly 5,000 men captured or disorganized (2, 3, 4). General McClellan was rewarded by a call to Washington after the Bull Run disaster late in July. He was succeeded in western Virginia by Rosecrans. The reinforced Confederate troops were reorganized by General William W. Loring, and Lee was assigned by Richmond to overall direction in western Virginia. He soon organized the Army of the Northwest under Loring and the Army of the Kanawha under Floyd (5, 6). He remained with Loring through September and then moved down to the Kanawha.

Prompt and loyal cooperation failed to follow (7). Lee did not yet have the great prestige or the ability to manage difficult lieutenants that helped him two years later. Floyd and Wise were flambuoyant politicians of national renown, and Whiting ("Old Blizzard") was an old one-armed dragoon from the frontier who, having outranked Lee in Mexico, now firmly defended his prerogatives even as they disappeared. Lee's position as the superior in the area was needlessly made difficult because the nature of his command was not shown by the records (8). This appears to have been one of Jefferson Davis' earliest important equivocations.

After the death of General Garnett, this area had become the responsibility of the Confederacy rather than of Virginia, and regiments were sent in from Tennessee, Georgia, North Carolina, and Arkansas. General Loring had as his brigade commanders Generals H. R. Jackson, S. R. Anderson, D. S. Donelson, and Colonels William Gilham, William A. Taliaferro, and J. S. Burks. He concentrated in the general area of Monterey and Huntersville in July. Here Lee joined him on August 3rd. A cold rain that began on July 22nd continued for twenty successive days and intermittently for nearly six weeks. Loring not taking the initiative, Lee carried out his own reconnaissance and planned an attack for September 12th. Preliminary troop movements requiring the cooperation of Loring and Jackson were to begin on the 9th (2). The Union opponent now was General J. J. Reynolds, Rosecrans having gone to the line of the Kanawha where the threat appeared greater.

The juncture of Lee's columns did not materialize as planned, and after probing disclosed an alert enemy, Lee called off the attack. Not only were the Union troops ready, but the Confederates were cold and hungry, the officers resistant, and morale low. The planned offensive was an utter fiasco. The demoralized army retreated to Valley Mountain and other camps well to the rear.

Lee attributed the failure to the rain and to the will of God (2). Freeman added to these an alert enemy, tangled terrain, the exhaustion of supplies, and an excessively long and difficult line of communications. Railhead was far back on the Virginia Central railroad. Lee was confirmed as a full general on August 31st, and a month later he departed for the Kanawha. His first campaign and battle had ended ingloriously, and the Kanawha effort also fizzled out later. In the meantime, the Richmond papers had reported great victories. After three months of frustration, Lee was assigned to South Carolina early in November. Loring wintered in the mountains further east. The Confederate western regiments were sent home after the fall of Fort Donelson in February. For practical purposes the border from 1861 ran along the main Allegheny chain. Neither Lee nor Loring wrote any official report.

## The Role of Epidemic Diseases

Communicable diseases helped greatly to defeat the Army of the Northwest. In his approximately nineteen regiments, Loring had about 15,000 men, a number greater than Reynold's force. Some of the regiments were very new and none were more than a few months old. But nearly half of these men became sick at the same time. Not only were they unavaible for combat but they required nursing care, consumed badly needed food, helped to break down the supply lines, clogged the rear, and disorganized their units by their absence. The chief diseases were measles, diarrhea and dysentery and, later, typhoid fever and pneumonia. Malaria was also present in some regiments, probably brought with them from farther south. Diphtheria, rheumatism, and other diseases were also troublesome at times in some units.

General Lee learned that his army was sick when he arrived. He wrote to Mrs. Lee on August 4th (9):

> The soldiers everywhere are sick. The measles are prevalent through-out the whole army, and you know that disease leaves unpleasant results, attacks on the lungs, typhoid, etc., especially in camp, where accommo-dations for the sick are poor.

Chaplain Quintard of the First Tennessee, a former physician, joined his regiment on August 23rd at Valley Mountain, Virginia and found much sickness (10). General Loring's chief of artillery and inspector general wrote that nearly one-third of the army was rendered *hors de combat* by sickness within a few weeks in August (11); all of the camp diseases were highly prevalent. Colonel Walter Taylor, who spent four years with Lee, later said that the troops were sorely afflicted with measles and a "malignant type of fever, which prostrated hundreds of each command; and being entirely destitute of proper food and other supplies" (4). At no time thereafter did he see conditions so bad. One North Carolina regiment of 1,000 men was reduced to one-third this size before it came under fire, and one-half of the army was ineffective. One regiment had only 200 able for duty.

In 1861, measles promptly erupted in most regiments in their first camps. In western Virginia all of the regiments were relatively new, and many of them brought this disease with them. The Sixteenth Tennessee had also malaria and typhoid fever, and it left a trail of sick men wherever it moved (12). The First Tennessee had developed measles in camp and to it typhoid was added in Virginia so that "... we filled the hotels at Warm Springs" (13). They ran short of army rations but ate local cattle and blackberries; nevertheless, they were in a "sad plight" from hunger and bare feet. Colonel Robert Hatton's Seventh Tennessee had mumps and measles in camp and dribbled off many cases en route to Virginia (14). Still, by August 12th there was much sickness: "It is caused by excessive, continued rains, flooding our camp, wetting the men and everything in their tents. Another cause is, they are fed almost exclusively on fresh beef, and that with not half enough salt." Far more important, by August 23rd their camp site was, he said, ". . . like a Tennessee hog pen." In November, over 5,000 were still sick in the hospitals of the rear. Over the period of the entire campaign, from June to October, nearly every man must have been sick at least once, but all-inclusive figures are not available.

Regarding the sickness in the Sixteenth North Carolina, ". . . its horrors have never been half told" (15). Their surgeon and assistant surgeon having both been disabled by sickness, two privates in the ranks, both physicians, were detailed for medical service. In January, 1862, the commanders of two brigades and nine regiments in the Army of the Northwest wrote to General Loring about the past and present suffering (16) :

> It is unnecessary to detail to you, who participated in it all, the service performed by the Army of the Northwest during the last eight months. The unwritten (it will never be truly written) history of that remarkable campaign would show, if truly portrayed, a degree of severity, of hardship, of toil, of exposure and suffering that finds no parallel in the prosecution of the present war, if indeed it is equalled in any war.

The situation was bad and one repercussion was the appointment of a special committee of the Confederate congress to investigate the medical department (17). Their report, dated January 29, 1862, found the situation in western Virginia especially bad. The climate was wet, cold and changeable, the transportation difficult, tents insufficient, and food inadequate. There were no hospitals except buildings taken over and converted. During retreats transportation for the sick was inadequate and the mortality great.

General Lee realized that the medical factor was far greater than he had previously conceded when he wrote to his wife on September 1 (9) :

> We have a great deal of sickness among the soldiers, and now those on the sick-list would form an army. The measles is still among them, though I hope it is dying out. But it is a disease which though light in childhood is severe in manhood, and prepares the system for other attacks. The constant rains, with no shelter but tents, have aggravated it. All these drawbacks, with impassible roads, have paralyzed our efforts.

Here is recognition that intercurrent disease had been an important factor in stopping his effort to regain central western Virginia. His offensive a few days later failed from intrinsic causes, namely, too many sick soldiers. There was no reduction in the sick lists between September 1st, when he wrote, and September 13th, when his campaign in the center was abandoned.

The health of the opposing Federal force was also bad, but this was not a factor in determining the outcome of the campaign as the Confederates from their own loss of strength and organization had to retreat without a test of arms.

During McClellan's campaign in June and July, the principal disorders, according to his medical director (18), were diarrhea, dysentery, intermittent fever, and rheumatism. The Eighth Ohio experienced an exceptionally virulent measles at Camp Dennison and a "low type of fever," called by the soldiers the "disease of Camp Maggotty Hollow," in July and August in Virginia (19). This disease was probably typhoid fever. At one time, 300 men were in the camp hospital when their surgeon was absent sick. Their plight was so bad on August 18th that another regiment had to be substituted when they were called upon for military duty. The men of the Sixth Ohio suffered severely from bowel disorders (20). At the time of General Lee's advance in August, the eight opposing Union regiments and some smaller units under General J. J. Reynolds had been reduced to about 4,000 effectives by sickness (21). Dysentery and other diseases prevailed (21b). They were in no condition to stop a vigorous thrust.

The reported cases of disease in the entire Federal Department of Western Virginia for the four months of July-October, 1861, numbered 20,279, with 150 deaths (22). The mean strength for the entire department ranged from 10,377 in August to 25,047 in September, but only part of these soldiers confronted Lee. The most common diseases were acute and chronic dysentery and diarrhea, malaria, typhoid fever, acute and chronic rheumatism, and measles. The peak of the measles epidemic had been passed by this time. The respiratory infections increased in the cold autumn months. It is of interest that a large outbreak of epidemic jaundice followed about thirty to sixty days behind the typhoid curve.

Surgeons R. R. McMeens of the Third Ohio and R. N. Barr of

the Thirty-sixth Ohio regiments left vivid accounts of the medical situation. McMeens (23) had to deal with outbreaks of severe and protracted rubeola, parotitis, pneumonia, and diarrhea. Most of the cases were treated in an open barn on bunks of straw; the diet was meager. For the measles he relied on Eberle's mixture of muriate of ammonia as an expectorant and on diaphoretic ptisans. The pneumonia, some of it of the "typhoid type," he combatted with veratrum viride and by blistering; also, as needed, calomel, opium and ipecac, quinine and spirits nit. dulc. or Doveri. In "inflammatory cases," he applied the lancet with decided benefit. For the after-treatment he administered a decoction of senega. For the diarrheas and dysenteries, mostly "catarrhal" in type, he found the sulphate of magnesia and tart. antimony of Tripler best. Typhoid remittent and intermittent fevers prevailed in September, October, and November. In the two latter months alone, the regiment had forty cases of typhoid, which he treated with Hope's mixture and emulsion of turpentine. The first long march in the mountains in June had revealed the disabilities not observed at enlistment; these included hernias, deformity from old fractures, cicatrices from wounds, epilepsy, and general debility.

Surgeon Barr's experiences with the Thirty-sixth Ohio were even more dramatic (24). On a long march in the hills, a number of men developed "hernia inguinalis," from which two died. In the four months from September to December, 1861, the regiment had 1,002 on the sick list, of whom twenty-seven died. This figure included only forty-nine wounds and injuries. Thirty-one were diagnosed as dysentery, 110 as diarrhea, 27 as diphtheria, 143 as catarrhus, 7 as phthisis pulmonalis, 11 as typhoid pneumonia, 109 as rubeola, and 3 as erysipelas. The largest group, 344 cases, included all forms of "idiopathic camp fever" of which 233 were febris typhoides, 49 intermittens, 31 continua, 18 typhus, 11 remittens, and 2 febris congestiva. Surgeon Barr found quinine and other antiperiodics ineffective. In the fever cases, he administered a mild laxative consisting of gr. IV to V of calomel with about half that much ipecacuanha followed in four to five hours by castor oil and turpentine. Then he gave camphor and opium, and later a tonic. He wrote a fine clinical description of his main troublesome "camp fever." His colonel was cooperative, the campsite was cleaned up, and good food obtained, but the location was unhealthy so that by December 1st, the average daily sick list was 240. As prophylaxis he finally issued two ounces of whiskey daily to those on duty and to the nurses, "to keep them nursing." Surgeon Barr was promoted to a less stressful position in 1864, as the Surgeon General of the State of Ohio.

A number of regimental historians were not impressed by disease, failing even to mention it (25, 26, 27, 28, 29), although from the overall statistics and the official records it is known that these regiments did not escape. This evasion was in keeping with the times, and it reflects not callousness to suffering but familiarity with the commonness and the inevitability of disease and the acceptance of this fact. Lieutenant Colonel R. B. Hayes (later President) was with the Twenty-third Ohio through this campaign, but not until October 3rd did he first mention sickness in his diary or home letters, although they had already lost nearly 150 men (30).

## Reasons for the Epidemics in This Theater

Can reasons be recognized to explain the exceptional effectiveness of illness in stopping this campaign? The severe effects resulted both from the large amount of disease and the breakdown in medical care. In retrospect seven factors appear to have converged, summating their effects to produce this result. The chief diseases were measles, diarrhea and dysentery, typhoid fever, pneumonia, and, in some regiments, malaria. The responsible factors were as follows:

1. All regiments were new.
2. Nearly all regiments were rural in origin.
3. The weather was exceptionally wet and cold.
4. Camp sanitation was unusually bad in some regiments (in a microbiological sense).
5. Hospital facilities, segregation, and medical supply were bad.
6. Many colonels and surgeons lacked experience in even the field sanitation of that day.
7. The terrain was peculiarly and exceptionally unfavorable for good camp sanitation.

These new regiments composed of young, rural recruits developed much measles simultaneously. The complications and sequels in the respiratory tract were exceptionally severe and numerous because of the unseasonable wet and cold weather, the poor accommodations for the sick, the inadequate nursing, and the bad food. Moreover, the measles was made more serious by concurrent upper respiratory tract infections and other debilitating diseases, both common under the epidemiological conditions that existed here. The entire Department of Western Virginia (Union) reported only 1,101 cases of measles during the six-month period of July through December, 1861 (22). The corresponding Confederate figures have not been found, but they were probably far larger. Never again did measles so critically harm armies because after 1861 their regiments were not all simultaneously new.

In western Virginia, as in most places, diarrhea and dysentery soon made an appearance in most regiments. The simple efficacy of sterilizing by heat or chemicals of things destined to ingestion, or of avoidance by adequate sanitary measures were unknown. In this area camp sanitation was unusually poor in some regiments, and there was flooding of campsites. The hilly terrain favored the rapid drainage of surface water from camps into water supplies at lower levels. Surgeon Brown in 1894 described the fecal contamination by run-off of gushing, clear, sweet water as the major cause of the disaster of 1861 (31). Also the soldiers foraged and ate food under unsanitary conditions many times. Most of the regimental surgeons and many of the colonels were inexperienced in field sanitation in 1861. Some of them had served in Mexico, where the problem of camp disease had also not been solved. With a large susceptible population, a plentiful supply of virulent microbes, means for their contamination of food and water, and ignorance of their presence and importance, it is not surprising that the enteritides should have flourished. In fact, things could hardly have been better for them.

Typhoid fever in the field was disseminated by many of the same methods as dysentery. In western Virginia its distribution by regiments was spotty, many escaping for awhile. Consequently, its influence on the August-September campaign was less; many cases came after that time. The reported number of Union cases in the six-month period of July-December was 2,089, but the peak (755 cases) came only in November (22). This figure is probably inaccurate as it included only 147 deaths; many of the serious cases were probably reported in the categories of their complications. The occurrence of the decubitus ulcers and suppurative parotitis in typhoid patients shows that the treatment was not ideal (24).

Pneumonia was common in western Virginia both as a primary disease and as secondary in others, especially in rubeola and typhoid fever. Except for the smallpox cases, no attempt was made in the field hospitals to separate the wounded or the different infectious diseases from each other. Under such conditions the aerogenous respiratory tract infections flourished, as the debilitated were especially susceptible and in the cold months ventilation was likely to be poor and overcrowding common. Good nursing was lifesaving more often in pneumonia than in most diseases, but expert care seems to have been exceptional here. In the malnourished and in cold, wet weather, sore throats and colds could progress to bronchitis and pneumonia. The number of pneumonias in the campaign is unknown, as this term was not used in the official Union compilations. The cases of pneumonia were classified under common continued fever, inflammation of the lungs and pleura, acute and chronic bronchitis, catarrh, and in other categories.

Malaria was a problem in some Confederate and Union regiments. It seems that much if not most of it was brought with them, and conditions were unfavorable for a major epidemic. The cold weather and the altitude must have suppressed the size of the mosquito population that summer. The peak prevalence of malaria usually came in September, but in western Virginia ice formed already in one camp in the night of August 14-15 (2). The leaves changed color early that summer and frost was seen in another camp in October (21b). Despite the mosquito suppressing factors malaria disabled many soldiers. In the entire Department of Western Virginia (Union), 2,569 cases of intermittent fever (quotidian, tertian, quartan, and congestive) were reported in the six months from July to December (22). In addition, some of the 2,026 reported as remittent fever may have been malaria. Corresponding data from the Southern army are not available but a few regimental accounts describe the disease as serious.

Rheumatism was described in many reports as common; while not communicable and rarely the cause of death, it helped to embarass military operations. At that time, the serious rheumatic fever was

still included in this category. In the entire Department of Western
Virginia (Union) 969 acute and 687 chronic rheumatisms were
reported for the six months of July through December (22). The
occurrence of so many cases during the summer months shows the
harshness of the life here. No doubt some had existed prior to enlistment and others were spurious, as chronic rheumatism was a favorite
claim by malingerers. Nevertheless this was an important disease in
the Union army and, no doubt, also among the Confederates.

Little information is available on the health in Loring's regiments
after the collapse of the offensive in September.

In 1861, fanciful causes were often given for these diseases. Thus
General Thomas A. Morris wrote McClellan that the prevailing
diarrhea was caused by the diet solely of fresh beef without bread
or salt (32). Surgeon J. J. B. Wright, McClellan's medical director,
attributed the diseases to inexperienced officers who did not know
how to care for raw troops (18). One officer in July wrote that "The
sickly months are now on us" (21b), correctly recognizing a seasonal
factor without understanding its operation. One surgeon conceded
that camp hygiene was more important than surgery, but his regiment
suffered greatly nevertheless (24). Colonel Taylor of Lee's staff
attributed both the measles and the camp fever to the excessive rains.
Lee himself wrote home about the sickness that "They bring it in
themselves by not doing what they are told. They are worse than
children, for the latter can be forced. . . ." (9). The surgeon of the
Forty-sixth Virginia blamed the measles ". . . to exposure and fatigue
incident to rapid and forced marches" (33). Some of these views contain a fragment of the truth but not its essentials, and corrective
measures could not be taken.

Long after the war a former Confederate surgeon wrote from
hindsight and the newer knowledge of bacteriology about this experience (31). This part of Virginia had been considered healthy because
of high altitude, perfect drainage, and its clear spring water. Nevertheless, the army became "desolated" by typhoid fever, septic dysentery,
and pneumonia. The cause of the epidemics was found to be purely
"excremental" in character, the copious rains washing the excreta,
deposited on the surface, into the springs and fountains. Note that

the method of transmission of pneumonia was not yet understood when
this was written in 1893.

It is probable that the medical services failed fully to use even the
knowledge then available. Some of the regiments lacked medical
officers because of sickness, ambulances, field-hospital equipment,
medical stores, and ordinary shelter and food. The failure to detect
and discharge even men with hernias is hard to understand. The
ignorance about health matters of some of the commanders, who often
were virtual dictators over their commands including the medical
officer, was abysmal. One colonel, whose regiment was in bad health,
wrote to his wife on November 7, 1861 (14):

> You know my horror of medicine. . . . Do not, on any account, permit
> my boy, Reilly, to be dosed by a doctor. If he is, the chances are all
> against his life—against his being any account, if he is not *killed*.

This son lived in malarious country. Was he to be deprived of quinine
if he developed chills and fever? This was the same colonel who had
described his campsite as resembling a hog pen. His medical ignorance
was not exceptional, and it must have handicapped his surgeon.

## Aftermath

Coming so early in the war, the ultimate repercussions from this
campaign were complex and great. Military activity practically stopped
in western Virginia, late in 1861, as the weather became worse and
disease continued its steady attrition . Union forces held the country,
but small scale guerilla activity occasionally erupted. From the area
Generals John Fremont and Robert H. Milroy advanced their columns toward Stonewall Jackson in the Shenandoah Valley early in
1862, and General George Crook operated toward the Virginia and
Tennessee Railroad bridges in 1864. In 1863, the loyal people, having
seceded from secession, organized the State of West Virginia at
Wheeling.

Few military reputations were made in this area and a number were
lost. McClellan was the chief winner, becoming the general-in-chief of
all armies on November 1st as the successor to General Scott. It can
be argued that the advancement was not soundly deserved, and that
McClellan as well as the cause were hurt by the promotion. His

successor, Rosecrans, appears not to have received adequate credit for his good work against Garnett and Floyd, and he eventually made his reputation in battle at Stone's River. Generals J. J. Reynolds, Thomas A. Morris, and Newton Schleich did not prosper. General Jacob D. Cox was long retained against his wishes in the Kanawha valley. He was finally transferred to the Twenty-third Corps of the Army of the Ohio, with which he wound up in 1865 near Raleigh under Sherman. His brand as a political general seems to have harmed more than helped him. The numerous Federal colonels who obtained experience included Robert H. Milroy, E. Dumont, James B. Steedman, Robert L. McCook, E. B. Tyler, Rutherford B. Hayes, B. F. Kelley, and others. Most of them became generals and performed good service without achieving military distinction.

General Robert E. Lee left the area early in November under a cloud of criticism (2), and public confidence was not restored until the Seven Days' battles in the following June. General Garnett, a promising professional, was lost to the Confederacy and his chief subordinate, Colonel John Pegram, was long under criticism for his surrender at Beverly. General Wise went off a few months later and lost Roanoke Island to Burnside, and General Floyd helped surrender Fort Donelson to Grant at about the same time. Generals Loring, S. R. Anderson, H. R. Jackson, D. S. Donelson, and the colonels rendered some good service.

From the viewpoint of military medicine no known advances in knowledge or practice came from this large, disastrous experience. The great, if not untoward, amount of disease seems to have been regarded, as was expressed by General Lee, as an act of God or as bad luck. In a sense, it was as no medical or military knowledge then known could have prevented most of it. In one modified form or another the experience was repeated in a number of subsequent campaigns described in this book. In another connection it has been shown that commands (regiments, brigades, and divisions) whose commanders were physicians had health records no better than did the commands of others (34). These officers were not all ignorant or criminally negligent, and one must conclude that the sanitary, hygienic, and medical measures necessary to keep a command healthy in the field, under all conditions, simply did not exist.

There is little profit in speculating on the consequences of a Confederate victory in western Virginia in 1861. If they could have maintained themselves there, the use of the upper Ohio River and of the Baltimore and Ohio Railroad would have been interdicted. The State of West Virginia could not have been organized in 1863. Pittsburgh and the line of the Pennsylvania Railroad eastward to Harrisburg could have been raided, leaving intact only the northern line of communication to the west. Stronger Union forces would likely have been thrown into the area, making it a major theater of operations and delaying the advance into the South along the Tennessee, Cumberland, and Mississippi Rivers. The area was not suitable for large military operations, and it favored the side approaching from the west as they were nearer their bases. Epidemic disease aided the Union here just as later it would help the South elsewhere.

These regiments had sustained a great attrition without having felt the shock of battle. Losses of this type would continue, but some of these regiments met again at Shiloh, Corinth, Perryville, and elsewhere. For those who survived it, the experience in western Virginia was only a conditioning.

General Lee's letter of September 1st to his wife resembles that of General James A. Garfield (to be quoted in chapter 4) to Mrs. Garfield in that both gave important facts about disease in their home letters not found in their official correspondence, although this information was of the greatest military importance. This principle, that militarily pertinent facts about disease were sometimes suppressed, needs to be recognized in medical-military historical studies.

## References

1. NICOLAY, J. G.: *The Outbreak of Rebellion.* New York, Charles Scribner's Sons, 1882, 226 p.
2. FREEMAN, D. S.: *R. E. Lee, A Biography.* New York & London, Charles Scribner's Sons, Vol. 1, 1934.
3. PORTERFIELD, G. A.: A narrative of the service of Colonel Geo. A. Porterfield in Northwestern Virginia in 1861-1862. *So. Hist. Soc. Papers, 16*:82-91, 1888.
4. TAYLOR, W. H.: *Four years with General Lee.* Bloomington, Indiana Univ. Press, 1962, 218 p.
5. LEE, R. E.: *O.R., 5*:192.
6. LEE, R. E.: *O.R., 5*:810.

7. *O.R., 5* and *51.*

8. *O.R.,* 5:1.

9. LEE, R. E., JR.: *Recollections and Letters of General Robert E. Lee.* Garden City, Garden City Publ. Co., 1926, 471 p.

10. QUINTARD, C. T.: *Doctor Quintard, Chaplain C.S.A. and Second Bishop of Tennessee.* Sewanee University, University Press, 1905, 183 p.

11. LONG, A. L.: *Memoirs of Robert E. Lee.* New York, Philadelphia, and Washington, J. M. Stoddart & Co., 1887, 707 p.

12. HEAD, T. A.: *Campaigns and Battles of the Sixteenth Regiment, Tennessee Volunteers.* Nashville, Cumberland Presbyterian Publ. House, 1885, 488 p.

13. TONEY, M. B.: *Privations of a Private.* Nashville, published by the author, 1905, 133 p.

14. DRAKE, J. V.: *Life of General Robert Hatton.* Nashville, Marshall & Brucer, 1867, 458 p.

15. CLARK, W. (Ed.): *Histories of the Several Regiments and Battalions From North Carolina in the Great War 1861-1865.* Goldsboro, N.C., Nash Bros., Vol. 1, 1901.

16. *O.R., 5*:1046-7.

17. *O.R.,* Series IV, *1*:883-891.

18. WRIGHT, J.J.B.: *Med. and Surg. Hist.,* Vol. I, Part I, Appendix p. 13-14.

19. SAWYER, F.: *A Military History of the 8th Regiment Ohio Vol. Inf'y.* Cleveland, Fairbanks & Co., 1881, 260 p.

20. HANNAFORD, E.: *The Story of a Regiment.* Cincinnati, published by the author, 1868, 622 p.

21. KEIFER, J. W.: *Slavery and Four Years of War.* New York & London, G. P. Putnam's Sons, 2 vols., 1900.

21b. BEATTY, J.: *The Citizen-Soldier; or, Memoirs of a Volunteer.* Cincinnati, Wilstach, Baldwin & Co., 1879, 401 p.

22. *Med. and Surg. Hist.,* Vol. I, Part I, p. 73-84.

23. McMEENS, R. R.: Letter from Meredith Hospital, Nashville. *Cincinnati Lancet and Observer,* 5:348-356, 1862.

24. BARR, R. N.: Army diseases. *Ohio Med. and Surg. Jour., 14*:95-116, 1862.

25. GRAYSON, A. J.: *History of the Sixth Indiana Regiment in the Three Months' Campaign in Western Virginia.* Madison, Indiana, Dourier Print, No date, 52 p.

26. HORTON, — and TEVERBAUGH, — : *A History of the Eleventh Regiment (Ohio Volunteer Infantry).* Dayton, W. J. Shuey, 1866, 287 p.

27. SPEED, T.; KELLY, R. M., and PIRTLE, A.: *The Union Regiments of Kentucky.* Louisville, Union Soldiers and Sailors Monument Assn., 1897, pp. 274-281, 282.

28. WITTKE, C.: The Ninth Ohio Volunteers. *Ohio Arch. and Hist. Quart., 35*:402-417, 1926.

29. WOOD, G. L.: *The Seventh Regiment: A Record.* New York, James Miller, 1865, 304 p.

30. WILLIAMS, C. R.: The Life of Rutherford Birchard Hayes. Columbus, *Ohio State Arch. and Hist. Soc.,* Vol. 1, 1928...
31. BROWN, B.: Personal experience in observing the results of good and bad sanitation in the Confederate States Army. *Va. Med. Monthly, 20*:589-599, 1893-4.
32. *O.R., 2*:221.
33. *O.R., 5*:116.
34. STEINER, P. E.: *Physician-Generals in the Civil War.* Springfield, Charles C Thomas, 1966, 194 p.

# III

## The South Carolina Coast in 1861-1862

A FEDERAL MILITARY CAMPAIGN was started on the South Carolina coast in 1861 that would last more than three years, have relatively few combat casualties, cost many thousands of lives from disease, but gain little advantage. It was the first major Union offensive after the humiliating defeats at Bull Run in July, and Wilson's Creek in August. Under General Winfield Scott's direction, the strategy of isolating the South had been adopted. The need for a suitable naval base for the blockading fleet was one reason for this campaign. At the same time, a coastal base could help an army mount attacks on Charleston, Savannah, and other ports, or disrupt communications in the interior. Beyond these military reasons were political and psychological factors not well formulated. Northern civilians and soldiers needed a victory to boost morale and Charleston, the heart of secession, seemed a prime target. It was known that this coast was unhealthy for whites in warm weather, so the expedition had to be timed for winter. When it had to be carried over through the following summer, it exacted a penalty. Savannah and Charleston were blockaded until they surrendered in the last months of the war, but the blockade was never fully effective. In the meantime, sizeable bodies of rival soldiers neutralized each other for years, while being steadily ravaged by disease. Federal attempts in 1862 to take Charleston and to sever the Charleston and Savannah railroad were stopped, in part, by epidemics. It is the present purpose to describe and document the role played here by disease in the first year.

### Health During the Assembly and Landing

Under a presidential target date of October 1, 1861, about a dozen regiments were finally assembled on or near the grounds of the Naval Academy at Annapolis (1, 2). Brigadier General Thomas W. Sherman, an old artillery captain, had been appointed the com-

[67]

mander. Nearly all the troops were new, untrained, and untested. Because of keen competition from General McClellan for the new regiments, Sherman had to solicit the governors of the northeastern states for a share. They sailed on transports on October 21st for Fortress Monroe. Here they were delayed for a week, awaiting the assembly of the fleet and additional stores, arms, and soldiers.

The mighty armada of about seventy-seven vessels finally departed Hampton Roads under sealed orders on October 29th, under the command of Commodore Samuel F. Dupont. Aboard were about 15,000 soldiers organized into three brigades which were led by Brigadier Generals E. L. Viele, I. I. Stevens, and H. G. Wright. They were carried in thirty-three transports escorted by men-of-war. Tugs, cargo ships, and small craft sailed along. The transports included steamers and sailships—ocean-going, coasters, river boats, and ferries. The sailships and smallest craft were towed by steamers. A terrific storm beginning on November 1st dispersed the fleet, sank several vessels (including one loaded with beef cattle), and caused the heaving overboard of some valuable equipment and supplies, including the entire medical stock of Kidwell's disinfectant (3). Some cavalry horses died or were swept overboard (4).

The original sites for the landings, at Bull's Bay, South Carolina and Fernandina, Florida, had become known to the Confederates, so the destination was changed to Port Royal Harbor, South Carolina (1), the most capacious south of Hampton Roads. The fleet began to assemble off the bar on November 4th, when the entrance was sounded and buoys placed. The gunboats entered on the 5th, and the warships on the following day. The entrance was guarded by two forts—Forts Walker and Beauregard. They were reduced by the warships in a six-hour bombardment on November 7th, and occupied by soldiers sent ashore in lighters on the 8th. In this action, General T. F. Drayton of Charleston, commanding on Hilton Head island, came under the guns of his brother, Captain Percival Drayton, commanding the *U.S.S. Pocahontas* (5).

The campaign seemed a great success. The days were warm, the air balmy, and the palmettos and orange groves green. Butterflies met the soldiers even in November. That this signified the survival also of disease-transmitting insects was not recognized.

The troops were fairly healthy although they carried the germs of several communicable diseases (3). Some of the regiments were so new that they were not yet through their "conditioning" by the usual childhood diseases of the recruit camps, chiefly measles and mumps. Overcrowding in the transports spread the infection to many of the remaining susceptibles (4, 6). The Sixth Connecticut had had a dozen deaths from "congestion of the brain" (meningitis?) late in September (7), and this disease later reappeared. Although they were new soldiers, they had already been exposed to unsanitary conditions on many occasions. For example, the Seventh Connecticut had been fed on October 8th at the Soldier's Rest, a large pavilion for troops near the railroad station in Washington, where the catering was by contractors: Flies lit on their food, maggots infested the boiled beef, and insects crawled from the hardtack. Therefore, they drank the coffee with closed eyes (8).

Several of the regiments had camped for about ten days in September and October on Meridian Hill in Washington, a campsite then already started on its infamous record of spreading the enteric and other pathogens to the passing regiments. Here some contracted dysentery, typhoid fever, or malaria (3). At Annapolis they had acquired catarrhs, fevers, and derangements of the digestive system— the common camp diseases of new troops. Smallpox appeared in the camp of the Forty-fifth Pennsylvania (9). The same disease broke out in the Eighth Maine three days before sailing. The victims and contacts were isolated, and this regiment and those camped nearby were vaccinated. It was impossible to get enough vaccine from the surgeon general for the entire command. The next case in the Eighth Maine developed aboard ship on October 31st. Three months later, the disease again appeared in the crew of this ship and in the Eighth Maine ashore (3). After the storm of November 1st, many men of the Fiftieth Pennsylvania developed a "fever of low grade" consequent, supposedly, to the contamination of their water or food supply. These preceding experiences were not auspicious omens for a healthy campaign.

## Hunter's Engagement at Secessionville

The Union expedition spent a month establishing a base on Hilton

Head island, after which the troops spread through the Sea Islands
aided by the patrolling gunboats. These islands extended from
Savannah to Charleston and beyond in both directions. They were
numerous, low, and flat. The smallest were uninhabited, tidal, and
marshy; the largest, over ten miles long, had prosperous plantations
on which rice and a special cotton were important products. The
islands were separated by sounds, large tidal rivers, bayous, and creeks.
Fresh and salt water swamps and marshes were found in many places.
One Northern physician was impressed by the low flat islands, large
mud banks, tall rushes, numerous birds and insects, and the inter-
minable creeks in which the tides ran in every direction (10). The
inhabitants included about 7,000 whites and 32,000 Negroes (11).
The owners had fled to the mainland before the Nationals landed and
the contrabands were celebrating. The largest town was Beaufort,
on Port Royal Island, a beautiful, semi-tropical place used as a health
resort. The Federal military designation for the area (South Carolina,
Georgia, and eastern Florida) was later the Department of the South
and for its troops, after reinforcements arrived, the Tenth Army
Corps (12). The topography of the area posed many health problems.

Defense works had been built on a few of the islands but, except
for those protecting Charleston and Savannah, they offered little
resistance to the spread of Sherman's forces in December. General
Robert E. Lee, in charge of the department that winter, withdrew to a
defense line on the mainland (5). By using the Charleston and
Savannah railroad near the coast, Confederate troops could be quickly
transferred from one threatened place to another, permitting a strong
defense by relatively few men. After Lee departed in March, 1962,
most of the Southern regiments were transferred to the acutely threatened points in Virginia and Mississippi, where they were soon in
battle. Sherman contented himself with sending a few raiders to the
mainland, occupying undefended Fernandina and Jacksonville in
Florida, and supporting an attack on Fort Pulaski in the Savannah
River, which fell in April.

The Confederates justified the reduction of their troops by the
supposition the Union threat would cease during the warm weather
because of the danger from disease. Thus, Governor F. W. Pickens
wrote, on May 23, 1862, to General John C. Pemberton, who succeeded Lee as the departmental commander (13): "It is too late in

the season for the enemy to send any land force to invest Charleston regularly, but they send their gunboats any day into the harbor. . . ." Lee, from Richmond, independently pleaded of Pemberton on May 31st for more troops on the basis that (14) "At this season I think it impossible for the enemy to make any expedition into the interior." A few days later, after the Battle of Fair Oaks near Richmond, Jefferson Davis added his opinion (15): "Decisive operations are pending here in this section, and the climate already restrains operations on the coast." Here was military planning based on knowledge of the capabilities of "natural" disease in warfare in this area.

General David Hunter, a sixty-year-old former army paymaster, major, and outspoken abolitionist, succeeded Sherman in the departmental command early in April, presumably because he would be more aggressive. For ordering the emancipation of the slaves in the department he was declared by the war department in Richmond not only a public enemy of the Confederate States but also an outlaw (16). By land and ship, Hunter concentrated his troops on James Island in June for an attempt to take Charleston by land. The regiments that crossed other islands to reach James Island suffered many disease casualties.

During Hunter's temporary absence from the command his substitute, Brigadier General Henry W. Benham, marched to within five miles of Charleston. Here he was stopped on June 16th by a gallant defense of a prepared position in what became known as the Engagement at Secessionville. The Union losses, the largest in combat in this department during 1861-1862, were 683 (107 killed, 487 wounded, 89 missing) (17). The corresponding Confederate figures were only 204 (18). For his precipitate action, General Benham was arrested and sent north.

Colonel Daniel Leasure, a physician from New Castle, Pennsylvania (19), commanding an infantry brigade in a charge, vividly described how some of these casualties came about (20):

> . . . we entered the range of a perfect storm of grape, canister, nails, broken glass, and pieces of chains fired from three very large pieces on the fort, which completely swept every foot of ground within the range, and either cut the men down or drove them to the shelter of the ravine on the left.

Hunter still had a large army and, although he had been repulsed, the enemy's position was vulnerable and an advance to Charleston seemed possible. Nevertheless, he withdrew his army from James Island in July, giving as his reason the threat of disease. On June 27th he wrote to General Wright (21):

> Hearing from Washington that there is no probability of our receiving re-enforcements, and it being all-important to provide for the health of the command in the sickly season approaching, I have determined to abandon James Island, in order that the troops may be placed where, in so far as practicable in this climate, they may be out of the way of malarious influences. . . .

In justifying his retrograde movement to Secretary Stanton, Hunter gave as reasons his need for more transportation and reinforcements ". . . and the increasing sick list from the command is another argument not to be overlooked (22).

General Hunter wrote to Stanton in greater detail about the role of disease two weeks later, when his troops were back at Beaufort and North Edesto Island (23):

> . . . all possible precautions being taken to secure their health and comfort, and with results fully meeting my most sanguine expectations. No epidemic fevers have yet appeared in any portion of the command, though the great numbers of men prostrated on James Island by bilious and low typhoid fevers and the increasing sick list, attributed to malarial debility, gave warning of what might be expected had the occupation of our position there been continued.

General Wright reminded Hunter on July 9th that "The actual sickly season has not, however, I presume, fairly been entered upon" (24).

It is clear that sickness and the threat of even more disease was an important factor in the failure to renew the drive toward Charleston and in the withdrawal of the troops from James Island.

## Mitchel's Campaign to Pocotaligo

General Hunter was succeeded in the departmental command on September 17th by Major General Ormsby M. Mitchel, an astronomer, lecturer, and mathematician. His reputation aroused little apprehension among his opponents who wrote (25): "He is known to be more fussy than dangerous and addicted to predatory excursions."

At this time the sick list was about ten per cent of the command (8), but during a month, twenty-six per cent were entered on the list, showing that the turnover was rapid. Despite the unhealthy season, Mitchel planned to take the offensive. His first large engagements came on October 22-23, near Pocotaligo, during an attempt to sever the Charleston and Savannah railroad. In a stretch of thirty miles this road had six miles of wooden bridges and trestles, all highly vulnerable. The expedition was repulsed rather easily, and a sustained offensive was not pressed because "At this season of the year I did not deem it prudent to expose the troops upon the main-land for a longer period" (26). The Federal casualties had been about 340 (26), while the Confederates lost only 163 (27).

General Mitchel had not accompanied this expedition. Yellow fever had broken out in the department on August 29th (28, 29), and he died from this disease on October 30th after an illness of only four days (30). Of the three departmental commanders of 1862 (T. W. Sherman, Hunter, Mitchel), he was the most aggressive. If he had lived, it is unlikely that he would have remained idle long. After this check by disease, military affairs lapsed under apathy in this department. Mitchel had the strength to destroy the railroad, and only the half effort—half because of fear of disease—caused the failure and the withdrawal. Yellow fever also prevented him from making plans for the coming cool season. Thus, disease distinctly influenced military operations on three occasions within a year in this department.

## Diseases in the Union Forces

Diseases, both imported and indigenous, by threat and by their occurrence, handicapped the operation, almost from the day of landing, far more than this brief account indicates. Their types and frequency varied with the season, the island, the number of troops concentrated in an area, the length of their stay, their prior history, the insect vectors, and other factors.

Potential insect vectors were numerous in numbers and types. Beside the vermin in the hardtack and the body lice brought with them (7) there were clouds of house flies and mosquitoes abounding in nearly every department. Here, in addition, were sand flies, gnats, and fleas. On several islands the fleas caused "blotches on the skin"

(8). They were great pests, interfering with sleep and persisting through most of the winter (8, 9). One soldier wrote that (9) "We could smoke away the gnats, smash a mosquito and scald the 'graybacks,' but the ubiquitous, elusive flea—he was too much for us." Another soldier thought there was no practical importance to killing them because for each a thousand more were left (8). Thus vectors existed for malaria, yellow fever, dengue, typhoid fever, dysentery, typhus fever, and other diseases.

Indeed, some of these diseases soon reinforced the measles and the prevailing colds. General Stevens suffered a severe attack of bilious fever from which he recovered only slowly (31). Deaths became so numerous that the playing of funeral marches was forbidden. General Mitchel, who had been campaigning in Kentucky and Tennessee, realized soon after his arrival that he would have to fight not only rebels but also disease (32). The effective methods for combatting yellow fever were not known, and he died of this infection before he could improve the health situation.

The overall disease picture for the Federal Department of the South was compiled after the war (33). The published figures pertain to the entire department, but as the regiments on the Sea Islands comprised most of the personnel of the department, the data approximate the situation here in the Tenth Corps. The sick list for the twelve months, November, 1861 through October, 1862, totalled 52,178 and the deaths 724 (Table V). During this time the mean strength varied from a low of 13,145 in August, 1862 to a high of 21,242 soldiers in April. The combat casualties were few and most of the diagnoses represent disease. Inasmuch as the troop turnover in the department was low, it is clear that every soldier, on the average, had been sick several times within the year. In most months, between twenty-five and thirty-three per cent of the command was on the sick list. Medical casualties of this size were inconsistent with high military efficiency.

Diarrhea and dysentery were the most common diagnoses, with 12,284 examples during the year. These diseases never disappeared, and they peaked that summer in June (1,555 cases). Cholera morbus, in a separate category, occurred in 424 soldiers, and was fatal only in one. Intermittent fever, with 3,866 diagnoses but only 96 deaths,

TABLE V

Major Diseases in the Department of the South (Federal)
November 1861 through October 1862*

| Year and month | Mean strength | Total wounds and diseases | Diarrhea and dysentery | Malaria | Re-mittent fever | Epidemic catarrh and bronchitis | Typhoid and common continued fever |
|---|---|---|---|---|---|---|---|
| Nov. 1861 | 13,225 | 4,481 | 972 | 179 | 220 | 621 | 251 |
| Dec. 1861 | 17,016 | 5,872 | 872 | 285 | 214 | 764 | 192 |
| Jan. 1862 | 18,571 | 5,029 | 766 | 337 | 192 | 450 | 184 |
| Feb. 1862 | 16,228 | 3,451 | 596 | 179 | 147 | 197 | 58 |
| Mar. 1862 | 17,821 | 3,764 | 665 | 156 | 183 | 150 | 138 |
| Apr. 1862 | 21,242 | 4,817 | 1,278 | 256 | 211 | 153 | 274 |
| May, 1862 | 16,230 | 4,563 | 1,438 | 363 | 244 | 100 | 159 |
| June, 1862 | 16,336 | 4,602 | 1,555 | 278 | 130 | 71 | 187 |
| July, 1862 | 14,203 | 3,804 | 1,250 | 178 | 187 | 143 | 68 |
| Aug. 1862 | 13,145 | 3,802 | 1,084 | 291 | 453 | 188 | 85 |
| Sept. 1862 | 13,837 | 3,623 | 883 | 611 | 534 | 159 | 40 |
| Oct. 1862 | 14,980 | 4,370 | 925 | 753 | 573 | 197 | 36 |
| Totals | | 52,178 | 12,284 | 3,866 | 3,288 | 3,193 | 1,672 |

*Compiled from *Medical and Surgical History of the War of the Rebellion.*

ranked second. Included in this category were the quotidian, tertian, quartan, and congestive types. The mortality was high only in the latter. This disease reached a low point in March and peaked in October. Probably the great majority were malaria. Remittent fever ranked third with 3,288 examples. In the last four months of this period, some of these cases were recorded as typho-malarial fever (255 cases). The true nature of these two categories is unknown, but they were probably not all typhoid because only twenty died. The monthly distribution curve and the mortality resembled those of malaria. The differential diagnosis between intermittent and remittent fevers was uncertain in those days when the clinical thermometer was rarely used and no other objective test was available.

The respiratory infections collectively (epidemic catarrh, acute and chronic bronchitis) numbered 3,193. These were infections predominantly of the winter months. It is of interest that acute and chronic rheumatism, with 2,754 victims but no deaths, ranked fifth, and that its seasonal curve resembled that of the respiratory infections but lagged behind them about a month. Typhoid fever ranked only sixth in relative frequency but first in mortality (1,672 cases and 145 deaths). It was always present. These figures include some cases reported as "common continued fever," which reduce the average mortality for the group. In seventh place was the jaundice group, with 1,276 examples and no deaths. This disease peaked in July and August. Several regimental histories describe it as epidemic in form and as relatively mild, in agreement with the low mortality. Many of these soldiers were eating local shellfish.

Other infectious diseases included yellow fever (372 cases, 79 deaths), measles (749 cases), mumps (300), syphilis (151), gonorrhea (206), consumption (222), inflammation of the brain and meninges (175), inflammation of the lungs (203), smallpox and varioloid (128), and typhus fever (7 cases). On a percentage basis, the mortality was highest in yellow fever (21 per cent). These cases all occurred in the late summer. Measles disappeared from the command after April, presumably because of a lack of any more susceptibles, but smallpox remained troublesome among the contrabands (34). The venereal diseases decreased during the year, reflecting the relative isolation from cities. The meningitis cases were scattered in time, but they followed crowding in confined spaces. The pneumonia was chiefly a disease of winter. One soldier in the Forty-fifth Pennsylvania died suddenly after eating oysters (9).

The enteric diseases were everywhere but not uniform. They broke out whenever the troop concentration was large and static. For the year ending June 30, 1862, the rate per 1,000 mean strength in the Department of the South was 730 cases (35). Thus, three men out of four had been on the sick list with this disease during the year. Because some infections became chronic and protracted, the military handicap must have been sizeable. Among the six Federal military departments in the Atlantic Region submitting figures for that year, this department stood highest. The Middle Department, with headquarters at Baltimore, was lowest, having a rate of 445 cases per 1,000 mean strength. However, in the Central Region west of the Appalachians, three departments out of six reporting had higher rates than the Department of the South. These high figures were: Department of the Gulf, 1,637; Department of the Tennessee, 1,469; and the Department of the Cumberland, 1,084. The Department of the Gulf included the troops of General Ben Butler's expeditions to New Orleans, Baton Rouge, First Vicksburg, and in the garrisons. The other two departments embraced the Fort Donelson, Shiloh, and First Corinth campaigns; their dysentery occurred chiefly between the Battle of Shiloh and the aftermath of Corinth.

Thus, the rate of dysentery was high in this department but not excessive by the standards of that time. Its prevalence seems to have varied from one unit and island to another. It appears to have been high on the larger islands with many troops and where the drinking water was taken from streams. In some camps, water was drawn from wells. Water was struck by digging down only a few feet. Such water often had a low potability because of bad taste and appearance, but it was usually safe. This safety appears to have been an incidental benefit of the unusual method used in constructing the sinks which, for convenience, were built out over tidal water, as at Hilton Head. Bad water was sometimes used because of negligence, ignorance, or military necessity. On one interisland trip by ship, the Sixth Connecticut from kerosene barrels drank water three months old that was nauseating and foul, that was so thick it could be lifted on the finger, and that discolored sea water when they were mixed (7). Surgeons Jacob H. Scheetz of the Forty-seventh Pennsylvania, David Merritt of the Fifty-fifth Pennsylvania, Joseph L. Mulford of the Forty-eighth New York, William W. Brown of the Seven New Hampshire, and others left interesting observations on this group of diseases (36). All described it as relatively mild and as having a low mortality. When postmortem examinations were made, they always revealed a severe ulceration, thickening, and contraction limited to the large intestine.

Typhoid fever was a major military liability, whose size is not exactly known because of the problems in correct diagnosis, reporting, and compiling. Together with typhus fever and "common continued fever" it comprised the continued fevers. Typhus may be disregarded for statistical purposes because it probably accounted for only one or two per cent of the group. The common continued fever category probably included some mild typhoids, some paratyphoids, some atypical and inadequately treated recurrent malaria, and some other diseases. At the same time, some of the typhoid cases were statistically lost by inclusion with the large "remittent fever" category, some members of this group exhibiting ulcerated Peyer's patches at autopsy examination. The common continued fevers in this department through the four years showed an annual rate of 72 cases per 1,000 soldiers (37). Thus, in the four years, nearly one-third of the men would have this disease. Among the ten Federal military departments in the Atlantic Region, four had higher and five had lower rates. The Department of the East stood lowest (27 cases per 1,000) and the Department of Washington highest (105 per 1,000). The former had only a few troops, in established old garrisons. Washington got the new regiments and serially crowded them into old, contaminated camps. Among the twenty-three military departments in the entire country, the infection rate in the Department of the South ranked seventh. The considerable mortality rate and the extended period of military incapacitation combined with a sizeable rate of infection to make this disease an important military liability.

The pattern of disease sometimes varied between islands, even adjacent ones. For example, the Seventy-ninth New York at Bay Point was healthy in December, but across the bay at the Hilton Head base the hospitals were full with fevers and dysentery, and funerals were depressing by their great frequency (38).

An epidemic of "yellow jaundice" struck the Sixth Connecticut during the summer of 1862 while they were encamped near Beaufort, regarded as a relatively healthy place (7). "All seemed afflicted with it more or less, which was about as comfortable to endure as sea-sickness." The statistics for the department show 1,276 cases of jaundice in the twelve months from November, 1861 (33). It increased gradually from eight examples in November, 1861 to a peak of 260 in the following July, with a slow decrease thereafter. Inasmuch as the mortality was low it is probable that this disease was infectious hepatitis rather than Weil's disease or the jaundice secondary to biliary tract obstructions. The yellow fever epidemic came later, and it had a high mortality, so the diseases were not confused.

Although it was not named in the military correspondence, yellow fever was probably the disease most feared. Its mysterious origins, rapid spread, high mortality, and abrupt disappearance after the first frost gave "yellow-jack" tragic, dramatic impact. It was imported when soldiers of the Seventh New Hampshire were brought from Key West, where the disease was current, to the army base at Hilton Head. The first examples appeared on August 29th and, after the appropriate incubation period, indigenous cases rapidly broke out and the disease spread. Four members of General Mitchel's staff came down. He took them to Beaufort by steamer, became sick that evening, and died on October 30th (30). This was the first outbreak of this dreaded disease in Northern soldiers during the war. It returned in greater strength in 1864. Before the war yellow fever had visited the South Caroline coast only occasionally, and it did not spread far in the Confederate army or in the civilian population this time. It seems always to have been imported, although this was long disputed.

The cited official statistics do not reveal the full disease picture as the regimental officers saw it. For example, the Sixth Connecticut had a severe epidemic called "spotted fever" with a number of deaths early in 1862 (7). They had been crowded aboard a filthy ship for some days. Every man, from the colonel down, became infested with lice so large they were described by a German soldier as "shust like wheat," and the men were landed briefly once to wash and bathe. The epidemic was so severe that the regiment was placed in an isolated island rest camp, where it soon recovered. The term spotted fever was used variously for cerebrospinal meningitis and typhus fever. Another synonym for typhus was "ship fever." The exact diagnosis of this epidemic is unknown. As only seven cases of typhus fever were officially recorded during this time in the entire Department of the South (33), this outbreak did not go into the record as typhus. The death in this regiment from "congestion of the brain" several months earlier together with other circumstances suggest it was meningitis. Moreover, the Ninety-seventh Pennsylvania had a death at about the same time from "ship fever" (38). As the disease was fatal in a few hours, this was probably a meningococcemia. Another soldier in this regiment died a month later of ship fever after a four-day illness.

In this department bilious fever was the most common diagnosis made that does not appear in the official disease tables. For example, "black bilious fever" became common in the First Massachusetts Cavalry that summer (4), and one of its surgeons was sent home with it. The true nature of this outbreak is unknown. Bilious remittent fever was mentioned by nearly all of the surgeons who left a record as being the predominant fever that spring (36). Unfortunately, none of them left a precise description. It is probable that these cases were tabulated in the *Medical and Surgical History* as remittent fever, later called typho-malaria. There is inconclusive evidence that many were either typhoid or malaria or both. Some may have belonged to the paratyphoid group.

About 100 men out of 400 in the Forty-fifth Pennsylvania dropped out of a review on July 9th from heat prostration (9). They had been marched several miles in deep sand under a fierce heat. Their temperatures were not recorded and it is not known whether the condition was sunstroke or heat exhaustion.

The great and persistent attrition in a regiment by disease is illustrated by the experience of the Ninety-seventh Pennsylvania (6). The regimental historian was a dentist serving as a combatant. In October, 1862, when the regiment was already quite small, 500 men were on the sick list at one time. On July 4th, four died. Among thirty-five deaths in which the cause is stated, only one resulted from combat. Yellow fever accounted for thirteen, typhoid for six, diarrhea and congestive fever for four each, and ship fever for two deaths. The remainder, one each, were attributed to measles, climatic fever, congestion of the brain, remittent fever, and diphtheria. Intermittent fever and chills were always present.

## Disease Among the Confederates

Less information about disease is available among the Confederate defenders, but it is known to have been common. Lieutenant Colonel John G. Pressley of the Twenty-fifth South Carolina wrote of the regiment for the week of July 23-31, 1862, when it was encamped on James Island (39):

> The health of the regiment growing worse. Our medical staff were kept very busy, and we heard of the death of several of our comrades in the general hospital in Charleston. The regimental hospital was constantly full. It was distressing to see the shortened line of the regiment on dress parade. Some of the companies had scarcely a platoon of men fit for duty.

On August 1st he reported fever cases (*i.e.* malaria) on the increase and becoming more virulent. He hoped to be permitted to leave the island during the sickly season. The health of the regiment was much better by November. In the first year these soldiers had measles, diarrhea, malaria, and typhoid fever like most new soldiers (40). When one company was alone on a small island without a surgeon, its captain held the sick call:

> As malaria was the cause, either immediate or remote, of nearly every case of sickness, the most common dose was ten grains of quinine. . . . I had the satisfaction of knowing that my prescriptions were approved by the Doctor in every case but one. To that one, instead of the usual dose, castor oil had been given. The Doctor said that was a mistake, and administered an emetic.

A comparison of the amount of malaria in the Federal Department of the South with the Confederate Department of South Carolina, Georgia, and Florida was made for the nineteen-month period January, 1862 through July, 1863 (41). According to this compilation the Confederates had 41,539 and the Union 14,842 cases. In both groups the majority of cases were intermittents of the quotidian and tertian types. These figures cannot be expressed as risks or rates of infection because the respective size of the military populations is unknown. The number of troops on both sides varied from time to time, and, serving with the Confederates at times were South Carolina and Georgia state units. However, for June, 1862 the Confederates present for duty numbered 23,375 and the present and absent were 35,656 (42); the figures for July were 18,689 and 31,015 (42). The corresponding Federal figures for June were 18,715 and 23,880 (43), and for July 13,293 and 18,533 (43). If these figures are representative, the rate of malaria infection must have been several times higher in the Southerners. On the other hand if there was any substantial underdiagnosis, it would likely have been by the Northern medical officers, who were less familiar with the protean features of malaria.

The monthly return for the Confederate Department of South Carolina and Georgia always showed a wide gap between the number "present for duty" and the "aggregate present and absent." For example, for May, 1862, 34,112 were listed as present and absent (44) but only 18,097 as present for duty. Thus, half the soldiers on the rolls were absent from their companies. In general, major causes for such absence were wounds and disease. In this department there had been few wounds. It is probable that many were away at home or in the general hospitals because of sickness. A fifty per cent absence was not unusual in 1864, when many were away recovering from wounds, but it was distinctly unusual in the first half of 1862.

General Beauregard, who replaced Pemberton in the command of the department in the autumn, wrote on October 3rd that in its Georgia portion ". . . the troops are already prostrated by disease, as General Mercer reports" (45).

It seems likely that the Confederates suffered as much or more from disease as the Federals. Their main advantage was a knowledge of the unhealthiest spots. Military necessity, however, required both sides sometimes to disregard such knowledge. In the prevention and treatment of disease, neither side had any advantage. With respect to natural and previously acquired immunity, there was probably little difference.

## Résumé

The questions can now be answered whether the fear of infectious diseases in this region as a military liability was justified and, if so, what they were. From the Union viewpoint, inasmuch as one departmental commander died of yellow fever, General Stevens suffered from bilious fever, 52,178 soldiers were sick and 724 died, the fears were not groundless. The apprehension was caused by the known occasional but unpredictable eruption of yellow fever and by the regular visitations of the cosmopolitan camp diseases, dysentery and typhoid fever, and, more important in this area, malaria. The element of malnutrition to the point of scurvy, present in some other armies from the middle of 1862, was not a cofactor here where the army ration was easily supplied by ship and supplemented by local seafood, fresh fruit and vegetables, and sometimes by fresh meat and poultry.

The knowledge and fears of Generals Scott, T. W. Sherman, Hunter, and Mitchel were soundly based. For the warm months, these commanders were about as aggressive as the medical conditions warranted, except for brief campaigns, and more aggressive than the Confederate leaders expected. In the cool months, greater efforts would have been warranted. When the offensives on James Island in June and at Pocotaligo in October were abandoned, the threat of disease was given as a factor in both instances. With monthly morbidity rates of over twenty-five per cent of the command, military effectiveness could be maintained only partially. For this condition, the introduction of additional troops could have compensated only in part because the units, if new, would have had the high susceptibilities of all recruits, and the increased troop concentration would have facilitated even greater spread of some of the communicable diseases.

From the Confederate viewpoint the management of their medical-military problem was good. Jefferson Davis and Generals Lee and Pemberton underestimated the courage, aggressiveness, or foolhardiness of their National opponents. Their objectives, however, were defensive and at this they succeeded. Many thousands of Northern soldiers were neutralized or lost by 1865. The Confederates also paid a big price in disease casualties, the size of which is, however, not accurately known.

One must conclude that "natural" diseases played an important part in the warfare in South Carolina in 1862.

# References

1. VIELE, E. L.: The Port Royal Expedition, 1861. *Mag. Amer. Hist., 14*: 329-340, 1885.
2. STEVENS, H.: Military Operations in South Carolina. *Papers Mil. Hist. Soc. Mass., 9*:111-157, 1912.
3. COOPER, G. E.: *Med. and Surg. Hist.,* Vol. I, Part I, Appendix p. 230-233.
4. CROWNINSHIELD, B. W.: *A History of the First Regiment of Massachusetts Cavalry Volunteers.* Boston & New York, Houghton, Mifflin & Co., 1891, 490 p.
5. CAPERS, E.: *Confederate Military History* (C. A. Evans, Ed.), Vol. 5, *South Carolina.* Atlanta, Confed. Publ. Co., 1899, 424 p.
6. PRICE, I.: *History of the Ninety-seventh Regiment Pennsylvania Volunteer Infantry.* Philadelphia, Published by the author, 1875, 608 p.
7. CADWELL, C. K.: *The Old Sixth Regiment, Its War Record, 1861-5.* New Haven, Tuttle, Morehouse, & Taylor, 1875, 227 p.
8. WALKLEY, S.: *History of the Seventh Connecticut Volunteer Infantry.* No city, no publisher, 1905, 226 p.
9. ALBERT, A. D.: *History of the Forty-fifth Regiment Pennsylvania Volunteer Infantry, 1861-1865.* Williamsport, Pa., Grit Publ. Co., 1912, 530 p.
10. DALTON, J. C.: Dalton Letters, 1861-1865. *Proc. Mass. Hist. Soc., 56*:354-495, 1922-23.
11. DENISON, F.: *Shot and Shell: The Third Rhode Island Heavy Artillery Regiment in the Rebellion 1861-1865.* Providence, Third R. I. H. Art, Vet. Assoc., 1879, 368 p.
12. *O.R., 14*:380.
13. *O.R., 14*:517.
14. *O.R., 14*:528.
15. *O.R., 14*:534.
16. *O.R., 14*:599.
17. *O.R., 14*:51.
18. *O.R., 14*:90.
19. STEINER, P. E.: *Physician-Generals in the Civil War.* Springfield, Charles C Thomas, 1966, 194 p.
20. *O.R., 14*:72.
21. *O.R., 14*:47.
22. *O.R., 14*:43.
23. *O.R., 14*:107.

24. *O.R., 14*:109-110.

25. *O.R., 14*:638.

26. *O.R., 14*:144-147.

27. *O.R., 14*:180.

28. *O.R., 14*:382.

29. *O.R., 14*:384.

30. SMILEY, T. T.: The Yellow Fever at Port Royal, S. C. *Boston Med. Surg. Jour., 67*:449-468, 1863.

31. STEVENS, H.: *The Life of Isaac Ingalls Stevens.* Boston and New York, Houghton, Mifflin & Co., 2 vols., 1900.

32. MITCHEL, F. A.: *Ormsby Macknight Mitchel, Astronomer and General.* Boston and New York, Houghton, Mifflin & Co., 1887, 392 p.

33. *Med. and Surg. Hist.,* Vol. I, Part I.

34. *O.R., 14*:390.

35. *Med. and Surg. Hist.,* Vol. I, Part II, 80-82.

36. *Med. and Surg. Hist.,* Vol. I, Part II, 80-82.

37. *Med. and Surg. Hist.,* Vol. I, Part III, 203.

38. TODD, W.: *The Seventy-ninth Highlanders New York Volunteers in the War of the Rebellion 1861-1865.* Albany, Brandon, Barton & Co., 1886, 513 p.

39. PRESSLY, J. G.: Extracts from the diary of Lieutenant-Colonel John G. Pressly of the Twenty-fifth South Carolina Volunteers. *So. Hist. Soc. Papers, 14*:35-62, 1886.

40. PRESSLY, J. G.: The Wee Nee Volunteers of Williamsburg District, South Carolina in the First (Hagood's) Regiment. *So. Hist. Soc. Papers, 16*: 116-194, 1888.

41. *Med. and Surg. Hist.,* Vol. I, Part III, 107.

42. *O.R., 14*:575-576, 591-592.

43. *O.R., 14*:362, 367.

44. *O.R., 14*:529.

45. *O.R., 14*:619.

# IV

## Eastern Kentucky in 1861-1862

A CAMPAIGN IN eastern Kentucky during the first winter of the war dragged to a close in the spring with a partial Union victory. Of the three Federal objectives only two had been achieved, but the Confederates had won neither of theirs. On both sides the aims were both military and political. Severe epidemic disease had embarrassed the campaign and was one reason for its termination. On several occasions, about half the men of some regiments were on the sick report. Other adverse factors were the inexperience of the two leaders, both politicians, the great difficulties in supply and communications, and the lack of military realism in some of the objectives. The operation had to be conducted in the severe winter months, when the other armies were quiescent, in an area having poor roads. Both commanders graduated to their respective legislatures in Washington and Richmond later in the war.

### The Military Problem

The area in dispute was essentially the valley of the Big Sandy River and its tributaries and their headwaters in a range of the Cumberland mountains near the Virginia border. It consisted of wooded hills and narrow deep valleys with some subsistence farms on the flats. Starting south from Catlettsburg on the Ohio River, the county seats, all hamlets, were Louisa, Paintsville, Prestonburg, and Piketon (or Pikeville). This border country had already experienced civil strife in November when Brigadier General William Nelson with a small force of Ohio and Kentucky troops had defeated Colonel John S. Williams near Prestonburg and Piketon, and had forced his withdrawal through Pound Gap into Virginia. Both sides had been after recruits and local subsistence but found them meager.

The present campaign began in December, 1861 by the almost simultaneous assignment of new opposing leaders with small forces to the area (1, 2, 3, 4, 5, 6). In Richmond, Humphrey Marshall was made a brigadier general and was ordered to Prestonburg to organize the assembled men, to recruit others, and to defend that frontier for the Confederacy from a base in southwestern Virginia. There was great concern for the salt-works, the lead mines, and the railroad to the west in this region (3, 7). With the Kentucky troops, two western Virginia regiments, a battery of six field pieces, and some cavalry units, he would have the equivalent of a brigade of over four regiments—from 4,000 to 5,000 men. This force was sometimes designated the Army of Eastern Kentucky. The operation came under the supervision of General Albert Sidney Johnston at Bowling Green (7), but communications with him were tenuous, and Richmond retained a dominant interest if not control.

The Union campaign began on December 17th when Brigadier General Don Carlos Buell at Louisville assigned to Colonel James A. Garfield the new Eighteenth Brigade of the Army of the Ohio, and instructed him to support the people in the Big Sandy valley by operating against the rebel forces collecting there (8). Garfield was to supply himself by the river and by local purchases if possible. Buell had little interest in this area but he was forced to make this commitment by pressure from Washington. President Lincoln wanted to aid and encourage the loyal mountain people in Tennessee and Kentucky, not realizing the almost insuperable physical difficulties facing an expedition in the winter months. General McClellan had backed the Lincoln policy (9), but in addition he hoped the Virginia and Tennessee railroad, an important link with the West, could be severed. Buell assigned to Garfield's brigade the Fourteenth and Twenty-second Kentucky and the Fortieth and Forty-second Ohio regiments of infantry, some Kentucky and Ohio troops of cavalry, but no artillery. He thought artillery would be worthless in this hilly terrain.

## The Opposing Commanders

Marshall and Garfield provide a study in contrasts. At first glance the advantages appear to favor the Southerner, but in actuality Garfield won through greater leadership, energy, resourcefulness, and determination. Marshall was nationally known as a soldier, lawyer, farmer, and politician, the scion of a distinguished family. He had been graduated from West Point in 1832, forty-second in a class of forty-five. Resigning almost immediately to practice law, he had further military experience with the Kentucky militia and as the colonel of a regiment of Kentucky cavalry in the war in Mexico (10). Three terms in the U. S. House of Representatives were interrupted by a year as a commissioner to the Empire of China in 1852. In politics originally a Whig and admirer of Henry Clay, he had supported successively the Know-Nothings and the Breckinridge Democrats. He was a nephew of James G. Birney, the abolitionist editor and presidential candidate, and thus a cousin of the five Birney brothers, of whom two became Federal generals and three were to die in the war. At this time he weighed three-hundred pounds but carried himself and rode well (11). Two years later, when he was a congressman in Richmond, he was described as ". . . a great waddling mass of obesity, . . puffing like a porpoise" (12). During the time here under study, he wrote frequent and inordinately long and detailed reports to General Johnston and to the war department. These messages display erudition and industry but many inconsistencies, and they fail to convey a clear picture. After his defeats he complained bitterly to General Lee at having been falsely accused of intemperance (13).

Garfield, in contrast, was only thirty-three years old but already a teacher, preacher, lawyer, academy president, and politician (5). His reputation as yet was only local, but he had served for two terms in the Ohio senate, and he was an admirer and friend of Secretary S. P. Chase. His military experience had been limited to three months service at Camp Chase, Columbus, as an aide and as the colonel of a regiment which he had recruited (6). His selection by Buell to command virtually an independent expedition seems to have been based on political more than military considerations. Two members of Buell's staff, old friends of Garfield, had apparently recommended him. Buell had complained to Washington about the great dearth of trained officers in his department, and it is understandable that he should not have assigned a West Pointer to what seemed essentially an unrewarding police and political chore. At that time none of Buell's officers had combat command experience and neither did he. Garfield subsequently sat on the Turchin, Buell, and Fitz John Porter Boards in 1862-1863 and he served as the chief of staff to Rosecrans before taking his seat in Congress in 1864. During the war, another Ohio colonel thought that Garfield wore too many buttons on his coat, the splendor of the double row detracting from the splendor of his remarks (14). The same observer commented that even then when Garfield shook hands it suggested "vote early, vote right." Garfield's military correspondence beginning at this time shows a rapid comprehension of the military problems, practical planning for their prompt solution, and a sound understanding of the volunteer soldier. It will also be necessary to show that his reports were less than candid about disease.

## The Military Operations

Colonel Garfield promptly started the new Fortieth Ohio marching eastward from the bluegrass country at Paris through the hills to get behind the Confederates assembled at Paintsville. With the other three regiments eventually assembled on the Big Sandy, he pushed up the valley to Prestonburg. All his regiments were new and inexperienced, and the two Kentucky units were undersized as well. The Fortieth he described as little better than a Union-loving mob (15). Humphreys withdrew from Paintsville after a skirmish on January 7, 1862 (16), and Garfield, accumulating a few supplies, followed. Near Prestonburg they fought a four-hour action on the wooded slopes above a valley on January 10th that became known as the Engagement at Middle Creek (17, 18). The losses were slight on both sides, and it was possible to bring only a part of each brigade on the field because of disease to be described. Because the area was destitute of food, forage, and transportation, both forces withdrew. Marshall retired nearly to Virginia at Pound Gap and Garfield to Paintsville, where he controlled most of the valley and could be supplied by boat.

Garfield went into winter camp even as he wrote Buell on January 30th that he hoped to receive permission to pass the "gates of the mountain" and strike the great railroad (19). In view of his serious disease and supply situation, that hope seems unrealistic. However, McClellan also still retained this objective for him (20).

In February Garfield pushed up to Piketon. Here, on the 24th, Nature added physical disaster to disease. After two weeks of heavy intermittent rainfall and twenty-four hours of continuous downpour, the river quickly rose sixty feet to the highest point in known history, flooding the campsite and town and destroying food, stores, horses, and camp equipment. Under renewed pressure from Buell (21), Garfield advanced to Pound Gap where, on March 16th, he dispersed the last component of Marshall's army on Kentucky soil (22). By the winding valley, this point was about one hundred and fifty miles from the Ohio River—the source of all of his supplies.

In March Garfield heard that he had been promoted to brigadier general, the commission to date from his victory in January. On March 7th, he asked Buell for new orders because he had reached the limit of his instructions (23). Consequently on March 24th, he was ordered to report to Buell and his brigade was dispersed (24). Marshall was then back at Abingdon, Virginia where his brigade was badly depleted and demoralized. In May, however, it won a sizeable engagement in the Kanawha Valley.

## The Role of Disease

This campaign, then, ended in three months after one engagement and a number of raids and skirmishes but small combat casualties. At no time was even half of either force engaged. The morale was low on both sides, but lower among the Confederates. That disease played a major part in determining these facts is not apparent in the official records, already cited, or from Garfield's edited history of the campaign (2), but it is demonstrable from other sources. Marshall was more candid about disease than Garfield except when Garfield was writing to his wife. However, several surgeons made good reports through the official medical channels. In addition, the vivid home letters of Surgeon B. F. Stevenson of the Twenty-second Kentucky were published (25), and Surgeon John N. Beach of the Fortieth Ohio left much medical information in the regimental history, which he wrote (26).

General Marshall was able to organize only one new regiment in Kentucky (27). His Virginia soldiers were unhappy at having to leave their home country, and one balky colonel had to be arrested

(28); later the ten captains of this regiment petitioned to be sent to the rear where subsistence would be better and the regiment could recover its health (29). Twenty per cent (200 men) had been left sick in Virginia, and in January, besides "ordinary inflammatory diseases incident to a winter campaign" (*i.e.* respiratory tract infections), fully half the men were suffering from dysentery and diarrhea. Marshall reported 3,000 men on December 30th (30), but a few days later, out of 1,915 present for duty, many were actually not fit because of measles and mumps (31). On the day of battle (January 10), only 1,600 were able for duty (32). By January 15th, many needed hospitalization, which was not available, for measles and mumps (32). On January 20th the command was in "bad condition," fewer than half being available for duty (32). Three days later, 400 men in his new Kentucky regiment were suffering from measles and mumps; in February, many had coughs and fever (33).

The military ineffectiveness resulting from this sickness was candidly reported by General Marshall to Johnston and to Richmond. Disease had reduced the effective size of his command far below its paper strength. Its efficiency was further reduced by low morale resulting from inadequate subsistence and shelter, heavy snow and rain, deficiencies in shoes and clothing. On January 23rd he was immobilized and ". . . shall have to be as quiet as possible until the diseases have run their course" (32). At first he thought that with large reinforcements he could strike into central Kentucky, but he finally decided an invasion would be impractical until May 1st, when the grass would be up and the roads good (33). Therefore, he retreated back into Virginia. Marshall blamed Jefferson Davis for planning the campaign and then failing adequately to support it. In allocating troops Davis seems to have failed to have taken into account the inevitable large morbidity in new soldiers.

One observer was inclined to attribute the excessive sickness to the scanty rations (3). While malnutrition may well have been a factor in chronic dysentery, it would not greatly modify the infectivity of highly communicable diseases such as measles and mumps. No diagnosis of scurvy, one indicator of malnutrition, has been found for this area, although it soon made its appearance elsewhere.

Garfield's official correspondence is reticent about the health of his command. However, on January 17th he conceded that 207 troopers out of 300 in the First Kentucky cavalry were sick (15), and on March 7th he admitted that the "exposure" resulting from the flood in February had "largely increased my sick list" (23). Other sources describe a picture of disease more severe than that of the Confederates, although the suffering was not as great because of a slightly better supply situation.

Surgeon B. F. Stevenson, of the Twenty-second Kentucky, nominated for this position by Professor Austin Flint of Louisville, found seventy men from his regiment in a rear depot hospital at Ashland, Kentucky, when he was travelling to join up in January. Their diseases were chiefly measles, bronchitis, pneumonia, and typhoid fever (25). Forward at Louisa Court House he found many more sick. Finally, at the regimental hospital in the Piketon courthouse in February, most of the measles had disappeared but about fifty were down with mumps. Doctor Stevenson, like many other old practitioners, was surprised to find so many adults susceptible to both diseases. At one time each regiment had between sixty and seventy patients in its hospital but Stevenson thought that half the soldiers were unfit for duty. He cautioned on February 14th that "There is a much greater amount of sickness in camp than the world is aware of." The weather was bad and he had a number of pneumonias within four days. The flood in February submerged the town plateau, and on subsiding it left the entire valley under deep mud and sewage. By March 9th, typhoid fever was highly prevalent. The mortality rate was moderate but the victims remained "attenuated," feeble, and worn down for a long time. By this time, each regiment had a sick list of seventy or more present, but an additional 450 were in the depot hospital at Ashland and still others were sick at home. None of the regiments could muster half their nominal strength. Another medical officer of this regiment wrote that two to three hundred men had rubeola at the same time (34).

Surgeon John Beach of the Fortieth Ohio in general confirmed but expanded on Stevenson's findings (26). The Forty-second Ohio on leaving the Big Sandy valley in the middle of March, 1862, three months after departing Camp Chase at Columbus, had already lost eighty-five men by death. Beach's own regiment lost eighty-three by death and 153 from all medical causes in its first fifteen months of service, but ninety per cent of these occurred in the first four months after leaving Ohio. This loss, he thought, was not due to any epidemic but it resulted largely from "exposure" and the want of attention to proper hygiene, not defined. The chief causes of mortality were typhoid fever and diarrhea that peaked in their camp at Piketon.

In a medical report Surgeon Beach described the amount of sickness in the Fortieth Ohio as involving half the regiment at one time; the serious type being chiefly typhoid fever (1). As late as April 19th, fifty cases lay in the hospital at Piketon and new victims were still being admitted. He related this outbreak to the previous flood. In April and May this regiment had a great excess of dysentery and diarrhea as well.

The historian of the Forty-second Ohio described a big increase in sickness at Paintsville in January, only three weeks after they departed their barracks at Camp Chase (4). A second big increase came after the flood in February, which left a coating of slime in the valley. Late in March, when they were shipped to Cincinnati, nearly one-third of the men were on the sick list or in hospital at Ashland. Almost every supply steamer returning to the Ohio River from the upper Sandy took down hospital cases of pneumonia, measles, and fevers. Another member of the regiment recorded that in February they were ". . . suffering from all the chronic diseases which beset new soldiers in an unhealthy climate" (35).

Although Garfield did not admit to a high disease rate or mention its military consequences to his military superiors or in his history written during his presidential activity, he expressed great concern in his letters home (6). Thus, on March 10th he described his sick list consequent to the flood as fearful and alarming. In hospital at Ashland were over 400 men and he was sending down sixty more. Fifty had already died during the past month. Many men in his regiment had volunteered because of his personal influence, and he warned his wife not to mention this sickness outside the family. That his own feelings were involved is shown by his cry:

I declare to you there are fathers and mothers in Ohio that I hardly know how I can ever endure to meet. . . . I dare not tell you how small a number of that noble regiment can be mustered for duty. This fighting with disease is infinitely more horrible than battle. . . . This is the great price for saving the Union. My God, what a costly sacrifice.

There can be little doubt that the exceptional prevalence of typhoid and some of the dysentery was related to the flood a few weeks earlier. Apart from this epidemic, the morbidity was similar in the opposing armies. Although Garfield described the rise in the river as being sixty feet, others measured it up to seventy-two feet. The camps as well as the town were flooded, and food, supplies, and equipment were soaked or swept away. Of course the latrines and wells were flooded, their contents mixing. Regardless of whether open trenches or toilets of other types were used, the countryside, including the wells, the stored food, and the eating utensils were contaminated. Typhoid and dysentery had previously existed in the four regiments and every sizeable body of soldiers must have had carriers discharging these enteric pathogens. An epidemic would be expected following the catastrophe. If the Confederates would have found the strength to force the Federals from the area, they would have suffered in turn, as the polluted water was probably infective for many months.

## Aftermath

Neither side enrolled many recruits during the campaign, and the valley attracted little further interest during the war. The expressed desire of Garfield to use the upper Big Sandy as a base from which to cut the Virginia and Tennessee railroad seems unrealistic. He had an advantage over Marshall because of the river, navigable except at low water. Neither side could operate in force far from the river. A raid to sever the railroad, one short strike, would have made only temporary damage. Any small Union force attempting to hold a point could have been quickly overcome by a superior force brought up on the railroad from one or both directions.

The Eastern Kentucky campaign ended in March, 1862, when General Marshall withdrew into Virginia. He gave up because his little "army" had been depleted—cut down chiefly by disease. Garfield's brigade was not larger, but he had shown considerable audacity and greater tenacity and endurance. In fact, after the typhoid epidemic struck, his force had become smaller. The Fortieth Ohio, that remained in the area for some months longer, continued to have much enteric disease, and it is likely that the other regiments would have had similar trouble if they had remained. Marshall might have imposed his will in the valley if he had tried again. No statement has been found on the health of the civilian population after the flood. The inhabitants had previously been few and warfare had driven away many even of these. No moveable property was safe when soldiers foraged. On the night of the first encampment in the valley, hungry men of the Forty-second Ohio foraged some pigs and poultry. Colonel Garfield lectured the regiment the next morning on the sin of confiscation and paid the farmer out of his own pocket. The lesson did not last long.

The secretive attitude toward medical casualties practiced by Garfield was common—a fact that must be recognized in the military writing of that war. This attitude still exists among people who do not understand the infectious diseases. It explains the illogical abhorence to bacterial warfare expressed today. A bacterial infection like typhoid, being supernautral and irrational to them, was feared whereas a gunshot wound of the femur with a suppurating infection, also bacterial, was taken in stride even though its mortality was twice that of typhoid.

This campaign went almost unnoticed since, apparently, no reporters were present. It was overshadowed by General George Thomas' victory at Mill Springs in January, Grant's capture of Forts Henry and Donelson, T. W. Sherman's landing at Port Royal, Burnside's success at Roanoke Island, and Curtis' victory at Pea Ridge. In addition, before it ended McClellan had started toward Richmond, Butler for New Orleans, and Pope down the Mississippi. No medical or military lessons were learned. Cumberland Gap and the loyal mountaineers remained targets of Lincoln's worries and affections until the last winter of the war, absorbing sizeable military resources. Because relief was impractical, the people were finally placated, in part, by a political reward, so that Andrew Johnson eventually became the President.

# References

1. BEACH, J. N.: *Med. and Surg. Hist.*, Vol. I, Part II, p. 89.
2. GARFIELD, J. A.: My campaign in Eastern Kentucky. *North American Review, 143*:525-535, 1886.
3. GUERRANT, E. O.: Marshall and Garfield in Eastern Kentucky. *Battles and Leaders in the Civil War.* New York, Century Co., Vol. 1, 750, 1887.
4. MASON, F. H.: *The Forty Second Ohio Infantry.* Cleveland, Cobb, Andrews & Co., 1876, 306 p.
5. SMITH, T. C.: *The Life and Letters of James Abram Garfield.* New Haven, Yale Univ. Press, Vol. 1, 1925, 650 p.
6. WILLIAMS, F. D.: *The Wild Life of the Army: The Civil War Letters of James A. Garfield.* East Lansing, Michigan State Univ. Press, 1964, 325 p.
7. *O.R., 4*:495, 503, 518-519.
8. *O.R., 7*:22, 503-504.
9. *O.R., 7*:473, 389, 501, 511-513.
10. MARSHALL, HUMPHREY: *Dictionary of American Biography.*
11. MOSGROVE, G. D.: *Kentucky Cavaliers in Dixie.* Jackson, Tenn., McCowat-Mercer Press, Inc., 1957, 281 p.
12. WISE, J. S.: *End of an Era.* Boston and New York, Houghton, Mifflin & Co., 1899, 474 p.
13. *O.R., 10*: Part 2, 410-413.
14. BEATTY, J.: *The Citizen-Soldier; or, Memoirs of a Volunteer.* Cincinnati, Wilstach, Baldwin & Co., 1879, 401 p.
15. *O.R., 7*:32-33.
16. *O.R., 7*:21.
17. *O.R., 7*:29, 30-32.
18. *O.R., 7*:46-50.
19. *O.R., 7*:33-35.
20. *O.R., 7*:660.
21. *O.R., 7*:620.
22. *O.R., 10*: Part 1, 33, 34-35.
23. *O.R., 10*: Part 2, 17-18.
24. *O.R., 10*: Part 2, 65, 68.
25. STEVENSON, B. F.: *Letters from the Army 1862-1864.* Cincinnati, Robert Clarke & Co., 1886, 311 p.
26. BEACH, J. N.: *History of the Fortieth Ohio Volunteer Infantry.* London, Ohio, Shepherd & Craig, 1884, 243 p.
27. *O.R., 7*:46-50.
28. *O.R., 7*:40-42.
29. *O.R., 7*:52.
30. *O.R., 7*:42-44.
31. *O.R., 7*:45-46.

32. *O.R.,* 7:53-55; 55-57.
33. *O.R.,* 7:58-60.
34. MANFRED, H.: *Med. and Surg. Hist.,* Vol. I, Part III, 654.
35. HOPKINS, O. J.: *Under the Flag of the Nation,* Ed. by O. F. Bond. Columbus, Ohio State Univ. Press for the Ohio Hist. Soc., 1961, 308 p.

# V

## The Peninsular Campaign of 1862

### Introduction to the Peninsular Medical-Military Problems

In 1862, General George B. McClellan lost the Peninsular campaign whose principal objective was the capture of Richmond. His effort was stopped by a force that was smaller but better led. Because of a faulty intelligence system, he probably did not know the opposition was smaller. McClellan conducted a strategic offensive until he met resistance near Richmond, but he never took the tactical offensive from this point. He demanded reinforcements for an attack, but they were provided only in part. The number of troops he requested in June was smaller than his sick list. If his sick could miraculously have been made well, or if the sickness could have been prevented, McClellan would have had the numbers he thought he needed to resume the offensive. Epidemic disease was therefore an indirect but major factor in McClellan's failure to give battle, and thus, possibly, in the failure of the first offensive against Richmond.

McClellan's army retreated to Harrison's Landing on the James River after a series of defensive battles at the end of June. Sizeable combat casualties were now added to the increasing losses from disease. McClellan again requested reinforcements to resume operations, but his figures were not fully met. Once again the sick list was larger than his demands, so disease was against an indirect but important factor in his failure to renew the campaign.

As the defeated army lay at Harrison's Landing, its future was discussed. After the decision was reached not to reinforce, it was ordered North by General H. W. Halleck. The principal reason lastly given for withdrawing from the Peninsula was the threat of even more disease in the late summer and autumn months. The evacuation made another offensive impossible. Thus the threat of more disease was a factor in closing out the campaign.

Disease, then, critically influenced the Peninsular campaign at three points: It deprived McClellan of the number of troops he claimed he needed to take the offensive before June 28th; it repeated this effect in July and August at Harrison's Landing; and, the threat of even more sickness in the late summer and autumn months was one reason for abandoning the Peninsula. The evidence will be given in this chapter.

The army had suffered severely from communicable and other diseases in its training camps during the preceding months. It went to the Peninsula already reduced by disease but, of far greater importance, carrying the germs of great epidemics. This background facet of the picture will also be documented.

Finally, was Halleck's fear of autumnal disease and his decision justifiable? Because the army was moved away his hypothesis was not tested, and any retrospective opinion must be based on collateral evidence. Fortunately this is quite good, and it is presented in a following section.

The opposing Confederate army also experienced much disease in its training camps and during the ensuing campaign. The military consequences, however, were less serious than in the Union army for various reasons. The situation inherently favored the defense. As it turned out, the size of the Confederate army was less important than what McClellan mistakenly thought it to be. Many of the pertinent medical documents no longer exist, but the surviving evidence will be reviewed.

It is the purpose of this chapter, then, to present the disease picture of this campaign, its roots in the preceding winter, and its military consequences. The course of the war was altered at several points. Finally, the great influence of the diseases on the careers and relationships of the leaders will be considered. One of the conclusions is that ignorance or reticence about the number of casualties resulting from disease accounted for the different estimates of the size of this army held by McClellan and President Lincoln. The consequences of this misunderstanding were great.

## The Military Campaign

The Peninsular campaign extended from the landing of McClellan's army below Yorktown, in March-April, 1862, to its departure after the middle of August. The opposing armies were soon named the Army of the Potomac (Union) and the Army of Northern Virginia (Confederate). They were the greatly enlarged descendants of those that had fought at First Bull Run in the previous July. In the interim small components had met only in a few small engagements such as those at Ball's Bluff in October and Drainesville in November.

The growth and training of these armies had taken eight months, the campaign would occupy three, and the withdrawal nearly two more. Thirteen months was a long time in the life of an army in the days when the regiments began to melt away from disease almost from the day they rendezvoused in their home states.

Although these armies had not fought since the previous July, other armies had not been idle and the picture had changed. Following the Confederate victory over General Nathaniel Lyon in the battle of Wilson's Creek in southwestern Missouri in August, 1861, sizeable Federal victories had followed: At Carnifex Ferry, western Virginia in September (General Rosecrans); at Belmont, Missouri in November (Grant); at Hilton Head, South Carolina in November (T. W. Sherman); at Mill Springs, Kentucky in January (Thomas); on Roanoke Island and Newbern, North Carolina in February and March (Burnside); at Forts Henry and Donelson, Tennessee in February (Grant); at Valverde, New Mexico in February (Canby); at Pea Ridge, Arkansas in March (Curtis); at Shiloh, Tennessee in April (Grant, Buell); at New Madrid and Island No. 10 in March and April (Pope); and at New Orleans in April (Farragut, Butler). Some of these actions were sizeable and costly, but they had raised morale in the North while lowering it in the South.

Consequently, before McClellan fought his first battle in May, National footholds had been obtained on the North and South Carolina coasts, the Mississippi River had been opened nearly to Memphis, and the armies of Grant and Buell stood on the borders of the Gulf states. It is understandable that the North was impatient with the large idle army in Virginia and that pressure was brought on McClellan. It is true that in his capacity as the general-in-chief he had supported most of these advances, but while simultaneously building up the largest army for himself.

McClellan advanced up the Peninsula to Yorktown. Here defense works stopped him for a month while an attack was being prepared. The line was abandoned before this could be launched. In the chase up the Peninsula, a sizeable engagement developed between the Confederate rear and the Federal advance at Williamsburg on May 5th. The retreat continued to the region below Richmond where the main Confederate force had been constructing defenses. The Union army followed slowly, some of it sailing up the York river on transports. The two-day battle of Fair Oaks (or Seven Pines) developed on May 31st, only a few miles from Richmond, when General Joseph E. Johnston surprised a part of McClellan's army temporarily segregated by high water in the Chickahominy river. Johnston failed, was himself wounded, and had to be replaced by General Lee, who had up to then won no laurels.

McClellan had yet deliberately to open his first battle when he was struck by Lee on June 26th to begin what became known as the Seven Days' battles. These ended on July 1st, at Malvern Hill, with a Confederate repulse by the massed Union artillery. The Army of the Potomac took refuge at Harrison's Landing under the Federal gunboats. During these battles the army base had been transferred from the York to the James River.

During this time, an acrimonious if not insubordinate correspondence had passed with the Secretary of War in which McClellan accused Stanton of not wanting him to win. This charge was chiefly based on the withholding for the defenses of Washington of troops on which McClellan had counted. McClellan's army had been so greatly reduced by combat and disease that he felt unable to renew the attempt to take Richmond, now over twenty miles away. The Confederates were stirring, so General Pope was brought from the West to organize all of the scattered troops in northern Virginia for the protection of Washington. This force, eventually numbering about 60,000, was named the Army of Virginia.

McClellan's army was idle, he failed to advance, and plans had to be made for the future. Feeling the need for a military advisor, President Lincoln appointed as the new general-in-chief Henry W. Halleck, whose army group had recently taken Corinth, Mississippi from General Beauregard.

After Halleck had visited Harrison's Landing, the decision was made in Washington to withdraw McClellan's army. As its components came north in late August, they were made available to General Pope, and some fought at Second Bull Run. McClellan was placed in charge of the defenses of Washington. As Pope's defeated troops fell back on that fortified city, they came under McClellan's direction, and with them he fought the battle of Antietam in September.

## The Disease Picture Prior to the Campaign

### Union

The Army that General McClellan took to the Yorktown Peninsula at the end of March, 1862, had been assembled and trained on the Potomac river since the previous summer. The first battle of Bull Run had been fought on July 21, 1861 by General McDowell, in part with three-month regiments. When McClellan took command he found (on July 27, 1861) the Washington troops composed of 50,000 infantry, 1,000 cavalry, and 650 artillerymen (1). An urgent call had already gone out to the governors for more regiments and they soon poured in. The resulting rapid and large build-up is shown in Table VI (2). The large decrease between March 1 and April 30 is accounted for chiefly by the detachment of the two army corps (Banks' and McDowell's) that were left behind on the Potomac or in the Valley. The three that went to the Peninsula (Sumner's, Heintzelman's, Keyes') were later expanded to five corps (Porter, Franklin) by reorganization and accessions, including a part of McDowell's corps. After the Seven Days, a part of Burnside's command in North Carolina was added, as well as scattered smaller units.

Before going to Washington the regiments had trained in the camps of assembly in their state of origin for periods varying from a few days to as many months. Here sickness had almost invariably broken out. Measles, mumps, diarrhea, dysentery, respiratory infections, and sometimes typhoid fever were the most common infectious camp diseases. In Washington the regiments were at first assigned to the Capitol (the rotunda or the House chamber) or to the temporary camps at Bladensburg or Tenallytown. From May, 1861, fields on Meridian Hill, Kalorama Heights, and nearby farms on Seventh

TABLE VI

Numbers in the Army of the Potomac, 1861-1862*

| | Total present and absent | Present | | | Absent |
|---|---|---|---|---|---|
| | | For duty | Sick | In confinement | |
| ** Oct. 15, 1861 | 152,051 | 133,201 | 9,290 | 1,156 | 8,404 |
| Dec. 1, 1861 | 198,213 | 169,452 | 15,102 | 2,189 | 11,470 |
| Jan. 1, 1862 | 219,707 | 191,480 | 14,790 | 2,260 | 11,707 |
| Feb. 1, 1862 | 222,196 | 190,806 | 14,363 | 2,917 | 14,110 |
| Mar. 1, 1862 | 221,987 | 193,142 | 13,167 | 2,108 | 13,570 |
| † April 30, 1862 | 126,387 | 109,335 | 5,618 | 397 | 11,037 |
| ‡ June 20, 1862 | 145,813 | 105,825 | 11,037 | 364 | 28,587 |
| § July 10, 1862 | 144,886 | 89,549 | 16,644 | 273 | 38,420 |
| Aug. 10, 1862 | 149,758 | 99,048 | ——— | ——— | 50,710 |

* Compiled from the *Official Records, War of the Rebellion.*
** The figures October-March include the army corps of McDowell and Banks.
† Includes McCall's division but not Dix.
‡ Includes Franklin's command.
§ Includes two brigades of Shields, absent, 5,354.

Street and elsewhere became the principal campsites. Some of these sites were poorly drained, the sewage and garbage disposal was primitive, and the drinking water came from small, exposed streams. Sickness soon increased in nearly all regiments and it reached epidemic proportions in some. After they were fully equipped and partly trained, the regiments were assigned to the Army of the Potomac up, down, or across the river, where they were brigaded. Incoming new regiments occupied the vacated and polluted campsites, perpetuating and enhancing the disease problem.

The amount of sickness reported to the adjutant general at various times is shown in Table VI. Here the column for "present sick" represents the number ill in camp on the day the return was made and not the cumulative monthly total. To this figure must be added many of the officers and men listed as absent; they were sick at home, in northern general hospitals, or elsewhere.

The amount of sickness in the army treated in hospitals as reported by its medical director, Charles Tripler, for the months of October and November is shown in Table VII (3). In November this army contained 156 regiments, six battalions, twenty batteries, and eight general hospitals, and its average strength was given as 142,577 officers and men. Therefore, in each month about one-third of the

TABLE VII

Sickness in the Army of the Potomac, 1861

|                                            | *October* | *November* |
|--------------------------------------------|-----------|------------|
| Average strength                           | 116,763   | 142,577    |
| No. under treatment in field or general hospitals | 38,248 | 47,836 |
| Returned to duty                           | 27,983    | 35,915     |
| Died                                       | 295       | 281        |
| Remained under treatment                   | 7,443     | 9,281      |
| Medical discharges                         | 510       | 618        |

complement was sick in a hospital. The sick in quarters or on duty are not included. Surgeon Tripler classified about one-third of these cases as serious. This level was maintained throughout the training period (4). Thus, in the nine months from August, 1861 through April, 1862 each soldier was sick on the average, three times. The reported deaths were few, but it is known from other sources that some of those receiving medical discharges eventually died. Also, some of those remaining under treatment eventually died; this category includes some cases of dysentery and tuberculosis in which death might be long delayed.

Sickness of this amount must have interfered with training, undermined health, and lowered morale. Its only good feature was that in some diseases it conferred immunity, partial or total, temporary or permanent. In view of the tendency after the middle of 1862 to attribute much of the infectious disease to the malnutrition of scurvy, it is noteworthy that this vast amount of disease in 1861 occurred long before any trace of scurvy was noticed.

As another measure of sickness, the report of Surgeon Tripler made about six weeks later on the amount in twelve brigades is useful (Table VIII). He made this report in an attempt to show that the figures of the adjutant general of the army, ultimately derived from the reports of the company commanders, were too high. The sick ranged from 29.75 down to 9.17 per cent in the records of the adjutant general but only 14.5 to 3.4 per cent in those of the medical director. Thus, the figures of the adjutant general averaged about double those of the medical department. The range between brigades was quite large in both sets of figures. Tripler did not explain the large discrepancy between the two reporting systems. It is probable that the company captains had included all men sick in quarters and

TABLE VIII

Amount of Sickness in the Brigades,
Army of the Potomac, 1862*

*Per cent sick*

| Brigade | General William's Table, Jan. 10 | Brigade surgeon's reports | | |
|---------|-----------------------------------|---------------------------|---|---|
| Slocum's | 14.34 | 6.8 | of Jan. | 21 |
| Howard's | 12.44 | 9.3 | " | 18 |
| Richardson's | 11.19 | 6.7 | " | 18 |
| Jameson's | 10.95 | 6.4 | " | 18 |
| French's | 9.6 | 6.3 | " | 11 |
| Morell's | 9.17 | 3.4 | " | 18 |
| Hancock's | 17.1 | 10.9 | " | 18 |
| Brooks' | 29.75 | 14.5 | " | 11 |
| Brannan's | 9.36 | 5.8 | " | 11 |
| Steinwehr's | 11.8 | 5.2 | " | 18 |
| Palmer's | 12.56 | 6.5 | " | 22 |
| Sykes' | 9.95 | 6.5 | " | 25 |

*Official Reports, Vol. 5, Appendix page 107-111.

absent on medical leaves, while the medical officers counted only those in the regimental and general hospitals. In this case, the figures of the adjutant general better portray the amount of sickness and military ineffectiveness. By either system, the amount of illness was large considering that these were spot checks.

Although the amount of sickness shown in Tables VII and VIII seems large, Surgeon Tripler assured McClellan that ". . . this is the most healthy army the world has ever seen." He diagnosed the chief diseases as continued, remittent, and typhoid fevers, measles, diarrhea, dysentery, and various forms of catarrh (5). The chief scourges of armies in the field have always been chronic diarrhea and dysentery, but he added:

> I am happy to say that in this army they are almost unknown. We have but 280 cases of chronic diarrhea and 69 of chronic dysentery in the month of November. No other army that has ever taken the field can show such a record.

He failed to include the numerous cases of acute enteritis, which may become chronic, or to mention that these bowel disorders tended temporarily to fall off during the cold weather.

As to measles, of which 1,331 cases were reported in November, Surgeon Tripler noted that it always occurs in irregular (*i.e.* volunteer) troops when they first assemble, but that it runs through a regiment, then disappears:

I don't consider its propagation under these circumstances as due
to contagion. On the contrary, it springs up from local causes . . .

Note that this remarkable conclusion was made about one of the
most contagious of all diseases and long so regarded even at that date.

All fevers in November numbered only 7,932 cases, 4,051 of them
remittents and typhoids. Typhoid of this amount, Tripler thought,
was not of any great moment. This indifference is hard to understand
in view of the sizeable mortality and the long period of convalescence
in the severe examples that survived.

Brooks' brigade, which had the most sickness (29.75 per cent) in
Table VIII, had suffered chiefly first from measles and later from
remittent and typhoid fevers. This was hard for Tripler to understand because the inspector of hospitals reported their camp police
good, clothing good, and tents good. Two regiments with poor tents,
moreover, had the least sickness! Many times during the four years
were medical officers with set, preconceived, wrong ideas to be similarly
perplexed by the discrepancy between the camp neatness and hygiene
and the amount of fever. Nobody, however, seems to have critically
investigated the reason by direct or by statistical observation and
analysis.

With the winter and spring, Tripler warned, typhus and typhoid
fevers and pneumonia would increase as they arise from foul air,
bad clothing, imperfect shelter, exposure to cold and wet, imperfect
drainage, and badly policed camps. The manure of horses must be
got rid of or the men would get sick, he wrote (5). Travel to
Washington and Georgetown should be prohibited as it brings on
smallpox. Also "It is notoriously unsafe to travel over any railroad
in the country at the present day unprotected." This statement is
confirmed by other sources.

Tripler concluded his report of January 4, 1862 to McClellan by
stating that the health of the army was improving and left little to be
desired. This contention is not supported by the figures already
given or by those that follow, published in the *Medical and Surgical
History* (6). Tripler's report is valuable in displaying the state
of knowledge of military field practice at the time, and in explaining
the disease that followed on the Peninsula.

By using standards other than Tripler's this army cannot be called healthy because the number of diagnoses of disease and injuries of all types combined numbered 247,747 in the nine-month training period from July 1, 1861 through the following March (6). The mean strength, the number of diagnoses, and the deaths for each month around Washington are recorded in Table IX. According to this compilation there were only 1,958 deaths during the period. However, the general hospitals of the Atlantic Region had 1,401 deaths during this time. These must have included many patients sent from the Army of the Potomac. Also, it is known that some soldiers went home with fatal diseases. The total figures include 988 gunshot wounds, 222 of them fatal. Most of these were received in camp accidents or in small affairs between the pickets and patrols. Other smaller categories of trauma also are included in the total diagnoses and deaths but the principal items were medical disorders.

TABLE IX

Total Diseases and Deaths in the Army
of the Potomac, 1861-1862*

| Month | Mean strength | Total diagnoses | Total deaths |
|---|---|---|---|
| July | 17,709 | 8,488 | 71 |
| August | 50,508 | 21,636 | 72 |
| September | 85,408 | 26,809 | 86 |
| October | 113,204 | 31,641 | 166 |
| November | 133,669 | 36,851 | 263 |
| December | 152,759 | 37,829 | 418 |
| January | 167,267 | 35,310 | 393 |
| February | 153,308 | 28,915 | 333 |
| March | 126,588 | 20,268 | 156 |
| Totals | | 247,747 | 1,958 |

*Compiled from *Medical and Surgical History, War of the Rebellion.*

The common communicable disease categories in the same nine-month period are shown in Table X. The most common was epidemic catarrh and acute and chronic bronchitis combined; these respiratory tract infections totalled 46,988. An epidemic gradually built up from 623 cases in July to a peak of 10,418 in January. By June, 1862 the number was down to 610. There were only eighteen deaths. Most of the deaths that resulted from the complications in the lower respiratory tract were probably classified elsewhere, as with "inflammation of lungs" (*i.e.* pneumonia), of which 2,613 examples with 242 deaths

TABLE X

Principal Communicable Diseases in the Army of the Potomac,
1861-1862*

| Month | Epidemic catarrh and bronchitis | Acute and chronic diarrhea and dysentery | Inter-mittent fevers | Common continued and typhoid fevers | Remittent fever | Measles |
|---|---|---|---|---|---|---|
| July | 623 | 3,450 | 165 | 140 | 62 | 272 |
| August | 1,412 | 1,186 | 1,607 | 628 | 584 | 365 |
| September | 2,054 | 5,844 | 3,514 | 941 | 1,340 | 462 |
| October | 3,864 | 7,134 | 3,984 | 1,338 | 1,756 | 518 |
| November | 6,933 | 6,314 | 3,011 | 2,119 | 1,922 | 930 |
| December | 9,132 | 4,447 | 2,151 | 1,692 | 1,474 | 1,488 |
| January | 10,418 | 3,910 | 1,170 | 1,482 | 982 | 927 |
| February | 7,980 | 3,151 | 793 | 1,195 | 1,148 | 751 |
| March | 4,572 | 4,574 | 993 | 670 | 664 | 272 |
| Totals | 46,988 | 40,010 | 17,388 | 10,205 | 9,932 | 5,985 |

*Compiled from *Medical and Surgical History of the War of the Rebellion.*

were recorded. Most of these pneumonia deaths also occurred in the winter months.

This army, without orders from the top, built winter quarters by regiments in the late fall. Many of the huts lacked adequate ventilation, heating, and living space, and in them airborne infections must have been easily spread. Streptococci and other agents pathogenic for the pharynx and the nearby mucus surfaces must also have been distributed by the contact of food with the inadequately cleaned eating utensils and cooking ware used by these amateur housekeeping groups. For example, in addition to the numerous respiratory infections were 462 cases of "inflammation of the internal ear" and 517 of "otorrhea." Curiously, only 72 cases of scarlet fever (four deaths) were recorded during this time. It is known that this was one of the historical periods of low scarlet fever prevalence, but these extremely low figures seem incredible in view of the large amount of epidemic catarrh, rheumatic fever, etc., then prevailing. It seems probable that many examples of scarlet fever went unrecognized. Possibly some were called croup, measles, or black measles. Diphtheria, membranous croup, and putrid sore throat were not even mentioned in the diagnostic tables of the period.

In this relation meningitis is of interest. It was not recognized as a major problem. This disease was reported under the headings of "inflammation of brain" and "inflammation of membranes of brain." Forty-five cases (seventeen deaths) of the former and sixty-five (seventeen deaths) of the latter were reported. In view of the absence of examination of the cerebrospinal fluid and the infrequency of necropsies, such a separation into two groups has a questionable value. These categories must have included the cases secondary to ear infections and to tuberculosis, the primary meningococcic type, syphilitic meningitis, and others. The low mortality in view of the absence of any effective therapy is remarkable, and it raises serious questions on both groups. Possibly some of the hopelessly ill were transferred away.

In the nine months 907 cases of consumption were diagnosed. Sixty were fatal, but some additional cases probably died at home as the mortality was known to be high. The early and nonpulmonic forms were not reported. Rubeola was a common precursor. Whooping cough was then not reported as such, but some of the bronchitis sounds suspiciously like pertussis. Scrofula was diagnosed in 286 soldiers. None died while under army observation. Some of them were probably bovine tuberculosis.

The army was not free from any of these various airborne infections when it went to the Peninsula.

The second largest disease category in Table X, 40,010 cases with fifty deaths, was acute and chronic diarrhea and dysentery. This mixed etiological group of enterocolitis cases probably included both bacillary and amebic dysentery as important components. A number of them later developed hepatic and other visceral abscesses, indicating an amebic origin. After the army was built up, the low month was February with 3,151 examples. From this point the disease increased every month, reaching 7,564 cases in June, 1862. The subsequent catastrophe on the Peninsula is understandable from these figures as many of these patients remained with their regiments as sources of infection. Cholera morbus, of which 1,315 cases (three deaths) were reported during this time, is not included in the dysentery figures. Some of these men probably had an acute staphylotoxin or metal (zinc, cadmium) food poisoning.

The third largest disease group was the intermittent fevers, supposedly malaria. It included the quotidian, tertian, quartan, and
congestive types. Among the 17,388 cases only forty-five died—
chiefly in the congestive type. The number of new cases dropped
greatly during the winter months but never stopped. Many carriers
of the malaria parasites must have been taken to the Peninsula that
spring, and the disease increased greatly.

No other internal parasite was recognized as a big problem. Worms
(489 cases, no deaths) were fairly common. They were not classified
but they were probably chiefly ascarids. External parasites included
the ubiquitous lice and the common army itch, often thought to be
scabies.

Typhoid and the common continued fevers together numbered
10,205 of which 797 died. In a related category, remittent fever, were
9,932 examples with only forty-five deaths. Inasmuch as overt typhoid
fever had a mortality of about twenty-five per cent both in and out
of the army, the common continued and remittent groups must have
been diluted by examples of some other disease (such as paratyphoid
fever) then not diagnosed, or by malaria. Typhus fever, another
"continued" fever, was not always distinguished from typhoid, but
during the same nine months only 173 patients with this disease
(thirty-nine deaths) were recorded. As regards both morbidity and
mortality, typhoid fever was an important uncontrollable disease that
built up to peaks in the autumn, but it was never absent from armies.
The long incubation period and the existence of healthy carriers
were unknown, so many hidden sources of infection were carried along
when the army moved.

Measles was also common during this period (5,985 cases). Among
the communicable diseases here mentioned it ranked second in mortality. The deaths resulted from the complications and sequels such
as bronchopneumonia and tuberculosis so that the full harmful effects
were not immediately apparent. It became axiomatic that army
measles, like army itch, never got well. The largest number (1,488)
occurred in December. New regiments were still joining the army that
month. For June, 1862, only twelve new cases were reported. It was
never again troublesome except if groups of recruits joined up. Since
German measles was not recognized as a separate disease it was

probably included with the rubeolas, accounting for the wide range in virulence described for this disease. The dreaded black measles was mentioned a number of times in the unofficial writings.

The importance of smallpox was not exaggerated by Surgeon Tripler. It appeared every month, adding up to 380 cases with seventeen deaths. These figures may include some chicken pox, not separately reported, to explain the exceptionally low mortality.

Of far greater importance were the venereal diseases. Syphilis, with 3,545 examples, was nearly as common as gonorrhea (4,086). However, there were also reported 183 strictures of the urethra and 916 instances of orchitis, not otherwise specified. The late visceral lesions of syphilis and the joint and other internal changes of gonorrhea were not recognized. The frequency of the venereal diseases varied directly with the proximity and accessibility to cities. They fell sharply each month on the Peninsula. "Ladies fever" caused more trouble in some other armies than in this one.

Another common communicable disease during the initial training period was mumps. This army had 1,786 cases in nine months. The frequency dropped sharply to forty-six cases in June, 1862, and mumps was not again bothersome.

Jaundice was reported in 3,400 soldiers. As there were only four deaths, this seems to have been chiefly infectious (viral) hepatitis rather than Weil's infectious jaundice or the secondary jaundice of stones, tumors or cirrhosis. Some comments on this disease in the memoirs and unofficial histories characterize it as deep, but painless and transient. It was both sporadic and in groups. It was present every month that winter and on the Peninsula.

Rheumatism is here mentioned briefly because of its great importance and its relationship to some infections. Acute and chronic rheumatism were a major problem in camp and field, especially during the winter months. This disease decreased in April, 1862, but in June there was a sharp rise. This may represent proximity to the battlefields of the Peninsula rather than a true increase because this was a favorite complaint with malingerers. In nine months, 15,517 cases and five deaths were recorded. This diagnosis included what today would be called variously rheumatic fever, rheumatoid arthritis, osteoarthritis, the arthritis of specific infections (gonococcal, tuberculous, etc.), and other diseases. Some of the gouty arthritis was probably included, although thirty-six cases of gout were separately reported under this diagnosis.

Surgeon Tripler used the standards of that day in calling this army "healthy" when it had 247,747 sick soldiers. Today the interference with training would be thought serious, and the reservoir of infection would be recognized as dangerous then and for the future. The soldiers and their folks at home were inured to high expectancies of infectious disease and uncomplaining in its presence.

The realities of the disease picture do not emerge as well from the statistics as from the experience of specific units. Thus an assistant surgeon described the principal diseases in Richardson's brigade for the months of October, November, and December, 1861 (7). Reference to Table VIII shows that this was one of the healthiest brigades. It was composed of the Second, Third, and Fifth Michigan and the Thirty-seventh New York regiments of infantry volunteers. Their mean strengths during the three months were respectively 927, 917, 923, and 729 (eight companies) soldiers. The men excused from duty for sickness in three months numbered 1,187, 756, 816, and 835. Thus, each man had been on the sick list once on an average. The principal diseases were as follows:

| | | |
|---|---|---|
| Catarrh | 709 | cases |
| Acute diarrhea | 573 | |
| Intermittent fevers | 502 | |
| Constipation | 221 | |
| Typhoid fever | 144 | |
| Acute bronchitis | 132 | |
| Rheumatism | 125 | |
| Continued fever | 89 | |
| Remittent fever | 75 | |
| Acute dysentery | 63 | |

Other diseases were present in lesser amounts. Discharges during the period had numbered 124 and deaths four. The high position of intermittent fever in northern men for these months is impressive. Note that all the diseases on this list except two are transmissable, an ugly portent for the army later on the Peninsula.

Dozens of regimental and other medical officers left accounts of their experiences that winter in the medical periodicals (8, 9, 10, 11), in regimental histories (12, 13, 14, 15, 16, 17), in personal memoirs and diaries (18, 19), in official reports (20, 21, 22, 23,

24, 25, 26, 27), and in other places. These accounts put some flesh on the bare bones of the statistics. Many of the medical officers shared these diseases with the men, showing again the impossibility of preventing them.

Surgeon J. M. Allen of the Fifty-fourth Pennsylvania summarized the situation for many when he wrote (20):

> This regiment is on duty in the valley of the Potomac. This region of Virginia is proverbial for almost every variety of miasmatic fever, and when the peculiar nature of the climate, hot days and cold nights, is taken into consideration in connection with frequent overflows and rank undergrowth, the cause may be easily explained. The diseases incident to the vicinity are remittent, intermittent, typhoid and congestive fevers, pneumonia, diarrhoeal and bronchial affections.

Despite the assurance of Surgeon Tripler, considerable official concern about sickness was expressed by the senior combatant officers. As early as September 14, 1861, General McClellan informed the secretary of war that the medical department was inadequate for the needs of an army of 100,000 (28). He stated that the care of the sick and wounded in the field and in hospitals must be under the commanding general, who should also appoint the medical director for his army. In November, General Hooker found it desirable to build log hospitals for his division, tents being thought inadequate in winter (29). General Banks wrote McClellan in November that sickness was increasing in his division: "Purging, vomiting, intermittent fever, camp fever, approaching somewhat the typhoid in character, are among the principal diseases" (30). He attributed them to cold rains, a wet camp on clay soil, and little sun. Medical Director Tripler advised McClellan in November regarding winter camps that (31)

> . . . unless by our system we can secure a tolerable ventilation, as well as protection against the rains, snow, and cold, we have reason to fear a prevalence of typhus and typhoid fevers among the troops.

This and other bacteriological nonsense shows that correct preventive measures were impossible.

There was even much question among the medical officers of this army regarding the correct diagnosis of the prevailing camp or Potomac fever. At least two commissions were appointed to investigate and recommend. In a day when many infectious diseases were diagnosed clinically by the character of the fever, but when thermometers were not yet used and no laboratory aids were available, diagnosis was a difficult problem. The specific question to be answered was whether this was typhus, typhoid, malaria, remittent, bilious, common continued, or some other fever.

The first board was appointed in October, 1861, by Brigadier General Darius Couch, to study an epidemic in the Tenth Massachusetts (32). This regiment had been encamped on Kalorama Heights and fields north of there in Washington. The commission concluded that the disease was both remittent and typhoid fevers. It generally began as a remittent but changed quickly into a typhoid type. This tendency to assume the typhoid character, they thought, was due to the depressed condition of the men because of the previous high prevalence of measles, to the exposure to various camp influences such as wet marshy soil, to the climatic change in coming from the high cold region of western Massachusetts to the warm district around Washington, and to overwork on picket duty and erecting forts. They recommended no change in the existing campsite (or water supply) but a reduction of the number of men in each tent from sixteen to ten and the issue of a daily allowance ". . . of those articles which medical experience deems best to invigorate and stimulate the system, and endow it with force to withstand whatever morbific influence is operating on this influence exclusively." Consequently, the regiment drew six barrels of whiskey and dealt it out a gill each day per man. The epidemic died out, probably far more from the lack of additional susceptibles than to the ethanol.

A more senior but confusing fever board was appointed by General McClellan on December 6, 1861. Note that this commission was appointed, not by the medical director of this army or by the surgeon general but by the commanding general (33), a man medically so unsophisticated that when he developed typhoid fever two weeks later he called in a homeopath (34). This board visited field hospitals and quizzed medical officers. They concluded that the prevailing fever was ". . . an intermittent or bilious remittent fever in its inception assuming in its course a typhoid type, or a typhoid fever primarily." They thought that although a certain number of cases of ordinary typhoid existed, the large majority were bilious remittent fevers which ". . . had assumed that adynamic type which is present in enteric fever." The cause of this bilious remittent fever was malaria resulting from exposure along the Potomac river in late summer and autumn. The typhoid, they thought, originated from blood-poisoning resulting from overcrowding, from the fatigue of excessive drill, from overexertion, from nostalgia, and from personal uncleanliness.

Remittent fever was on the approved diagnostic list but bilious remittent fever was not, then or later. It has been impossible to find a clear, unambiguous definition or description of this disease. Although malaria and typhoid were both moderately to highly prevalent, typhus also was present, and paratyphoid probably existed then, the board did not consider that some of these soldiers might concurrently be harboring several diseases. Statistically and clinically this was a real probability. Both boards thought that one disease changed into another one. Because of the failure to agree on the nature of this important disease, the term *typho-malaria* was coined and used in the records of the last three years of the war.

In looking at the health situation of this army at the end of March, when it moved down to the Peninsula, the germs of serious trouble if not disaster are evident. It is true that most of the soldiers were now immune to the infectious diseases of childhood, measles and mumps. Scarlet fever, pertussis, rubella, varicella, diphtheria, poliomyelitis, and meningitis were potential dangers that never materialized for reasons that remain unknown. Smallpox could break out, but it could not reach proportions of military importance because most of the men had been vaccinated. The common camp diseases, however, remained a threat. True, many soldiers were now permanently immune to typhoid fever because of an attack before enlistment or in the training camps. Possibly as much as half of this army was so protected. Enough susceptibles remained, however, to support and feed additional typhoid epidemics. Among many other regiments, the Eighty-third Pennsylvania, for example, was steadily burying men who died of typhoid both before and after their transfer to Yorktown (34b). Against dysentery and malaria the soldiers were not protected at all.

The seriously ill were left behind, but the moving army contained men in the incubation period, the healthy carrier state, and in the chronic stage of the various types and species of malaria, dysentery, paratyphoid, and typhoid fever. This army probably had the equivalent of hundreds of "Typhoid Marys" for each of the camp diseases. The Confederate army was similarly contaminated, and in retreating up to the environs of Richmond it would unwittingly pollute the country, streams, and wells that the Federal army would use. In the North "Chickahominy fever" would soon be a term of opprobrium even greater than "Potomac fever" had been that winter. The existing regulations on military hygiene, even if enforced, would be unable to prevent disaster, and the medical knowledge able to prevent it did not yet exist. The virulence of the infectious diseases would be enhanced by the inadequate, scorbutigenic diet issued there, where it could not be supplemented by foraging, packages from home, or visits to the sutler's tent as before. From McClellan down to the privates, many soldiers would pay a big price.

### Confederate

The opposing Confederate army wintered and trained in camps along the railroads in the general region from Centerville to Manassas Junction. After the battle of Bull Run it had been enlarged with new regiments. In March, 1862, under General Joseph E. Johnston, it moved to the vicinity of Richmond, and eventually it was merged with the smaller forces of Generals John B. Magruder and Benjamin Huger above Yorktown. Known as the Army of the Potomac during the first year, it later under Lee became famous as the Army of Northern Virginia.

The size of this army and of the military district on several dates is given in Table XI. On August 17, 1861, Johnston reported only 18,178 present at Manassas (35). A sizeable increase soon took place. A conspicuous feature shows the number present for duty to be only slightly more than half of those carried on the rolls (*i.e.* aggregate present and absent). Some of those absent were away in hospitals or on sick leaves. Leaves of absence for other reasons were not being liberally granted that winter. The absence of nearly half of an army was not rare in the later years of the war but it was unusual in the first year as in this instance. For comparison the situation

TABLE XI

Size of the Confederate Army of the Potomac 1861-1862*

| Dates | Present for duty | Effective total present | Aggregate present | Aggregate present and absent |
|---|---|---|---|---|
| October, 1861 | 44,367 | 44,131 | 52,435 | ——— |
| November, 1861** | 46,281 | 51,943 | 63,928 | 82,553 |
| December, 1861** | 61,898 | 62,112 | 76,331 | 98,051 |
| February, 1862** | 47,306 | 47,617 | 56,392 | 84,222 |
| February, 1862† | 35,960 | 36,267 | 42,860 | 60,062 |

*Complied from the *Official Records, War of the Rebellion.* Later known as the Army of Northern Virginia.
**Includes the Potomac, Valley, and Acquia Districts; the latter two were small.
†Potomac District alone.

in McClellan's army at this time can be calculated from the data in Table VI.

The large amount of sickness came to the attention of the Confederate Congress, and a special committee made an investigation and reported on January 29, 1862 (36). They found an excessive amount of disease, for which the preparations in camp and hospitals were inadequate. A large proportion of the troops had contracted measles, in which the mortality was high. The prevailing diseases were camp fever, measles, pneumonia, diarrhea, and dysentery. Some regiments had much typhoid in which "All of them partook of the depressing character of the camp fever, being of a typhus tendency." They found the number of medical officers inadequate for the needs. Some regiments had no surgeon or assistant surgeon so a private, who happened to be a physician, had been detailed from the ranks to treat the sick.

A serious military effect of disease is shown by the numerous requests that winter and spring in the *Official Records* from General Johnston to the war department for additional senior officers: They were, he said, needed during this important training period to replace officers on sick leave and to compensate for the numerous junior officers absent for the same reason. Johnston's requests were not filled.

The medical records for the period are incomplete but it is reasonably certain that the disease picture resembles that of the Union opponent. On August 17, 1861 General Johnston reported from Manassas that of 18,178 present, 4,809 were sick (35). This figure is nearly twenty-five per cent, even without including those on sick leave or sick in the general hospitals away from the army. Johnston told Jefferson Davis the troops would be healthier if they had bacon four times each week instead of only twice. In September he proposed to ". . . remove the troops from the unhealthy valley of Bull Run . . ." (37). At about the same time, General Magruder was demanding more quinine at Yorktown, where the Fifth North Carolina, 1,150 strong, had only 190 fit for duty (38). General G. W. Randolph, a grandson of Thomas Jefferson and soon to be the secretary of war, wrote in August that ". . . this infernal war took me from my books, my home, and everything I love, to swelter in the pestilential marshes of the Peninsula" (39). These two comments are of great interest in view of the medical-military decision faced by the Union authorities a year later on this spot.

The reported Confederate cases of illnesses numbered 148,149, for the nine-month period July, 1861 through March, 1862, when the average strength of this army was 49,394 men (40). This averages over three illnesses per soldier, a figure resembling that found for the opposing army.

The types of disease seem to have resembled those in the Union army. General John B. Gordon, then a major in the Sixth Alabama, wrote that they ran the whole catalog of babyhood and boyhood diseases except teething, nettle-rash, and whooping cough, and some had the latter (41). He thought it amazing to see the large number of country boys who had never had measles. This army had 8,617 cases of measles in three months (July-September, 1861), but only eight in the following February (42). The Thirty-fifth Georgia had to be withdrawn from picket duty in January, 1862 until they had recovered from measles and other camp maladies (43). At the same time an Alabama regiment had to be withdrawn from the front because of total disablement by sickness (44).

Diarrhea and dysentery were a major problem as in the Federal army. With an average mean strength of 49,394 soldiers this Confederate army in nine months had 36,572 cases (45). The monthly distribution of these cases is shown in Table XII. The rate of infection was lower in the Confederate than in the Federal army during the summer of 1861, but the drop was less that winter. At the Chimborazo

Hospital in Richmond the mortality from diarrhea and dysentery was nearly ten per cent of the 10,503 admissions (45). Because of the high mortality rate, it is probable that the admissions here contained an exceptionally high proportion of severe cases—those that had not done well in the field hospitals. This disease, therefore, killed many and disabled more.

TABLE XII

A Comparison of Diarrhea and Dysentery in the Union
and Confederate Armies of the Potomac, 1861-1862*
(Cases per 1,000 mean strength)

| Dates | Confederate | Federal |
|---|---|---|
| July, 1861 | 145 | 195 |
| August, 1861 | 138 | 122 |
| September, 1861 | 59 | 68 |
| October, 1861 | 65 | 63 |
| November, 1861 | 61 | 47 |
| December, 1861 | 70 | 29 |
| January, 1862 | 78 | 23 |
| February, 1862 | 83 | 21 |
| March, 1862 | 92 | 36 |

*Data from *Medical and Surgical History,* Vol. I, Part II, p. 27.

Malaria was also of major importance to the Confederates. A comparison with the Federal problem during this period is given in Table XIII. The rates of infection or relapse were similar in the period under study, including the winter months. In general, malaria was more prevalent but less fatal among Southern than Northern troops. Probably the Southern physicians were more familiar with its treatment.

Typhoid fever, the major serious camp scourge of armies, did not

TABLE XIII

A Comparison of Malaria in the Confederate and Federal Armies
of the Potomac, 1861-1862*
(Cases per 1,000 mean strength)

| Dates | Confederate | Federal |
|---|---|---|
| July, 1861 | 29 | 13 |
| August, 1861 | 67 | 43 |
| September, 1861 | 60 | 57 |
| October, 1861 | 54 | 51 |
| November, 1861 | 38 | 37 |
| December, 1861 | 29 | 24 |
| January, 1862 | 17 | 13 |
| February, 1862 | 15 | 16 |
| March, 1862 | 19 | 12 |

*From *Medical and Surgical History,* Vol. I, Part III, p. 103.

spare the Southern force. The rate of infection and a comparison with the opposing Nationals is shown in Table XIV. These data essentially represent typhoid fever because the amount of typhus was negligible and many of the "common continued fever" cases were mild typhoids in reality. The size of the increase in the late summer and autumn of 1861 was greater in the Confederate than in the Union army. The monthly average rates per 1,000 strength were twenty-three and ten cases respectively. The Southern cases totalled 1,133 during the nine-month period (40). Of 2,153 treated at Chimborazo Hospital during a longer period, 885 (41 per cent) died. There were 1,619 deaths among 6,245 cases treated in general hospitals outside of Richmond between January, 1862 and February, 1863. Because the most serious cases were transferred to the general hospitals whenever practical, the mortality rate was higher there than in the regimental hospitals. Surgeon Edward Warren described hospital conditions when he was assigned to the University of Virginia in August, 1861 (46). Here the regular and improvised hospitals in a large area overflowed with the wounded and sick from the Bull Run campaign. Surgeons, nurses, supplies, blankets, etc. were few. They were burdened with 1,200 cases of typho-malarial fever.

TABLE XIV

A Comparison of Typhoid, Typhus, and Common Continued Fevers
Combined in the Confederate and Union Armies of the Potomac,
1861-1862*

(Cases per 1,000 mean strength)

| Months | Confederate | Federal |
|---|---|---|
| July, 1861 | 10 | 8 |
| August, 1861 | 42 | 12 |
| September, 1861 | 45 | 12 |
| October, 1861 | 27 | 11 |
| November, 1861 | 25 | 16 |
| December, 1861 | 17 | 11 |
| January, 1862 | 11 | 9 |
| February, 1862 | 9 | 8 |
| March, 1862 | 6 | 5 |

*From *Medical and Surgical History,* Vol. I, Part III, p. 206.

An occasional regiment reported "good health," but this is a relative term that requires interpretation today. The First Maryland was such a healthy unit according to its commander, Bradley T. Johnson (47). In the fall and winter of 1861-1862 in camp on Bull Run it had no mumps, measles, or whooping cough, although its service was hard. It lost less than ten men from typhoid fever, but it had some pneumonia and rheumatism ". . . from sleeping on the snow."

From this survey it is apparent that the Southern Army of the Potomac had many cases of the major acute communicable diseases. The basis for potential trouble in the summer campaign of 1862 resembled that in the Federal army, already described. If one army should be struck harder than the other, disease might become a crucial factor in the outcome.

## Losses in Combat

The size of McClellan's army on several dates is given in Table VI. As the footnotes show, accessions of troops arrived several times on the Peninsula. Losses from disease were continual and from combat intermittent, while the return of the convalescents and the exchanged prisoners was irregular. Because of the fluctuations the figures on size are approximations.

The size of Lee's Army of Northern Virginia on July 20, 1862, after the Seven Days, was reported as follows (48) :

| | |
|---|---|
| Aggregate present and absent | 119,242 |
| Aggregate present | 78,891 |
| Present for duty | 57,476 |

These figures omit those troops present in the state of Virginia but assigned to the Department of North Carolina. They also omit Jackson's two divisions (Ewell's and Jackson's) which were under Lee's command at this time and ought to be included. The figures show that fewer than half the soldiers on the rolls were present for duty. Exclusive of those in Jackson's corps, 61,766 men were absent wounded, sick, in prison, as deserters, on leave, and for other causes. Unfortunately, it is impossible accurately to count the total medical casualties among the absentees.

Both armies were large, and Lee's reached nearly its all-time peak when Jackson joined on June 27th at Gaines' Mill. At this time the Union army was already shrinking because of sickness. The total size is not very significant during the Seven Days because neither army was wholly engaged at any time. Some units fought several times and others not at all.

TABLE XV

Combat Casualties in the Peninsular Campaign*

| | Federal | | | |
| --- | --- | --- | --- | --- |
| | Killed | Wounded | Missing | Total |
| Williamsburg, May 4-5 | 456 | 1,410 | 373 | 2,249 |
| Fair Oaks, May 31-June 1 | 790 | 3,594 | 647 | 5,031 |
| Seven Days, June 25-July 1 | 1,734 | 8,062 | 6,075 | 15,849 |
| Totals | 2,980 | 13,066 | 7,095 | 23,141 |
| | Confederate | | | |
| Williamsburg | | 1,570 | 133 | 1,703 |
| Fair Oaks | 980 | 4,749 | 405 | 6,134 |
| Seven Days | 3,478 | 16,261 | 875 | 20,614 |
| Totals | | 27,038 | 1,413 | 28,551 |

*From Miller's *Photographic History,* Vol. 10, p. 142.

The number of combat casualties on the Peninsula is shown in Table XV. The number was large on both sides. The totals include some of the losses incurred between the battles. The number of Confederate killed and wounded was larger than the Union figure because they fought on the offensive. They took more prisoners (some of them wounded) because they were usually advancing and they held most of the battlefields. For this reason, a high proportion of the wounded came under their care. Some of the Northern soldiers listed as missing had actually been killed or wounded but not recovered. Many of the prisoners and wounded were restored to duty during the campaign or later, but such numbers are unknown and cannot be treated statistically. Confederate Surgeon Lafayette Guild on July 3rd wrote that he was caring for 4,700 Union wounded and sick (49).

Despite the large losses neither army was disorganized. Confederate morale was high because they held the battlefields and the threat to Richmond had been relieved. The spirits of the Northerners were low at first because of the loss of men, ground, and material. A widespread depression and listlessness was recorded. It may have resulted in part from the prolonged dietary deficiency which in some showed as a frank scurvy. It disappeared at Harrison's Landing within a few weeks after the diet improved.

## Disease on the Peninsula: Confederate

The disease in the Confederate army during the period April to August, inclusive, is poorly documented, but it is known that many were sick as well as wounded. On June 13th, Jefferson Davis ordered the surgeon general to comb the hospitals at Danville, Farmville, Huguenot Springs, and Lynchburg for convalescents who could return to duty (50), showing that dispersal had been wide if not large. General Lee found it necessary to remind the medical officers that they could not issue a pass except in the extremity of battle, but only sign certificates of professional opinion as a basis for military action by others (51). It is likely that this meant that leaves were hard to get.

Writing of the operations for the period April 15-May 19 when he was in the command, General J. E. Johnston said that "The great fatigue and exposure incident to their service told very severely upon the health of our troops. In three days, ending May 3, about _____ sick were sent to Richmond" (52). The figure must have been large enough to have military importance as it was censured. Of the siege at Yorktown, General Magruder wrote that "The medical officers deserve the highest commendation for the skill and devotion with which they performed their duty in this sickly country" (53). General D. H. Hill's division, soon after arriving near Gloucester Point, crowded its hospitals with the sick (54). In battle at Fair Oaks he lost 2,936 men on May 31st, but by June 16th he had more than that number again absent sick or without leave (55). General Samuel Garland's brigade of five regiments and a battalion (about 5,500 at full strength) entered that fight, their first, with only 2,065 men (56). One regiment, the Fifth North Carolina, had only 180 for duty.

General James Longstreet wrote to Governor Letcher of Virginia two days before the beginning of the Seven Days' battles that his command had twenty-three Virginia regiments, one battalion, and seventeen batteries that should number about 32,000 men, but actually only 20,000 were on the rolls. Of these about 7,000 were absent, leaving less than 13,000 with the army. The largest regiment contained 691 men, the smallest less than 100 (57)—this at a time when the war was only fourteen months old. A few days earlier Surgeon S. G. Welch of the Thirteenth South Carolina had written to his wife from camp near Richmond that many men were sick and they were dying by the thousands (58).

A Richmond memorialist, Mrs. Sally Putnam, wrote later (59):

The month of July of 1862 can never be forgotten in Richmond. We lived in one immense hospital, and breathed the vapors of the charnel house. . . . Every family received the bodies of the wounded or dead of their friends, and every house was a house of mourning or a private hospital. . . . Sickening odors filled the atmosphere, and soldier's funerals were passing at every moment. . . . Our best and brightest young men were passing away.

She was writing of the sick and wounded of the recent weeks.

Although the losses of this army cannot be quantitated, it is certain that they were large. The damage to its morale, however, was less severe, as these men fought well during the Seven Days' battles and again in August and September at Cedar Mountain, Second Bull Run, and Antietam.

## Disease on the Peninsula: Union

The documentation of the sickness in the National force is also incomplete but it is certain that the amount was large. One survivor thought the sick list was almost the army (60). In Table XVI are listed 124,027 illnesses with 1,940 deaths in five months, compiled by the medical department: The mean strength of the army as here reported is smaller than in McClellan's figures (Table I). It appears to represent the number of men able for duty because if the sick are added, the figures are like those of McClellan's adjutant general. To achieve the mean strength shown for July, the corps of Burnside that joined from the southern Atlantic coast was probably added. The drop in mean strength and sickness in August probably represents the detachment of the Fourth corps, which was left behind when the army was shipped north, and it never rejoined. The relatively low

TABLE XVI

Sickness on the Peninsula in 1862, Federal Army*

| Month | Mean** Strength | Number of Cases | |
|-------|-----------------|-----------------|-------|
| | | Sickness | Death |
| April | 71,259 | 16,694 | 116 |
| May | 72,536 | 18,896 | 497 |
| June | 78,733 | 24,690 | 705 |
| July | 106,069 | 42,911 | 371 |
| August | 69,320 | 20,836 | 251 |
| Totals | | 124,027 | 1,940 |

*From *Medical and Surgical History*, Vol. I, Part I.
**Figures exclude McDowell, Pope, troops around Washington, etc.

mortality must be explained by evacuation to Northern hospitals of many of the very sick. Many shiploads had been sent, and many deaths occurred there that summer and autumn.

The principal infectious disease was the enteritis of acute and chronic dysentery and diarrhea, of which 48,912 examples were recorded in five months. The largest number (19,776) came in July. This figure includes the epidemic at Harrison's Landing, which was widespread but mild. The intermittent fevers (7,715 cases), typhoid fever (2,805 examples with 279 deaths), jaundice (1,161 cases), and many others were also present. The respiratory tract infections were now infrequent.

Probably every regiment leaving the Potomac carried with it the microorganisms of communicable diseases, and more were contracted *en route*. The Third Michigan embarked at Alexandria on March 14th and then lay at anchor between there and Washington for about thirty hours before proceeding (61). Their surgeon noticed:

> The water of the Potomac, always muddy and dirty, is at this point pretty well mixed with the drainings of sewers and filth of every kind from Washington, which at the present time, between citizens and other civilians and soldiers, must have a population of over 100,000. This was the only water our men had to drink from the time we embarked, and in less than twelve hours it began to show its effect in diarrhoea and dysentery.

By the time they reached Fort Monroe, 150 cases had been treated. The Eighth New Jersey was aboard another ship for seven days and had a similar experience with bad water (24).

The unhealthiness of the Peninsula was soon widely recognized. After one month a surgeon wrote in his dairy (18):

> Everything soaked with rain, chilly and cheerless. But we are gradually becoming amphibious. Four weeks' inundations have failed to drown us out, and rheumatism has not yet anchylosed our joints.

Surgeon Alfred S. Castleman of the Fifth Wisconsin vividly described the series of diseases in himself and his large regiment that within a year reduced it to 227 muskets in line, feeble, emaciated, and spiritless (19).

The U.S. Sanitary Commission, which first evacuated sick by ships on April 25th, eventually transported away 8,000 patients (62). The quartermaster service claimed it removed ninety per cent of the total. This would give a figure of 82,000 evacuations for sickness and wounds, which seems large, but it is a possibility as nearly half again that number were sick. This number if sick simultaneously would have ruined the army. However, the sickness was staggered over a period of months and the convalescents formed a return flow, sluggish but considerable.

General McClellan reported that disease increased from a previous eight per cent of the force to twenty per cent at Harrison's Landing. These are spot relative frequency figures and not cumulative totals. He conceded that military operations had placed the medical department in a very unsatisfactory condition. Supplies were short because they had been exhausted or abandoned. Many hospital tents had been destroyed or left behind. Medical officers were deficient in numbers or broken down by fatigue (63). In brief, McClellan recognized bad medical conditions and accepted responsibility for them. This attitude is commendable but it obscures the fact that the medical department shared in the blame—not for the casualties but for their inadequate care.

The report of Medical Director Charles S. Tripler (who served to Harrison's Landing) vividly described the medical situation (64). Although he emphasized the administrative problems and the combat wounds more than the diseases and he provided no overall figures, much of his information is pertinent. He conceded that some things had not gone well, and he blamed a part of his troubles on presumptuous sensation preachers, village doctors, strong-minded females, and volunteer medical officers who were not familiar with army administration. When the army first moved from its winter camps in March, it shed its sick by transferring them to general hospitals, and this was repeated on their subsequent moves. The unexpected and belated order of the President in March creating army corps upset his plans and required him to appoint corps medical directors from his staff, depriving him of his most experienced aides.

On the Peninsula Tripler arranged for large temporary hospitals at Fortress Monroe, Yorktown, and at White House Landing on the York river. The overflow was transferred to hospitals in Washington, Georgetown, Alexandria, Annapolis, Baltimore, Philadelphia, New

York, and Boston. Steamers hurriedly fitted up as transports or hospital ships with a capacity up to 900, some of them provided by the Sanitary Commission, plied the waters from the York and James rivers to the North. One acted as a receiving ship. A hospital storeship did not arrive until late in April.

As early as April 7th, Tripler recognized a large swamp near the Union camps below Yorktown as potentially "malarial poison" if the weather should turn warm. Malarial and typhoid fevers soon appeared. By April 17th, 315 sick were shipped to Annapolis, and on April 29th more embarked. By May 4th, over 1,200 sick were collected from one corps, which had shown only 232 on its sick report. On May 9th, 950 were sent away but 2,000 more remained in the hospital at Yorktown. The embarcation of the wounded from the battle of Williamsburg of May 5-6 was not completed until the 11th, and most of the sick of that period had to be left behind in temporary hospitals. To provide space, 225 sick men were sent North from Yorktown on May 11th and 500 more on the following day. From the White House hospital 260 were sent to Boston on May 16th but 1,020 remained. At this time scurvy began to make its appearance. It was troublesome thereafter, greatly reducing the resistance of the sick and wounded.

Many more were sent North later in May, but the casualties from the battle at Fair Oaks on May 31-June 1 could not all be transported to the White House until June 7th. Some had then not yet received their definitive surgical treatment. Within a few days, early in June, 3,580 more were shipped to points as far as Philadelphia, Boston (450 sick), and New York. During this time the regimental field hospitals were nearly always full. The Yorktown hospital was now enlarged to a capacity of 3,000. So many dead horses and unburied rebels littered some campsites on the Fair Oaks battlefield that it was impossible for troops to occupy them. Tripler sent disinfectants to be strewn over the ground but the nuisance was not abated. It became necessary for him to disapprove leaves for surgeons because so many never returned. In the meantime a number of civilian physicians had joined and been assigned to duty. Some of the contract surgeons, of whom 100 were assigned, resigned. The last of the wounded from General Porter's engagement of May 28th at Hanover

Court House arrived at the White House only on June 19th; their evacuation had been delayed by the bad state of the roads. A receiving hospital was established on the railroad at Savage Station on June 16th, but when this point had to be abandoned two weeks later, about 3,000 sick and wounded had to be left behind to be taken prisoners. During this time many sick and wounded were leaving from the landing at White House, but on June 28th it was permanently cut off from the army, which changed its base to Harrison's Landing on the James.

Here the evacuation of the casualties began on July 2nd, and Tripler was relieved by Letterman on the following day. Departing at that time, he never received final reports of the casualties. His official report, submitted in February, 1863, concluded (64):

> During this campaign the army was favored with excellent health. No epidemic diseases appeared. These scourges of modern armies— dysentery, typhus, cholera—were almost unknown. We had some typhoid fever and more malarial fever, but even these never prevailed to such an extent as to create any alarm. The sick reports were sometimes larger than we cared to have them, but the great majority of the cases were such as did not threaten life or permanent disability. . . . The Army of the Potomac must be conceded to have been the most healthy army in the service of the United States.

Such indifference to the large amount of diarrhea and dysentery (48,912 cases) was a common attitude toward this disease at that time, but it was not good for a medical director of a large army. Tripler's statement that "No epidemic diseases appeared" cannot be accepted. The decision to replace him was made late in May or early in June, apparently as a consequence of the inadequate care given the large medical casualties at Fair Oaks. When he wrote he was on the defensive.

Tripler attributed some of his failures to the incompetence, the insufficient numbers, and the lack of enough authority of the medical officers. These factors existed but they in themselves did not explain the inadequate medical supply and service because Letterman with essentially the same personnel soon did much better. Tripler complained that he had to deal with the following:

> . . . all sorts of doctors—steam, electric, and even advertising quacks—

were sometimes commissioned as medical officers; men innocent of any such vulgar acquirements as orthography; men who had never even seen, much less performed, a surgical operation.

He further said that colonels had taken medical supply wagons to carry their baggage. He could not arrest incompetent surgeons because he had no replacements. His surgeons had the authority to prescribe for the sick but not to criticize the camp sanitation or to control their own ambulances and transportation. Surgeon Letterman soon corrected some of these defects, but Tripler thought the only remedy was to have a large standing army with only regulars as surgeons. In concluding his report, Tripler had a kind word of appreciation for only three of his six corps senior medical officers; all three were regular army officers.

Actually, the removal of casualties by the James River had begun several days before Tripler arrived. Major General Alfred Pleasonton of the cavalry took charge of the sick, wounded, and stragglers that arrived at Carter's Landing on June 30th (65). By 11:00 A.M., the *Stepping Stones* pulled out for Fort Monroe filled with 500 to 600 sick and wounded. Fifteen beef cattle were slaughtered to feed the soldiers. By the end of two days up to 12,000 had been cared for, about 5,000 of them stragglers.

Opposing the statements of Tripler regarding inefficient medical officers are many claiming that most of them were competent but poorly equipped and supplied. Surgeon George T. Stevens explained that the regimental surgeons were absolutely on their own in collecting, feeding, hospitalizing, and treating the sick and wounded while they were often destitute of medical and commissary supplies (17). Many thought the medical officers better prepared for their work than most (66, 67, 68).

Regarding the replacement of Medical Director Tripler by Letterman at Harrison's Landing, a representative of the Sanitary Commission wrote hopefully (62):

> Under the dry, taciturn, and impenetrable manner, promising nothing, of the new Medical Director of the Army of the Potomac, who, just after the battle of the Seven Days, relieved a predecessor of precisely the opposite qualities, was found to be concealed some influence by means of which whatever had before been impossible began to be thought possible, and to be tried for, after a few judicious dismissals had been made.

Surgeon Jonathan Letterman took over as the medical director on July 4th (69). He found the army "greatly exhausted." It had been marching and fighting for seven days and nights in pestilential swamps with heavy work, great excitement, scanty food, little sleep, and great depression. Its medical officers were exhausted. Scurvy was present and malaria was increasing. Reports of the number of sick were not available to him, but "After about 6,000 had been sent away on transports 12,795 remained." It was estimated that at least 20 per cent were sick. Medical supplies, equipment, and ambulances were lacking or insufficient. It rained on July 2 and 3, and the overflow of sick and wounded at the Harrison House lay out exposed. No food was available at first. Some beef stock was finally obtained and caldrons of soup were made day and night. Enough tents finally arrived to erect a 1,200-bed hospital. As fast as transports became available, men were shipped North. By July 15th, another 7,000 sick and wounded has been sent but 12,975 remained, making a total of nearly 20,000 for this period, with many more to come. Letterman tried to retain the sick and wounded with the army whenever possible because they became homesick in general hospitals among strangers.

By August 1st tents and ambulances were abundant but scurvy was serious. The chief commissary belatedly ordered potatoes, onions, cabbage, tomatoes, squash, beets, and fresh bread. The first antiscorbutics arrived on July 7th and potatoes and onions by the 20th. The medical purveyor issued 1,500 boxes of fresh lemons to various hospitals and troops. The full effect of a deadly malaria ". . . was now being fully manifest in the prevalence of malarial fevers of a typhoid type, diarrheas, and scurvy."

On Letterman's recommendation, General McClellan ordered that wells be dug where possible, that fresh vegetables be issued, that the food be prepared by companies rather than squads, that tents be raised daily and struck and moved to new ground weekly, that camps be near but not in woods, and that the men have a breakfast before marching; furthermore, the men should be compelled to bathe once a week; sinks should be used and six inches of earth filled in daily; similar holes should be dug for kitchen refuse; and all other refuse from stables and dead animals should be burned or deeply buried.

Under this regime, checked by frequent medical inspections, the scurvy disappeared but, surprisingly . . .

> In a few regiments the sickness increased; in some others it remained nearly stationary, and in others it decreased one-half. On the whole, the health of the army was improving.

On July 30th, the sick with the army still numbered 12,000. The improvement was greater than was indicated by the figures because the morale and spirits had improved and vigor had been reestablished. The sick and wounded prisoners from Richmond began to arrive, and 3,845 were sent North between July 15th and August 3rd.

Because the army was ordered in August to leave the Peninsula, shipments of the sick were resumed. Eventually, 14,159 more had to be sent away. On Letterman's request, General McClellan had ordered on August 2nd the formation of an ambulance corps, but this could not be carried out here. In fact, many ambulances, medical and hospital supplies, and equipment had soon to be abandoned at Yorktown and Fortress Monroe because of shortages in shipping, without the knowledge of the medical officers or over their protests. The divisions of this army that fought at Second Bull Run at the end of August were again almost destitute of medical facilities, and the miserable conditions were repeated.

In summary, Letterman's report disagrees with Tripler's on the amount of illness in the army around July 1st (20 per cent *vs* 8 per cent) and on the amount of scurvy. On these points the information from other sources (some to be cited) all agrees with Letterman's version.

For the scurvy, Doctor Letterman ordered the issuing not only of fresh vegetables but also of fresh soft bread to replace the hardtack (69). His reasoning has historical interest:

> The fresh bread was eagerly sought for by the men, as they loathed the hard bread, which they had used for so many weeks. This loathing was no affectation, for this bread is difficult to masticate, is dry and insipid, absorbs all the secretions poured into the mouth and stomach, and leaves none for the digestion of other portions of the food. The craving for fresh bread was founded in reason, and was not a mere whim.

Letterman was apparently not familiar with the research of an older medical officer, Doctor William Beaumont, published some years earlier. In extenuation it should be said that a number of surgeons noted pieces of undigested hardtack in diarrheic discharges. When the evacuations were half-hourly, the passage time was short.

Doctor Letterman expressed some honest dismay and amazement that his detailed orders of July 18th on camp sanitation (mentioned in part) had not been more effective. Many other medical officers in this and other armies expressed similar surprise. Surgeon J. T. Calhoun of the Seventy-fourth New York wrote (70) that at Harrison's Landing his camp had been a model in every respect, despite which excessive amounts of sickness, especially diarrhea and dysentery, had appeared. To his surprise, this disappeared as if by magic on the march to Yorktown in August when the men ate greedily the green field corn and unripe apples, both previously thought harmful. "I witnessed this effect in my own person," he added. The surgeon of the Eighth New Jersey had noticed on Meridian Hill much sickness despite an ideal campsite (24). The reason is obvious today. The measures ordered by Letterman were unable to stop any of the three main diseases. The measures were inadequate or wrong, and many were irrelevant to the microbiological problems. The regulations ordered did not effectively interrupt the chain of transmission, vulnerable today at several points, of any of the main diseases. Measures based on naked eye appearances were inadequate and microbiological concepts were as yet unborn. Nevertheless, Letterman did as well as was then possible.

For the retreat to the James, General McClellan assigned priorities that have current interest in view of the rapid weakening of his army by disease and malnutrition (71). To go were ammunition and subsistence, intrenching tools, and a reasonable amount of hospital stores. To be left behind or destroyed were tents, officer's baggage, the sick and wounded with attendants, subsistence and medical stores. These priorities reflect the great deficiency in ambulances. There were very few with this army, and it had gotten by so long only because of the chance presence of the railroad to their medical base at the White House. When the main artery was severed, the medical department found itself in deep trouble.

The sickliest periods coincided with the lengthy encampments at Yorktown, on the Chickahominy in May and June, and at Harrison's

Landing—periods when the army stopped in its own polluted environment. The division of Brigadier General Silas Casey, an old campaigner from the Frontier, suffered the most from disease at Yorktown and Fair Oaks. The corps commander, E. D. Keyes, requested an explanation, which Casey gave on May 28th (72): Since the previous September he had received at Washington and initiated into their duties about 120,000 men for other divisions. To fill his own division before departure he had taken eight new, untrained regiments, some unarmed and with new and incompetent officers. In the entire division he had no regular army officer and only one brigadier, also inexperienced. Without transportation, his troops had almost starved, and without shelter tents the ". . . exposure to the miasma of the Peninsula was a great source of sickness." Casey attributed half his losses to imperfect brigade organization, to eight new regiments, to some incompetent medical, field, and company officers, to insufficient medical supplies, and to the mismanaged logistics; the other half he blamed on sickness from unavoidable causes. Today this seems to have been a fair estimate.

Chickahominy soon became an infamous word; ". . . the mention of that name causes a shudder to run through the survivors of the Army of the Potomac, and brings sad memories to thousands of householders" (60). Because of its connection with disease and death in 1862 and again in 1964, many Northern soldiers left descriptions. Among them a New Hampshire surgeon wrote (12):

> The Chickahominy river . . . is a narrow, sluggish stream flowing through swamp land. This land is covered with a rank, dense, tangled growth of trees, reeds, grasses and water plants. Vines climb and mosses festoon the trees; the soil is productive, but its stagnant water is poisonous; moccasins and malaria abound; flies and mosquitoes swarm; turtles and lizards bask; cranes and herons wade; buzzards and polecats stink; bitterns boom, owls hoot, foxes yelp, wild cats snarl and all nature seems in a glamor or a gloom . . . here was to be the home of our New Hampshire men, who had never sniffed malaria nor breathed miasma. Here for two months they were to dwell in the midst of alarms' in 'this horrible place,' during the very hottest days of the Southern year.

After Yorktown, the Fair Oaks area, which bordered on the Chickahominy, became odious among the soldiers for sickness, both in the two weeks before the battle and the month after. To the usual effects of crowded camps on poorly drained terrain in hot weather were added those from a poorly policed battlefield—dead horses and mules and about 3,000 improperly buried men. One regimental surgeon wrote of its atmosphere as composed largely of "poisonous gasses" (73). Another likened it to camping on a graveyard (24). They dug wells up to forty-five feet deep without finding good water, and in four weeks this regiment lost nearly a hundred from sickness and death. General Hooker, ordered on June 2nd to encamp his division on the battlefield, protested that it was impossible to occupy that ground because of the stench (74). He was required to camp there nevertheless, and four weeks later General Heintzelman reported the bad consequences in the Third corps to McClellan (75). The Second corps also was required to camp here. Its medical director after four weeks noted (76):

> ... the command, enveloped in malaria, illy supplied with antiscorbutics, much exposed to the weather, and almost nightly harrassed by the enemy, suffered much from intermittent fevers, diarrhoea, and scurvy.

To the usual horrors were added the shortage of food and supplies after the battle. To one field hospital General Sedgwick contributed two cavalry horses. Led away to a nearby woods, they were soon carried back as beautiful dressed beef, used for making soup for the wounded (77). (One wonders how long the First Cavalry Division in Viet Nam could subsist on its tanks.) General Thomas F. Meagher wrote that his brigade was startled on coming on the battlefield at ten o'clock on the night of the first day at seeing surgeons and chaplains with lanterns searching for the wounded and dead (77b). Another surgeon, exhausted by seven days of operations on subsistence sometimes reduced to mule soup and steaks, and required over his protests to camp in a swamp with his regiment, confided to his journal (18):

> As there is no spring near, we shall have to drink surface water. Of course, we shall get sick, but protest is unavailing. The only time I ever came near being placed in arrest was after remonstrating with the General for camping us in a marsh. When the engineers run their lines they are no respectors of hygienic conditions.

Many thousands of troops camped for a month on the Fair Oaks battlefield so vividly described on June 21st by a London reporter (78):

> There, the former abode of peace and beauty, we now see but a horrible desert, parched and dry, stumps of trees bristling the expense, trunks blackened with fire! Strewn amidst these ten thousand faggots embedded in the earth, the remnants of clothing—caps, boots, shoes, shirts, blankets, pools of stagnant water, broken arms, rations—food for maggots, horrid grinning heads of oxen, hides mosaic'd into earth by rains, mounds covering the plain, beneath which lie the remains of human-kind; bodies of gallant men, friend and foe, with a few inches of dust over them, and feet and hands here and there cropping out from their last resting-place. Boom! boom! The ear is startled with the report of cannon near by. . . . A rush of air in front of you, and myriads of flies darken your sight as you tread upon their banquet of putrescent vileness; the nostrils become filled with odours too foul as your foot slips upon the carrion grease, and you run, heart-sick, into the sheltering grove.

Buzzards circled overhead. Soldiers for a month had to drink surface water from this area.

The current concepts of the causes of the various diseases of the Chickahominy region were summarized by an observant surgeon (79): They included the sultry heat alternating with cold, severe rains, exposure in the swamps, labor in the trenches, the location of the camps on the battlefield, the bad water, the air rendered foetid by the emanations from the poorly made and numerous graves, and the constant excitement caused by proximity to the enemy. Another surgeon, after attributing the main causes of diarrhea to crowding of the camps and men, poor diet, salt meat in excess, want of fresh food, and badly kept sinks, added that "A well man will, I believe, sometimes get diarrhoea by sitting upon sinks used by patients affected by that disease" (70). In view of the great number of flies, this view was nearly correct for some cases. Today they would all more accurately be attributed to bacteria, protozoa, viruses, and malnutrition

The Union army arrived at Harrison's Landing in poor physical condition from disease, combat, loss of sleep, and undernutrition. The site was not ideal and it was too small. It was a plain bordered by low hills extending for three miles along the river and two miles deep, cut in several places by creeks. About 200 regiments had to camp here. One observer (80) thought that the country bred pestilence, the climate resembled that of Sierra Leone in Africa, and the air was filled ". . . with an impalpable dust which was actually a visible malaria." The army carried with it the sources of sickness ". . . which always accompany an army." In his regiment almost every man was soon sick. Another soldier thought there was no place known to geography and only one to theology hotter than Harrison's Landing. A number died of sunstroke. The only water in some places came from the river or the drainage from the marl beds. "Summer sickness" (*i.e.* diarrhea) was almost universal but not dangerous in the Philadelphia brigade (81). One lieutenant wrote that he drank so many wiggle-tails and polly-wogs he could hear frogs croaking all the time (82). Turkey buzzards blackened the air (83). Some regiments had their greatest amount of sickness here (12, 16, 84, 85, 86, 87, 88, 89, 90, 91), but in a few the health improved (92, 93). Besides the infectious diseases, many doctors noted the emaciation, lethargy, mental depression, and general weariness of the soldiers (12, 91). This may represent a malnutrition rather than an undernutrition.

One regiment, already in service for over a year, suffered its worst epidemic at the Landing (86). Eight days after their arrival, they were struck by dysentery that affected almost every man. Within two weeks, over 500 of the complement of 800 were sick. Their surgeon recommended that they be sent to a healthy place to recover but this respite was denied them until after the Second Bull Run campaign. By then they had only 185 for duty. This epidemic began when they forced to camp on an area washed ". . . by a little stream into which the filth of more than a city was daily emptied . . . by a woods used as a latrine by the army, and . . . where lay in putrescent death horses, mules and horned cattle."

General P. R. D. DeTrobriand, a French-educated officer, aptly summarized the conditions at Harrison's Landing (94):

> We were crowded together behind our intrenchments where the want of room was as prejudicial to the cleanliness as to the well-being of the soldier. Our camps were unhealthy. The water was of bad quality. The frightful heat of the month of July was scarcely tempered by the dreadful storms which came upon us so often in the afternoon. If the skies remained clear, a torrid sun cracked the earth in every direction, and from the openings exhaled fever-laden miasmas. In spite of the care taken to bury each day the animal matter of all kinds, an unhealthy odor infected the air around the tents, too thickly placed, in which the

heat, the vermin, and the flies left very little repose to the soldier. The flies were a veritable plague. They multiplied to an infinite extent, and their sharp stings tormented the men and covered the horses, who were powerless to defend themselves. Night alone brought any relief from the persecution.

Such were the camp conditions under McClellan who, of all the senior commanders of that war, left the highest reputation for good camp administration.

The filtration of the James river water through sand improved its appearance and taste but did not make it safe for drinking (95). The mechanical clarification of turbid water did not necessarily remove the microorganisms.

The same question on the nature of the prevailing fever arose on the Peninsula as in Washington the previous winter. A number of surgeons claimed that the fever at Fair Oaks, Cold Harbor, and Harrison's Landing was not a typical typhoid. One noticed that the course was shorter than that of ordinary enteric fever and rose-spots were rare (93). Surgeon George T. Stevens described the sudden burning fever, insatiable thirst, pains, delirium, parched lips, hot breath, sunken eyes, sallow skin, and "trembling" pulse (17). Surgeon J. T. Calhoun noted that it did not respond to quinine, had rather severe constitutional effects for a few days, but lasted less than a week (96). He thought it was a new disease, but reported it as typho-malaria. However, in one series of six deaths, autopsies revealed ulcerated Peyer's patches in all (97). In retrospect, it seems probable that several diseases existed: Some were true typhoid; the milder cases sound suspiciously like a paratyphoid; some might have been atypical malarias; others might have been a combination of several of these or of other diseases.

General McClellan and Doctor Letterman claimed that the health of the army was improving when it was ordered North in August. This may be true for many units but not for all. General E. D. Keyes of the Fourth corps wrote on July 21st that his corps was not better, as he knew from the inspection of several regiments every day (98). He also found a majority even of the generals "beginning to droop," and the men daily growing weaker in body and mind. He thought this due to the location, the small camp space, and the summer months. Also, a number of surgeons were impressed by the persistent bad conditions of the troops when they sailed away at the end of August. Surgeon Child noticed the barefoot boys, sallow men, threadbare officers and seedy generals; the diarrhea and dysentery; the yellow eyes and malarious faces (12).

It is well known that the Federal medical service was inadequate on the Peninsula, in part because of deficiencies in support by the commissary and quartermaster departments; the latter controlled all their transportation, including that for bringing them food. The medical and surgical casualties exceeded preparations if not expectations, some medical officers were inexperienced in military medicine, and the organization and facilities were defective for the large-scale field conditions encountered. The existing medical knowledge, low as it was, was not fully utilized, and much unnecessary suffering resulted. The medical department had to be renovated and reorganized. The Confederate medical service also was inadequate, but the suffering was far less because of the proximity to Richmond and because they held the battlefields and hospitals.

## A Comparison of Disease in the Two Armies

Did the Union army suffer proportionally more from disease on the Peninsula than the Confederates? It is probable that the Federal medical problem was more difficult because of greater distance from their bases, that their management of disease was poorer, that their soldiers suffered more, that adverse military effects were greater, and that the sickness and the inadequacies were later publicized and documented much more because of greater number of authors and the preservation of the official documents. More important is the probability that the actual incidence rates were higher because they occupied unhealthier terrain.

While the armies were in the vicinity of Richmond, the Confederates occupied higher, more favorable terrain, farther from the Chickahominy lowlands. Many camped on the watershed between the James River and branches of the York River. Their camps were scattered, and the resulting lower population density reduced the hazards of transmissable diseases. Jackson's corps later arrived from the Shenandoah Valley in good health, having been almost continually in motion for several months.

Although many parts of the Yorktown Peninsula were unhealthy during the war, it had previously been healthy for some years. The prevalence of malaria was said to have been high in the seventeenth and eighteenth centuries but much lower in the nineteenth under better drainage and more tillage (40). Warfare, by interrupting these things, by the use of wheeled vehicles in deep mud, by digging trenches, pits, and other defenses, by blocking streams, by destroying bridges, culverts, and drainage ditches, by greatly increasing the population density, by introducing many carriers, and by other measures might well have increased the malaria. Some of these same factors and others might have done the same for dysentery and typhoid fever.

Some of these hazards were recognized at the time, and one Union regimental historian expressed the fears of many (13):

> The rains and mud of the last days of May and beginning of June, were worth thousands of men to the enemy, as they compelled our army to rest astride the Chickahominy, unable to move either way. It gave him time to concentrate, while we were compelled to remain stationary, and let our men sicken in the swamps.

General John E. Wool, an old campaigner, predicted that this unhealthiness would actually be used by the enemy (99):

> The rebels will do all in their power to keep McClellan where he is with his army, in the hope that death and desertion will so thin his ranks that by fall his army will be reduced one-half.

A similar comment had earlier been attributed to General Joseph Johnston. When he was criticized in May for inactivity against the Yankees so close to Richmond, he answered (100):

> I *am* fighting, sir, every day! Is it nothing that I compel the enemy to inhabit the swamps, like frogs, and lessen their strength every hour, without firing a shot?

His passive bacterial warfare was effective as McClellan was then losing about a regiment a day.

In addition to occupying a more favorable terrain, the Confederate army could provide better medical care because it was within walking, riding, and driving distance of its capital city. It was nearer its base, hospitals, volunteer nurses, and food supply. Its communications were shorter if not better. The people of Richmond opened their homes and hearts to the sick and wounded, and the city for some weeks was a vast infirmary area. Even if the morbidity was as high as that of the enemy, the medical attention, nursing, shelter, and food were better. It seems important that there is no record of Confederate scurvy at this time. The great apathy, depression, and sagging morale described in McClellan's army had no counterpart in Lee's. The conditioning of the Confederates in their training camps had been more spartan. Medical Director Lafayette Guild concentrated the wounded Yankee prisoners at Savage Station by July 5th, where they had thirty Federal doctors but little food (101). They had, he wrote, ". . . been accustomed to such luxuries as coffee, tea, arrowroot, sago, jellies, etc., were disappointed in getting nothing but flour or hard bread and bacon."

In contrast, the Union army was farther from its bases, short of medical supplies and hospital stores. The presence of scurvy and the widespread emaciation prove the ration had been inadequate. Concomitant adverse effects on resistance to disease and on wound healing were probably very great. After green field corn became available in August and health improved, one colonel understood why the Johnnies fought so well (92): "Corn and bacon are far superior to hard tack and coffee, even with salt horse thrown in . . ." he thought.

Scurvy appears to have played a far larger role on the Peninsula than the statistics show. It was a cofactor in many other diseases. When it first appeared the diagnosis was officially denied, and only with the fully developed picture was the diagnosis finally conceded. Where a few cases were severe, many more were likely to be incipient, mild or early. Its dietary origin had been known for some time but by many not considered to be the sole cause. Because it often broke out synchronous with or following the camp diseases and sometimes had a similar epidemic type of prevalence curve, it was thought by many to have an infectious factor. Surgeon Frank H. Hamilton, a New York teacher, a textbook author on military medicine, and one of the corps commanders pointedly ignored by Medical Director Tripler, wrote (102) that scurvy broke out after a period of five or six months during which not a single full ration of fresh vegetables had been issued. He thought that 20,000 men might have been saved to McClellan's army if fresh vegetables had been furnished. These soldiers had been unable to supplement the diet by foraging and the package service from home was poor.

Medical Director Tripler minimized the amount and the importance of scurvy, but Letterman was more candid although inaccurate. He wrote of the army at Harrison's Landing that (103):

> Scurvy had made its appearance before its arrival there, the seeds of which had doubtless been planted some months previously, and was due not merely to the want of vegetables, but also to exposure to cold and wet, working and sleeping in the mud and rain, and to the inexperience of these troops in taking proper care of themselves under difficult circumstances. This disease is not to be dreaded merely by the numbers it sends upon the reports of sick. It goes much farther, the causes which give rise to it undermine the strength, depress the spirits, take away the energy, courage, and elasticity of those who do not report themselves sick, and yet are not well. They do not feel sick, and yet their energy, their powers of endurance, and their willingness to undergo hardship are in a great degree gone, and they know not why. In this way it had affected the fighting powers of the army, and much more than was indicated by the numbers it had sent upon the reports of sick.

It is apparent that Letterman was describing the effects not only of scurvy but of a broader, compound malnutrition, including other avitaminoses. Mixed in was a scorbutic component that responded to diet like scurvy.

The army ration formulated consequent to an act of Congress dated August 3, 1861 was (104):

12 oz. of pork or bacon, or 1 lb. 4 oz. of salt or fresh beef.
1 lb. 6 oz. of soft bread or flour, or 1 lb. hard bread, or 1 lb. 4 oz of corn meal.
To every 100 rations add:
    15 lbs. of beans or peas, and 10 lbs. of rice or hominy.
    10 lbs. of green coffee, or 8 lbs. of roasted coffee, or 1 lb. 8 oz. of tea.
    15 lbs. of sugar.
    4 qts. of vinegar.
    1 lb. 4 oz of adamantine or star candles.
    4 lbs. of soap.
    3 lbs. 12 oz. of salt.
    4 oz. of pepper.
    30 lbs. of potatoes, when practicable, and
    1 qt. of molasses, when practicable.

Desiccated compressed potatoes, or desiccated compressed mixed vegetables, at the rate of 1 oz. and ½ of the former and 1 oz. of the latter
to the ration, may be *substituted* for the beans, peas, rice, hominy, or
fresh potatoes.

There is ample evidence that even this marginal diet was not
always issued in the field or even in camp, that many soldiers detested
the desiccated vegetables and refused to eat them, and that the
salt beef and pork were often of inferior quality when issued.

Scurvy appeared later in Confederate armies but it was never
as severe as in the Army of the Potomac in 1862.

## The Decision to Abandon the Peninsula

The decision to order McClellan's army from the Peninsula involved
military, medical, political, and psychological factors. The medical
component was dual: Disease was not only a factor in the decision
made in Washington to withdraw the army, but it was also important
in causing the vacillation and low aggressiveness of the military leader
that was another reason for trying a new tack.

The decision was reached by the administration after about five
weeks of study. President Lincoln, disturbed by the conflicting reports,
had visited McClellan and other senior officers on July 8th (105).
Feeling the need for a military advisor, which McClellan had not
satisfactorily become when he had been the general in chief, Lincoln
summoned General Henry W. Halleck from Mississippi later in July.
Halleck also visited McClellan. After some prior correspondence, his
letter of August 6th explained the necessity of the withdrawal (106).
He accepted McClellan's figure of 90,000 as his effective force and
his last estimate of 35,000 reinforcements as necessary to make an
advance, and added:

> . . . it is entirely impossible to fill it until new troops could be enlisted
> and organized, which would require several weeks. To keep your army
> in its present position until it could be so re-enforced would almost
> destroy it in that climate. The months of August and September are
> almost fatal to whites who live on that part of James River.

To this statement, McClellan never replied. General E. D. Keyes,
commanding the Fourth corps, agreed with the analysis and decision
(107); he estimated the loss to the army from disease before reinforce-

ments could arrive as twenty per cent. Keyes recognized that the crowding of the army into a small space and the sickliness of the campsite was an important factor in its disease. Raw troops brought from the North as reinforcements at that season would ". . . melt away and be ruined forever." If the acute infectious diseases of childhood in new regiments were to be added to the camp diseases here prevailing, Keyes' estimate was about right. Keyes informed the President (108) on August 25th that twenty per cent of the army had been carried away sick and that by September 15th the army would be down to 10,000. Generals W. B. Franklin of the Sixth corps and John Newton, commanding a division, made the same recommendation to the President.

The evacuation resulted from a medical-military decision made entirely, as far as is known, without the participation of the surgeon general or of any other physician familiar with epidemics. It is possible that Medical Director Letterman was consulted. The administration had at hand the statistics on disease in this army up to that date. Halleck was himself mentally prepared to assess the disease factor, whether competent or not to do so: Shortly before coming to Washington from Corinth he had broken up his fine army group, as large as McClellan's, into small, less effective units because it was thought hazardous to chase after Beauregard in the swamps of Mississippi during the unhealthy summer and autumn months. His health problem there is considered in Chapter 6.

President Lincoln was puzzled at the way the army had melted away. After returning from his visit in July he sent McClellan the following analysis and questions (105):

| | |
|---|---:|
| Gone into McClellan's army | 160,000 |
| Number remaining | 86,500 |
| Therefore, number to be accounted for | 73,500 |
| Number killed, wounded, and missing in all battles | 23,500 |
| Remaining | 50,000 |
| Died | 5,000 |
| Therefore, alive but not with the army | 45,000 |

He pointed out that McClellan claimed he could go into Richmond with fewer that that 45,000. Where were they? What could be done in the future to prevent such loss.

Reference to McClellan's own figures (Table VI) shows that on

July 10th, 16,644 were present sick and 38,420 were absent for unstated reasons. The latter figure includes several thousand wounded convalescents. If the figures of Surgeons Tripler and Letterman and the comments of dozens of other medical officers are accepted, probably most of the 38,420 were absent on account of disease. The same comment applies to Lincoln's 45,000. The great tendency to overlook or minimize the disease factor and not to face it squarely eventually had come to a showdown when it was too late.

From the straight military viewpoints, Halleck had pointed out to McClellan that his army and Pope's were separated by a Confederate force of 200,000 (McClellan's own figure) which was larger than either and which was in a position to turn on each at will with overpowering strength to destroy them. Also, the number of reinforcements that McClellan thought necessary for an immediate advance were not available.

Militarily, McClellan had already passed his peak in the spring of 1862, although this was not realized then. For over four months he had been, as the general in chief, the main military advisor of the government, although he had not yet been tested in large scale combat. As a military advisor his value had been low in the generation of confidence, in his comprehension of the total problem, and in his management of the distant military departments. The subsequent field tests, on the Peninsula and at Antietam, revealed good training and camp administration but low aggressiveness and a tendency to perfectionism.

The psychological factor was harder to evaluate and document as it was not clearly verbalized. It has been stressed by Myers (109) and considered at length by myself elsewhere (110). McClellan's outlook at this time was bad, and it became worse under the stress of battle and an attack of dysentery in May. His physical condition (and, possibly, his mental vigor) was depressed until well into June and, possibly, through the Seven Days. In fact, the psychological factor became a neuropsychiatric problem. From the correspondence then passed and that revealed later a great mutual loss in confidence is clear. Some began to suspect the soundness of McClellan's military judgment, while others believed he lacked the will to take the offensive. Chief Quartermaster Rufus Ingalls wrote to Quartermaster General

M. C. Meigs on July 18th from Harrison's Landing that the army was in good condition and "All we require now is more men and generals full of health and desire to go into Richmond" (111).

In the matter of military judgment, McClellan's inactivity was caused, at least in part, by the paralysis resulting from his over-estimation of the size of the opponent's army. The figures of up to 200,000 enemy troops were provided to him by Pinkerton, the detective. His uncritical acceptance of these high figures suggests they were welcome to him. At the same time, General Meigs in Washington, on the basis of the identification of the Confederate units in the Richmond and Wilmington newspapers, calculated that Lee had about 152 regiments averaging 700 men, giving him a total of 105,000 (112). Even this figure was too large as the regiments no longer averaged that number. Knowledge of the military manpower potential of the South from the 1860 census and the probable size of the forces opposing the numerous other Union commanders should have given him a more likely figure. All of the Federal victories on the Mississippi, in Kentucky, Tennessee, North Carolina, South Carolina, and elsewhere had been won against opposition whose size became roughly known. McClellan was not faced by all the Confederates. His miscalculation prevented him from realistically facing his military problems, and it contributed to a reduction of confidence in his military judgment. President Lincoln's homely diagnosis of the "slows" was an apt lay term for a deepseated and serious disorder.

The Army of the Potomac and its commander were different from all others because they lived under the close scrutiny of many interested parties—the government, the press, the politicians, the parents, and others. Everybody felt this was his army. The large medical casualties in camp, the prolonged inaction, the unrealistic evaluation of the situation, and the uncertainty about the military plans and objectives produced a loss of confidence in the commander that was a factor in his estrangement from the government in July, 1862.

As a politician at this period, McClellan was both a leader and a victim, a craftsman and a tool. During his eight months in Washington he had made many powerful political friends, and enemies. Of some of the enemies he seemed unaware. When he requested permission of the war department to change the army corps and their commanders, which had been established by the President, Secretary Stanton granted permission (113). However, later that day a private letter from Lincoln warned:

> Are you strong enough—are you strong enough, even with my help— to set your foot upon the necks of Sumner, Heintzelman, and Keyes all at once? This is a practical and very serious question for you.

McClellan's reaction is not known, except that he did not remove these three old officers. Time soon did that for him. Two weeks later Lincoln informed McClellan that a large committee bearing a petition signed by twenty-three senators and eighty-four representatives had requested him (Lincoln) to restore General Charles S. Hamilton to his division; he wished to do this but not to rebuke McClellan (114). McClellan replied that Hamilton was not fit to command a division, and he was transferred elsewhere. McClellan's political aspirations were quenched in 1864 when he received little support in his presidential quest. Like General Grant he was politically naive, but Grant much later pinpointed his mistake (115) as political sympathies which made him a critic of the commander in chief and, later, his rival.

## Medical Validity of the Decision

Insofar as the fear of incapacitating infectious disease was a factor, how sound was the decision to end the Peninsular campaign? Chickahominy, swamp, and Peninsular fevers had already greatly reduced the size of the army and the efficiency of what remained at the time the decision was made. Would things have become worse that autumn, contrary to the cautious optimism of Medical Director Letterman? In the field, a problem such as this cannot be tried both ways to test which is correct.

The principal pertinent exhibits are (a) the trend of the epidemic diseases in this army up to its evacuation; (b) a projection of this trend according to the known seasonal and geographical behavior of the diseases concerned; (c) the fate of the Fourth corps, which was left behind; (d) the known behavior of camp diseases in new troops, such as would be required as reinforcements: (e) the experience of the same Union army in this area in 1864; and (f) the experience of general officers with disease. The information from these sources bears indirectly but it strongly supports Halleck's fears and justifies his decision.

The incidence of typhoid fever and of dysentery and diarrhea on the Peninsula since March had varied from one unit to another and from time to time but the general trend had been up. Malaria was definitely on the increase in July.

The seasonal statistical behavior of dysentery, malaria, and typhoid fever are valid evidence only if this geographical area and army conformed to the general pattern. It was found that they did.

The experience with dysentery during the four war years showed annual seasonal variations, with peaks in its prevalence rates in the period July to September and the lowest rates between January and March (116). The mortality rates were far lower and their peaks lagged about two months behind the prevalence, as would be expected from the clinical course of this disease at that time. The trend in the mortality rate was upward through the four years. These patterns apply to both the Eastern and Central Regions. According to this information the general probability was that the Army of the Potomac in early August, 1862 had reached its peak frequency of this disease for the year, *except if the local hazards were exceptionally bad.* This they had been up to then, and they were now not essentially improved. The water supplies were probably still fecally contaminated and the inordinate number of flies, to which apparently nobody objected, were still able to carry the infection in quantity from the open latrines to the food and water. The risk of contracting diarrhea during the war years was enormously greater in the army than in the civilian population (117).

The malaria prevalence rate through the four war years had annual peaks between August and October (118). The lowest rates were in February and March. The rates varied greatly (as much as fivefold) from one military department to another. On the east coast, the rate in the Department of Virginia was second only to that of the Department of North Carolina. From this evidence it is probable that the Army of the Potomac on the Peninsula, where population density, interference with drainage, and mosquito breeding had been great, would have continued to experience a great increase in this infection in September and October.

Typhoid fever (sometimes designated as continued fever) showed a more erratic seasonal variation than either dysentery or malaria. Apart from the big peaks in prevalence rates in November 1861 and 1862 (after many new troops had entered the service), it had annual peaks in July and lows in the late winter (119). The Army of the Potomac in August, 1862 was partly "seasoned," in the sense that it had gone through eight months of heavy exposure to this infection and many men were now immune. Nevertheless, it is possible that it would have run into serious trouble that fall. It had many carriers, and fecal contamination of its food and water was still easy by fingers or flies. The percentage of soldiers still susceptible is unknown. As in the case of dysentery and malaria, the soldier ran a far greater risk of contracting typhoid fever than the civilian (119).

In summary, it is likely that malaria prevalence rates would have increased on the Peninsula later that summer, and that dysentery rates would have remained high; the future typhoid rate was more uncertain.

The Fourth corps moved from Harrison's Landing with the army to Yorktown. Here it was assigned to garrison duty, covering a size-able area. Two divisions were soon sent elsewhere, leaving only one. This region had been unhealthy in April, when it was marshy and overcrowded. Now it was dry and pleasant. The army ration was supplemented with fresh fruit, melons, vegetables, oysters and crabs (91). The health improved greatly for a while, but with the rainy season malaria sickened nearly everybody despite the issuing of quinine and iron. On September 30th, when General Keyes' aggregate present and absent numbered 8,168, the number present for duty was 4,764 (120). That is, only about half the men carried on the rolls were present for duty. A separate report of the sick for this division has not been found, but in the Department of Virginia, which included Keyes' command, a mean strength of 17,985 in October had 6,289 on the sick list (121). Thus, in one month, over one-third of the command was sick. Considering that these troops were widely scattered and under better than average living conditions, this amount of disease suggests that a large army might have experienced much sickness. The inference from the experience of General Keyes is that McClellan could have encountered serious trouble.

Throughout the war new troops could expect much sickness. This experience was regarded by many medical and combatant officers as normal, necessary, and a true conditioning period. To General Lee is attributed the statement that he wanted no more raw recruits (122). They become sick immediately and prove a burden instead of a benefit. They should be kept in camps of instruction until better seasoned for the field. General Sherman expressed similar views to his wife in March, 1863 from Vicksburg (123):

> I see the whole North is again in agonies about the amount of sickness down here. . . . Only one man of the regulars had died since we left Memphis. My old regiments are all in fine health and spirits. Some of the new regiments have passed through the ordeal which afflicts all new troops . . .

If 35,000 recruits in thirty-five regiments would have been sent down to McClellan's camps in August and September, they would surely have been decimated several times over by disease. He would soon have been left with thousands fewer than he thought he needed, and the survivors would not have been fit for heavy field service for some months, and possibly not till the following spring. They would simultaneously have acquired the childhood and the common camp diseases. From this viewpoint, the winter spent by the Army of the Potomac on the Potomac had not been wasted.

These armies returned to the upper part of the Peninsula at the end of May, 1864. After only two weeks they moved on. The armies had been fighting and moving frequently for a month, they were composed of tested and screened veterans, and their health was then fairly good. Their health did not deteriorate here faster than before. However, because of the changed circumstances, this experience cannot be extrapolated to 1862.

If it was possible for soldiers to remain well in the army, the medical and general officers should have kept healthy because they had the best control over their living conditions and, supposedly, the most knowledge on sanitation. The experience of the medical officers shows the impossibility of preventing or avoiding sickness. Hundreds, if not thousands, of them were sick. In the Eighth Illinois cavalry one had typhoid, another had dysentery, the third doctor had to be evacuated to the rear, and a contract surgeon was finally brought in (16). In another connection (124) it was shown that medical officers had far fewer wounds and injuries than other officers but just as many diseases. Moreover, generals who were physicians serving in combatant capacities averaged as much sickness as other generals, other officers, and as the surgeons. No group had the requisite knowledge to keep healthy in the field.

Many generals were sick during this campaign. General McClellan had typhoid fever in Washington in December, 1861, dysentery in May-June at Fair Oaks and again in September at Antietam. His food and drink were fecally contaminated like that of most of his soldiers. No less than seven Federal and thirteen Confederate generals were wounded and two were killed during the campaign, but many more were sick. General McClellan grumbled at Harrison's Landing that he had more sick general officers than well ones. A partial list of the Union officers includes General W. H. Keim, who died of an acute camp infection, and the following generals who survived an illness: Daniel Butterfield (typhoid fever), Darius Couch (dysentery), N. J. T. Dana, John W. Davidson (sunstroke), W. A. Gorman, L. P. Graham, J. H. Martindale (typhoid fever), H. M. Naglee, and Francis E. Patterson. The Confederate sick list includes Generals W. S. Featherston, J. R. Jones, Wm. N. Pendleton (fever), G. W. Smith, Richard Taylor, and W. H. T. Walker among others.

This army was moved to northern Virginia at the end of August and into upper Maryland early in September. Its population density was greatly reduced most of the time, it was constantly on the move until late September, it advanced into country previously not contaminated by a large army, the countryside was drier, the weather was cooler, and commissary and medical stores were abundant. Under these conditions its diseases were materially reduced.

It is quite likely, therefore, from several lines of evidence that the Army of the Potomac would have continued to experience much, and even increasing amounts, of sickness if it had been retained on the Peninsula and reinforced by new regiments. The trends of the communicable diseases in this army, the known seasonal behavior of their prevalence rates, the large amount of disease suffered by the part of the Fourth corps that remained behind, the prompt outbreak of epidemics in most recruits, and the experience with sickness of the medical and general officers all strongly indicate that catastrophe was avoided by its recall. It seems that General Halleck was wiser than McClellan in this matter.

Disease on the Peninsula greatly influenced the outcome of the campaign, the course of the war, and the career of General McClellan. The Union strategic offensive was stopped by the Confederate strategic and tactical superiority, and it was not resumed because of existing and threatening epidemics. The armies fought elsewhere a number of times without any great change in the balance, but eventually the Union objective became the Confederate army itself and victory followed. McClellan was given another chance, but failing to satisfy his civilian superiors he was permanently shelved. These two armies faced each other for nearly three more years but they never again experienced so much disease.

## References

1. *O.R.*, 5:11.
2. *O.R.*, 5:12-13.
3. *O.R.*, 5: Appendix L, 111-113.
4. *O.R.*, 5:713-720.
5. *O.R.*, 5:76-113.
6. *Med. and Surg. Hist.*, Vol. I, Part I.
7. WILLSON, G. B.: Army ambulances—cases in the hospital of Richardson's Brigade. *Boston Med. and Surg. Jour.*, 65:542-544, 1862.
8. BREED, B. B.: Report of the Surgeon of the Eighth Regiment, M. V. M. *Boston Med. and Surg. Jour.*, 65:81-82, 1861.
9. BRYAN, J.: Cameron Regiment Dragoons. *Boston Med. and Surg. Jour.*, 65:313-316, 1861.
10. CROSBY, A. B.: A Month in a Volunteer Camp. *Boston Med. and Surg. Jour.*, 64:428-432, 1861.
11. WILLSON, G. B.: Letter from Surgeon Geo. B. Willson. *Boston Med. and Surg. Jour.*, 66:109-112, 1862.
12. CHILD, W.: *A History of the Fifth Regiment New Hampshire Volunteers.* Bristol, N.H., R. W. Musgrove, 1893, 228 p.
13. DAVIS, W. W. H.: *History of the 104th Pennsylvania Regiment.* Philadelphia, Jas. B. Rodgers, 1866, 364 p.
14. FISKE, J. C. and BLAKE, W. H. D.: *A Condensed History of the 56th Regiment New York Veteran Volunteer Infantry.* Newburgh, Newburgh Journal, 1906, 424 p.

15. FREDERICK, G.: *A Story of a Regiment, . . Fifth Seventh New York.* No city, Veterans Assoc., 1895, 349 p.

16. HARD, A.: History of the Eighth Cavalry Regiment, Illinois Volunteers. Aurora, Ill., No publisher, 1868, 368 p.

17. STEVENS, G. T.: *Three Years in the Sixth Corps.* New York, D. Van Nostrand, 2nd ed., 1870, 449 p.

18. BOMBAUGH, C. C.: Extracts from a journal. *Maryland Hist. Mag.*, 5:301-326, 1910.

19. CASTLEMAN, A.S.: *The Army of the Potomac.* Milwaukee, Strickland & Co., 1863, 288 p.

20. ALLEN, J. M.: *Med. and Surg. Hist.*, Vol. I, Part III, 154.

21. BRADLEY, W. A.: *Med. and Surg. Hist.*, Vol. I, Part II, 67.

22. CHAMBERLAIN, C. N.: *Med. and Surg. Hist.*, Vol. I, Part II, 67-68.

23. LITTLE, D.: *Med. and Surg. Hist.*, Vol. I, Part II, 68.

24. McKELWAY, A.: *Med. and Surg. Hist.*, Vol. I, Part II, 75-76.

25. MORRISON, W. B.: *Med. and Surg. Hist.*, Vol. I, Part II, 77.

26. VAN SLYCK, D. C.: *Med. and Surg. Hist.*, Vol. I, Part II, 66-67.

27. WARREN, J. H.: *Med. and Surg. Hist.*, Vol. I, Part III, 468.

28. *O.R., 5*:598-599.

29. *O.R., 5*:645.

30. *O.R., 5*:649-650.

31. *O.R., 5*:664-665.

32. NEWELL, J. K.: *Annals of the 10th Regiment, Massachusetts Volunteers in the Rebellion.* Springfield, Mass., C. A. Nichols & Co., 1875, 609 p.

33. *Med. and Surg. Hist.*, Vol. I, Part III, 364-372.

34. MEADE, G. G.: *Life and Letters of George Gordon Meade.* New York, Charles Scribner's Sons, 1913, Vol. 1, 242.

34b. HUDSON, A. M.: *History of the Eighty-third Regiment Pennsylvania Volunteers.* Erie, B. F. H. Lynn, No date, 139 p.

35. *O.R., 5*:790.

36. *O.R.,* Series IV, *1*:883-891.

37. *O.R., 5*:881-892.

38. *O.R., 51*: Part 2, 246.

39. *O.R., 51*: Part 2, 251.

40. BLANTON, W. B.: *Medicine in Virginia in the Nineteenth Century.* Richmond, Garrett & Massie, 1933, 258, 281, 292, 296.

41. GORDON, J. B.: *Reminiscences of the Civil War.* New York, Charles Scribner's Sons, 1903, 474 p.

42. *Med. and Surg. Hist.*, Vol. I, Part III, 649.

43. *O.R., 5*:1020.

44. *O.R., 5*:1023.

45. *Med. and Surg. Hist.*, Vol. I, Part II, 26, 31.

46. WARREN, E.: *A Doctor's Experiences in Three Continents.* Baltimore, Cushings & Bailey, 1885, 613 p.

47. JOHNSON, B. T.: *Confed. Mil. Hist.* (C. A. Evans, Ed.), 2:63, 1899.
48. *O.R., 11*: Part 3, 645.
49. *O.R.,* Series II, 4:798.
50. *O.R., 51*: Part 2, 570.
51. *O.R., 51*: Part 2, 577.
52. *O.R., 11*: Part 1, 275-276.
53. *O.R., 11*: Part 1, 403-411.
54. *O.R., 11*: Part 1, 601-606.
55. *O.R., 51*: Part 2, 572.
56. *O.R., 11*: Part 1, 961.
57. *O.R., 11*: Part 3, 614-615.
58. WELCH, S. G.: *A Confederate Surgeon's Letters to His Wife.* Marietta, Continental Book Co., 1954, 127 p.
59. PUTNAM, S. A.: *Richmond During the War.* New York, G. W. Carleton & Co., 1867, 389 p.
60. WARD, J. R. C.: *History of the One Hundred and Sixth Regiment Pennsylvania Volunteers.* Philadelphia, F. McManus, Jr. & Co., 1906, 455.
61. WILLSON, G. B.: Army Medical Intelligence. *Boston Med. and Surg. Jour., 66*:198-199, 1862.
62. U. S. Sanitary Commission: *Hospital Transports.* Boston, Ticknor & Fields, 1863, 18-167.
63. *O.R., 5*:26.
64. *O.R., 11*: Part 1, 177-210.
65. *O.R., 11*: Part 2, 48.
66. ELY, J. F.: First year's medical history of the Twenty-fourth Iowa. In *War Sketches and Incidents: Iowa Commandery of the Military Order of the Loyal Legion.* Des Moines, P. C. Kenyon, 1893, Vol. 1, 400 p.
67. GORDON, S. C.: Reminiscences of the Civil War from a surgeon's point of view. In *War Papers: Maine Commandery of the Military Order of the Loyal Legion.* Portland, 1898, Vol. 1, 352 p.
68. HART, A. G.: The Surgeon and the Hospitals in the Civil War. *Papers of the Mil. Hist. Soc. Mass., 13*:229-285, 1902.
69. *O.R., 11*: Part 1, 210-220.
70. CALHOUN, J. T.: *Med. and Surg. Hist.,* Vol. I, Part II, 73-74.
71. *O.R., 11*: Part 3, 272-273.
72. *O.R., 11*: Part 3, 197-198.
73. CALHOUN, J. T.: *Med. and Surg. Reporter, 9*:149-150, 1862.
74. *O.R., 11*: Part 3, 209-210.
75. *O.R., 11*: Part 2, 97.
76. HAMMOND, J. F.: *Med. and Surg. Hist.,* Vol. I, Part I, Appendix 64-65.
77. HAND, D.: In *Glimpses of the Nation's Struggle: Minnesota Commandery of the Military Order of the Loyal Legion.* St. Paul, St. Paul Book & Stationery Co., 1887, Vol. 1, 416 p.
77b. *O.R., 11*: Part 1, 776.

78. EDGE, F. M.: *Major-General McClellan and the Campaign on the York-town Peninsula.* London, Trubner & Co., 1865, 176-177.
79. WHITTINGHAM, E. T.: *Med. and Surg. Hist.,* Vol. I, Part I, Appendix 79.
80. PARKER, F. J.: *The Story of the Thirty-second Regiment Massachusetts Infantry.* Boston, C. W. Calkins & Co., 1880, 260 p.
81. BANES, C. H.: *History of the Philadelphia Brigade.* Philadelphia, J. B. Lippincott & Co. 1876, 316 p.
82. LANDON, W.: Fourteenth Indiana Regiment, Peninsular Campaign to Chancellorsville. *Indiana Mag. Hist., 33*:325-348, 1937.
83. STRONG, G. T.: *The Diary of George Templeton Strong.* Edited by A. Nevins and M. H. Thomas. New York, Macmillan Co., 1952, Vol. 3 462.
84. CUDWORTH, W. H.: *History of the First Regiment (Massachusetts Infantry).* Boston, Walker, Fuller, & Co., 1866, 528 p.
85. DAVENPORT, A.: *Camp and Field of the Fifth New York.* New York, Dick & Fitzgerald, 1879, 485 p.
86. KEPLER, W.: *History of the Three Months' and Three Years' Service.* Cleveland, Leader Printing Co., 1886, 287 p.
87. MARTIN, J. M. et al.: *History of the Fifty-seventh Regiment Pennsylvania Veteran Volunteer Infantry.* Meadville, McCoy & Calvin, 1904.
88. POTTER, W. W.: *Buffalo Med. Jour., 67*:69, 132, 199.
89. STOWITS, G. H.: *History of the One Hundredth Regiment of New York State Volunteers.* Buffalo, Matthews & Warner, 1870, 424 p.
90. WOODWARD, E. M.: *History of the Third Pennsylvania Reserve.* Trenton, MacCrellish & Quigley, 1880, 256 p.
91. HILL, J. A.: *The Story of One Regiment.* New York, J. J. Little & Co., 1896, 435 p.
92. HARDIN, M. D.: *History of the Twelfth Regiment Pennsylvania Reserve Corps.* New York, Published by the author, 1890, 224 p.
93. WOOD, C. S.: *Med. and Surg. Hist.,* Vol. I, Part II, 74.
94. DE TROBRIAND, R.: *Four Years with the Army of the Potomac.* Boston, Ticknor & Co., 1889, 757 p.
95. GRACEY, S. L.: *Annals of the Sixth Pennsylvania Cavalry.* No city, E. H. Butler & Co., 1868, 371 p.
96. CALHOUN, J. T.: The Chickahominy and Seven Pines. *Med. and Surg. Reporter, 9*:399-500, 1863.
97. BLISS, Z. E.: *Med. and Surg. Hist.,* Vol. I, Part I, Appendix, 86.
98. *O.R., 11*: Part 3, 331-333.
99. *O.R., 11*: Part 3, 330-331.
100. By an English Combatant: *Battlefields of the South.* London, Smith, Elder & Co., 1863, 2 vols. in one.
101. *O.R., 11*: Part 3, 633-634.
102. HAMILTON, F. H.: *A Treatise on Military Surgery and Hygiene.* New York, Baillìere Bros., 1865, 649 p.

103. *O.R., 11*: Part 1, 211.

104. *Med. and Surg. Hist., 1*: Part 3, 711-712.

105. NICOLAY, J. G., and HAY, J.: *Abraham Lincoln, A History.* New York, Century Co., Vol. 5, 241-242, 453-454.

106. *O.R., 11*: Part 1, 83.

107. *O.R., 11*: Part 3, 313-314.

108. *O.R., 11*: Part 3, 382-383.

109. MYERS, W. S.: *General George Brinton McClellan: A Study in Personality.* New York, D. Appleton-Century Co., 1934, 520 p.

110. STEINER, P. E.: Medical-Military Portraits of Union and Confederate Generals. In manuscript.

111. *O.R., 11*: Part 3, 326-327.

112. *O.R., 11*: Part 3, 340-341.

113. *O.R., 11*: Part 3, 153-154, 154-155.

114. *O.R., 11*: Part 3, 185.

115. YOUNG, J. R.: *Around the World with General Grant.* New York, Amer. News Co., 1879.

116. *Med. and Surg. Hist.,* Vol. I, Part II, 22, and Part III, 20.

117. *Med. and Surg. Hist.,* Vol. I, Part III, 14.

118. *Med. and Surg. Hist.,* Vol. I, Part III, 14, 20, 90, 97.

119. *Med. and Surg. Hist.,* Vol. I, Part III, 14, 20, 199.

120. *O.R., 18*:376.

121. *Med. and Surg. Hist.,* Vol. I, Part 1, 180-185.

122. JONES, J. B.: *A Rebel War Clerk's Diary.* Philadelphia, J. B. Lippincott & Co., 1866, Vol. 1, p. 168.

123. HOWE, M. A. D.: *Home Letters of General Sherman.* New York, Charles Scribner's Sons, 1909, 243.

124. STEINER, P. E.: *Physician-Generals in the Civil War.* Springfield, Charles C Thomas, Publisher, 1966, 194 p.

# VI

## The First Campaign for Corinth

ONE OF THE STRANGEST but most important large-scale campaigns of the Civil War was that for Corinth, from April to June, 1862 (1, 2, 3, 4, 5, 6, 7, 8). Two armies, both greatly enlarged since the bloody two-day Battle of Shiloh early in April, under new leaders faced each other for a month. Then, the Confederate army abandoned the town without giving battle. Thus, a "First Battle of Corinth" never materialized! The Union army made only a slight show of chase down into Mississippi. Then these armies, among the largest assembled during the war, again remained idle for nearly a month. Almost the entire military strength west of the mountains was concentrated here, so that a decisive battle would have had important consequences. It has been alleged that the Federal army group could have gone anywhere (2, 9). But, after minor skirmishes they slowly fragmented and dispersed. From them, four armies and other units were eventually organized, two by each side. One of the resulting Confederate armies was captured a year later at Vicksburg and the other survived longer only to be nearly destroyed at Nashville in December, 1864. These results might have been achieved in 1862. The soldiers not called into action at Corinth, fought bitterly at Iuka, Second Corinth, Perryville, Stone's River, Vicksburg, Chickamauga, Missionary Ridge, in the Atlanta Campaign, at Franklin, Nashville, and elsewhere.

How can this curious military behavior be explained? By some it has been attributed to the inexperience, timidity, and conservatism of the commanders, Generals Beauregard and Halleck. Actually, Beauregard had as much combat experience as any officer on either side but Halleck had never been in battle. It is the conclusion of this study that these factors existed, but that the main causative factor was a disease epidemic of major size and importance. Neither army was healthy, but Beauregard's already smaller force was reduced proportionally more than the Union opponent. Disease played a crucial part in Beauregard's evacuation of Corinth, and the threat of disease was an important factor in Halleck's decision not to follow down into Mississippi. Because the medical facts were stated but not stressed at that time and the data on the sickness are scattered, the disease factor in this campaign has not been emphasized. There was no terminal blood bath to give it drama and a name.

Decisions were made at this time that greatly influenced the course of the war, but this was not realized at the time. There seems to have been much drifting too, in which the fear and uncertainty introduced by poorly understood outbreaks and threats of disease played an important part. In General Scott's original anaconda plan for winning the war, the lower Mississippi River was to be reopened, but only after the autumnal frosts had killed the "virus" of the fevers below Memphis (10). Halleck and Beauregard found the fevers on the Tennessee and Tuscumbia Rivers to be just as bad as those of the Mississippi. The biology and role of the pathogenic microbes not being understood, these agents were able to wage potent warfare that stopped both armies.

## The Military Campaign

From the field at Shiloh, the Confederate Army of the Mississippi returned to Corinth, twenty-two miles from the river. Here they reoccupied their old camps and threw up defenses several miles out from the town. In a few weeks they were reinforced by Major General Earl Van Dorn with the Army of the West from Arkansas and by troops rushed from other places. General Beauregard commanded both armies, succeeding General Albert Sidney Johnston, who had bled to death at Shiloh. Corinth was a small town at the intersection of the Charleston and Memphis with the Mobile and Ohio railroads. It had military value only because of these roads.

Grant's Army of West Tennessee (hereafter called the Army of the Tennessee) reoccupied its camps on the Shiloh battlefield, while Buell's Army of the Ohio camped nearby. Major General Henry W. Halleck, the departmental commander, alarmed by the near catastrophe, arrived on April 11th, four days after the battle, to take over in the field. He sent for Major General John Pope, who had just captured Island No. 10 and was advancing on Fort Pillow and Memphis with naval support. Pope began disembarking his Army of the Mississippi at Hamburg Landing around April 21st. Halleck organized his three-army group into three wings and a reserve, and when the roads improved he belatedly got under way on April 29th, prepared to give battle at Corinth. Major General George Thomas directed Grant's Army of the Tennessee, and Grant was nominally the second in overall command but essentially a fifth wheel. Major General John McClernand commanded the reserve corps.

Halleck's jubilant forecast of May 3rd, to Washington, that he would be at Corinth in twenty-four hours proved far too optimistic (11). The intervening country was wooded, with scattered small farm clearings and a few villages. It was generally elevated but cut by streams in wide swampy bottoms. The roads were few, primitive and miry. The weather, which had been rainy in April turned only slightly drier and warmer in May. It was necessary to build bridges and new roads most of the way, corduroying some of them, and constructing cross roads to provide means for mutual support of the wings in case of need. At one time, pack mules had to be used to bring up supplies (4). The enormous health problems implied by these statements are evident. Halleck advanced slowly on a three-army front, latterly intrenching each night so that he arrived before Corinth only on May 29th. There had been small actions but no major engagement, and both railroads had been cut to the north and west. The combat casualties had been light, probably fewer than 500 on each side.

Corinth lay between two creeks on a low, wide ridge, the watershed between the Tennessee River and the Gulf of Mexico. Beauregard, facing a force more than twice as large as his, decided in agreement with his army and corps directors (Generals Bragg, Polk, Hardee, Van Dorn, Price, and Breckinridge) on May 25th to retreat to Tupelo, fifty-two miles south. On the night of May 29th, the Southern troops departed after destroying all supplies and ammunition they could not take along. To his surprise, Halleck discovered the town vacated on the 30th, and moved in. General Pope first and later Buell were sent in pursuit. They ran into some rear guards, but most of Beauregard's army group got away.

The entrance into the abandoned town was a depressing experience (12). It was an empty shell, a barren gift, a questionable victory. A sickening stench of the foul deserted camps and the smoke of burning houses, cotton, and commissary stores hung in the air. While some soldiers were elated, others felt mortified at the escape of the enemy. Some of the commanders vied for priority in the honor of having first entered the town (13), but Sherman wrote there was no honor in the event (2).

The excessive caution if not timidity of Halleck resulted, at least in part, from his lack of accurate knowledge about the number and condition of the enemy. There is no evidence that he made much effort to collect intelligence. Local loyal men should have been available for scouting one would think. It can be argued that Halleck did not make the wisest use of his vast forces. After the fall of Corinth, also, his dispositions did not employ his resources to their maximum. Nevertheless, when he was ordered to send 25,000 men to McClellan on the Yorktown Peninsula, he objected, saying this would result in the loss of Arkansas, or West Tennessee, or both (14). Beauregard was not beseiged at Corinth but neither could he withstand the threat of artillery or the severing of his communications.

## Military Aftermath of the Campaign

The Union commander had solved few problems. He had gained a town and a foothold on an east-west railroad, both nearly worthless to him, but the opposing army was intact. Memphis soon fell to naval action, and to the east, one of Buell's most aggressive divisional commanders, General O. M. Mitchel, threatened Chattanooga. Vicksburg was yet undefended. Halleck could have reopened the Mississippi, or strongly supported Mitchel with the object of freeing East Tennessee or going into Georgia, or offered battle to Beauregard, marching on to Mobile if successful. At the latter plan Halleck hesitated, giving as reasons the difficulty of effective pursuit (15), and the threat of disease in the swamps of Mississippi (16). Consequently he did nothing important.

Instead, Halleck fragmented his army group by occupying territory and reopening railroads of little or no immediate military value.

Buell's fine army was sent to the east, rebuilding the Charleston and Memphis railroad as it went. This line could not be used, however, because of its vulnerability at every point to raids from the south. Soon Buell would be required to make forced marches back to the Ohio River by the superior maneuvering of Bragg and E. Kirby Smith. Grant resumed the command of his District of West Tennessee with headquarters at Memphis. After Pope had been called east to head the Army of Virginia in June and Halleck summoned to Washington to become the general in chief in July, Grant was left in the virtual command of the area now depleted of over half its strength and much of the remainder dispersed. There was much soldiering that summer and fall in this theater, with many engagements and several sharp battles; the Confederates challenged at Iuka in September and at Corinth in October, but no major activity ensued until Grant began his six-month campaign on Vicksburg in November. Halleck had muffed one of the great opportunities of the war.

General Halleck was by formal education and early experience a military engineer. After this he became a mining engineer, railroad president, lawyer, political scientist, translator, and writer on mining and international law. These were the achievements of a gifted man but in contemplation rather than in action. His conduct and writing about this campaign clearly show a failure to evaluate and use the day to day emerging evidence. However, epidemic disease came to his aid and won him Corinth. On this reputation, without ever having led a soldier in action or witnessed a battle, Halleck became the general in chief of the National armies. This must be one of the strangest sequels of disease in history. Perhaps his subsequent failure to assume administrative responsibility and to grow, so that he had to be replaced in 1864, could have been anticipated had his psychology and the factor of disease in his elevation both been understood in Washington.

At Tupelo Beauregard's affairs also did not prosper. Van Dorn was ordered away to the Vicksburg defenses and took General John Breckinridge's Reserve Corps along. On June 17th, Beauregard went to Mobile on a surgeon's certificate for his health, leaving Bragg in temporary charge. Richmond promptly made Bragg's appointment permanent, stranding Beauregard without a command or an explanation for the precipitate, harsh treatment. Bragg soon started on his Kentucky invasion via Chattanooga, taking most of the troops and leaving only the smaller Army of the West for the protection of Mississippi. The Corinth campaign can be considered ended about July 15th. This area was never again of major importance although it immobilized and consumed many troops throughout the war.

Halleck had won a hollow victory and a promotion, Beauregard the increased disfavor of Davis and a demotion, Grant an opportunity to reopen the big river and achieve fame, Bragg and Pope major army commands, and Buell another chance to demonstrate the size of his talents. Van Dorn and George Thomas received temporary demotions. Over 80 Confederate and 115 Federal regiments and their thousands of officers had obtained some experience in the field. Thousands of soldiers had lost their health or their lives while others had gained immunities that would help them survive the war; most of them, however, were merely reprieved to face bullets and bacilli on other fields.

## Reasons for Confederate Evacuation of Corinth

The Confederate army experienced a large upsurge in disease at Corinth in the months of April and May, followed by a slight improvement after it moved to Tupelo in June. The Federal army, in contrast, had much sickness in April on and near the Shiloh battlefield. Health improved in May during the move on Corinth and, probably, because of the move. This followed the general rule that armies were healthier when in motion than when stationary and fouling their campsites and water supplies. At Corinth in June, sickness continued to decline in some Union regiments but to increase in others. In part, at least, this result was determined by the location of the camp.

The type and amount of disease is known moderately well for the Union army, considering the diagnostic difficulties of the time. The data are not so good for the Southern army, although figures are available for certain specific dates. Since there was a large patient turn-over, especially in the mild cases of diarrhea, such spot sampling yields poor overall figures. Nevertheless they provide some valuable information, supporting the statements of Beauregard.

General Beauregard wrote that he abandoned his position at Corinth because his army had been much reduced by disease and the enemy force had become disproportionate and too strong. He explained to Richmond that (17):

> The purposes and ends for which I occupied and held Corinth having been mainly accomplished by the last of May, and by the 25th of that month having ascertained definitely that the enemy had received large accessions to his already superior force, while ours had been reduced day by day by disease, resulting from bad water and inferior food, I felt clearly my duty to evacuate that position without delay.

Beauregard gave his reason for his retreat even more clearly in answering a direct question of Jefferson Davis' (17). Question No. 1 read: I desire to know what were the circumstances and purposes of the retreat from the Charleston and Memphis railroad to the position now occupied? To this Beauregard replied:

> The retreat was not of choice but of necessity. The position had been held as long as prudence and the necessities of the case required. We had received our last available re-enforcements. Our force was reduced by sickness and other causes to about 45,000 effective men of all arms, exclusive of cavalry ...

Beauregard claimed that his opponent was twice as strong, better disciplined, and more amply supplied in every respect. It is noteworthy that the disproportion in numbers had been produced in large part by casualties which resulted from disease and not firearms.

Davis' Question No. 4 was even more specific on the disease factor: What was the cause of the sickness at Camp Corinth? Would it have been avoided by occupying the higher ground in front? Has it been corrected by retiring to the present position? Beauregard replied:

> There were several causes for this sickness. 1st. The want of good water. 2d. The want of proper food, the salt meat furnished to the troops being often not fit to eat; also the almost total want of fresh beef and vegetables, beef having been furnished once a week or every ten days, instead of five times a week, as ordered . . . I will mention here that some of our own troops were affected with the commencement of scurvy. It is doubtful in my mind whether the health of the army would have been benefitted by the occupation of the hills referred to . . .

The present position at Tupelo was considered healthy, according to Beauregard, and the condition of his troops had improved by June 17th.

Beauregard's explanations seem valid only in part. No doubt some of the sickness resulted from poor water, but because of bacteria and not because of low potability. I know of no disease transmitted by unpalatable salt meat except, rarely, botulism but there was no acutely fatal disease of that type reported there. The lack of fresh vegetables was serious and a factor in the scurvy he reported.

It is pertinent to medical history to know how Beauregard arrived at his figure of 90,000 Union opponents. He knew that he had faced essentially three army corps and a reserve—information available in the newspapers. From this he estimated the number of divisions, brigades, and regiments. Then he calculated the total by estimating each regiment at 500 (17), which was about half of their original strength. Beauregard was an experienced campaigner who was realistic and, for that time, medically knowledgeable. Thus he knew that even regiments only one to twelve months old would have been reduced from 1,000 to an average of 500, largely by disease. His estimate was remarkably accurate. The rapid attrition by disease prevented both prolonged training periods and the maintenance of large stable armies, and it helped to deplete the manpower pools and end the war.

Was Beauregard's statement on the current size of his army correct, and what was his actual loss by disease? From his field returns the following figures are taken (18):

|     |                              | Aggregate | Effective total |
|-----|------------------------------|-----------|-----------------|
| (a) | Confederate force April 3, 1862 | 59,774 | 38,773 |
| (b) | After the Battle of Shiloh   | 64,500 | 32,212 |
| (c) | At Corinth, about May 28     | 112,092 | 52,702 |
| (d) | After arrival at Tupelo      | 94,784 | 45,365 |

The reduction in the effective total after the Battle of Shiloh is explained by his casualties, which numbered 10,699. The reduced figures at Tupelo are accounted for in large part by the detachment of McCown's division and the omission of the cavalry. As of May 28th, the Confederacy had provided over 112,092 men to this army but only 52,702 were now effective. What had happened to them?

The most significant figures are those for May 28th. The great increase in the aggregate represents the accession of reinforcements, including the Army of the Mississippi and other troops. The effective total was less than half the aggregate (*i.e.* all those carried on the rolls). About 59,390 officers and men were ineffective. This figure includes 18,390 present sick and 7,447 absent sick (19). Also 20,069 were absent with leave and 3,792 absent without leave. These two figures include many men on medical leaves, and some with disability who had left without permission. So many leaves for reasons other than disability would hardly have been granted at such a critical time. Many walking sick under treatment in camp are included among the effectives.

In the past this army had sometimes granted mass leaves of absence for convalescence and recruiting. Lieutenant Colonel Nathan Bedford Forrest's battalion of cavalry had, for example, actually been disbanded at the end of February, 1862. When they reassembled in March, they were able to organize as a regiment (20). How many, if any, of the 20,069 were absent at this critical time under a similar arrangement is not on record. Probably most of them were away for medical disability. If only half were absent for this reason, the medically disabled totalled about 36,000, the equivalent of between forty and seventy-five regiments at current strength.

Colonel William Preston Johnston, the aide sent by Davis to present his questionnaire to Beauregard, also inspected the army. His report on the medical department said in part (21):

> The medical department is in a state of great confusion and disorganization. Few of the acting surgeons have been regularly appointed. They have been assigned to duty by medical doctors, by generals, and even by colonels, or employed by contract. The position of these gentlemen is undefined, and the respect and consideration necessary to the performance of their duties is not shown to them. The returns are not regularly or properly made, and the requisite blanks and stationery are not properly supplied. The medical stores are said to be sufficient. . . . I did not examine the hospitals established in the rear of the army. The complaint in general is that they are conducted with little attention to order or system or to those details which render such places endurable. The superintendence of a large hospital is a business, and eminence in consultation is not the sole qualification for it. The relaxation of discipline and want of hospital accommodations which permitted the dispersion of the sick on plantations has saved many valuable lives. The

broad hospitality and unwearying kindness of the people of Mississippi were extended to our sick soldiers with a liberality so bountiful that the thanks of our whole people are due to them.

Colonel Johnston recognized the disease factor in the evacuation and candidly laid a part of the blame on both high and low places (22). Some of his etiological interpretations, however, will not hold up:

> Bad food, neglect of police duty, inaction, and labor, and especially the water insufficient, and charged with magnesia and rotten limestone, had produced obstinate types of diarrhea and typhoid fever. No sound men were left. The attempt to bore artesian wells had failed. With an aggregate of 112,092 the effective total had wasted away to 52,706 men. The sick and absent numbered 49,590, including officers. No sudden epidemic had smitten the camp; the sickness was the effect of causes evident from the day of occupation of the position, and increased with an accelerated ratio. The value of Corinth as a temporary base from which to attack the enemy was vast, but as it was untenable for permanent occupation on account of its unhealthfulness, it seems unfortunate that the army should have been retained there until a wreck only remained, to be crowded out by the steady pressure of the advancing, but cautious, foe.

Halleck now occupied the site and exposed his men to the same conditions.

In summary, Colonel Johnston agreed with Beauregard that disease had made it impossible for the Confederate army to retain Corinth, and that the evacuation was necessary. He thought Beauregard was wrong in having remained there is long as he had. Finally, he thought laxness in the medical department and in the enforcement of camp sanitation by regimental and higher commanders to be causal factors in the disease picture.

Horn conceded that an alarming amount and rapid increase of sickness created an enormous problem (6). Corinth had been flooded by over 5,000 wounded from the battlefield at Shiloh, who filled hospitals and homes. The overflow of maimed and suffering men lay on porches, sidewalks, and on the railroad platforms. To this horror was now added epidemics of typhoid fever, dysentery, malaria, and some measles. Corinth became one vast ward with 18,000 soldiers on its sick list. To the overburdening of the medical facilities was added a shortage of food and water. Beauregard may indeed have seen scurvy as he claimed. Many of the casualties were sent by railroad to the towns, plantations, and watering places of Mississippi. Corinth was described as a filthy place by the Union occupiers, and Halleck found it necessary to detail soldiers and prisoners to clean it up (23). The shortage of food was blamed on Doctor Northrop in Richmond, the commissary general. Beauregard bought large herds of cattle in Texas and Arkansas to supply the deficiency (7), substituted corn meal for a part of the flour in the ration, and used other measures. Some Tennessee soldiers were issued flour, sugar, molasses, beef, and rye for coffee, but they had no cooking utensils (24). It is surprising that morale held up so well.

## Disease in the Southern Army

The bad health conditions at Corinth were so impressive that many Confederate observers left comments. Thus, the Missouri brigades in Van Dorn's army, which had previously been unhealthy in Missouri and Arkansas, reported conditions even worse at Corinth (25). The Fourth Arkansas, arriving on May 4th, was soon reduced to less than half by "Camp fever" (26). The Kentucky "Orphan Brigade" was "seriously afflicted" (27). Lumsden's Alabama Battery of 170 men originally had six physicians on its rolls but it suffered severely nevertheless (28), and their sick overflowed the hospital tent to fill a church. Measles, pneumonia, erysipelas, typhoid fever, and diarrhea were most common. When they pulled out at the end of May, the battery had not enough well men to drive the horses so soldiers had to be detailed from a nearby regiment to help out. The Third Louisiana ate the hardtack and salt meat, drank the unpotable, scarce water, lived in rags and dirt, and felt gloomy and dispirited (29). In the Thirteenth Tennessee, many were given sick leave to recuperate for the summer campaigns (30). They improved greatly at Tupelo (31). The Nineteenth Tennessee drank "'seep-water" that collected in shallow holes and was soon full of wiggletails. A partial list of their deaths shows twenty-two, and many seriously sick were shipped to the rear (32).

A call went out for doctors, medical students, and nurses and many responded (6). Kate Cumming, who nursed at the Tishomingo Hotel hospital, found the wounded men lying on the floors, the air bad, and the floors filthy with blood and mud (33). The chief surgeon told her that the whole army was sick. The patients had one meal a day consisting of bad soup and bread. A practical nurse at the Baptist church hospital noticed much vermin, no cots, little bedding, and few blankets (34). After the evacuation she saw at Lauderdale Springs over 2,000 sick men, 1,800 of them typhoid cases. An unusually literate soldier summarized the picture (35):

> But an enemy invaded the heart of Beauregard's camp more terrible, more deadly than Halleck's vast host if it had doubled—it was the soldier's enemy, *disease*. The sultry sun, the putrid water, the unwholesome food, the low, swampy country, the unceasing duty, the long eternal battle, sapped the *elan* of the young volunteers, and filled the hospitals and grave-yards with the best blood of the South. Train after train carried the miserable sufferers southward, but train after train was still in demand, and the epidemic increased and the mortality was fearful.

The principal diseases were dysentery and typhoid fever. To these malaria would be added in June.

## Disease in the Northern Army and the Failure to Pursue

After the battle of Shiloh the Union wounded were evacuated by boat to Savannah, Cairo, and northern cities including St. Louis, Louisville, and Cincinnati. About 12,000 wounded and sick Federal and 1,000 wounded Confederates had been sent away by the end of the first week (36). Some had not yet had their primary operations because of the shortage of supplies and surgeons. Those remaining buried the dead—men, horses, mules.

Sickness, already common before the battle, increased thereafter, further crowding the medical facilities, although by May, 11,000 more had been shipped away (36). Because it was felt that too many sent to northern hospitals never returned, Halleck ordered the construction of a large general hospital behind each wing (*i.e.* army). Each of these three tent hospitals had accommodations for about 5,000. They were in addition to the regimental hospitals. All were soon needed.

At first the disease was mild and chiefly diarrhea and dysentery (12, 36, 37, 38, 39, 40, 41, 42, 43, 44, 45, 46, 47, 48). Nevertheless, when the order was given to prepare for the advance, the sick came to the Landing in great numbers (36):

> Many of them had been for weeks suffering from the diarrhoea peculiar to the Tennessee River. This is said to result from the large amount of animal decomposition which takes place on the mussel beds or shoals, a few miles above Pittsburg Landing. Whether this explanation be or be not correct, it is certain that almost every one drinking the waters of the river suffered from a profuse diarrhoea which resisted obstinately the ordinary therapeutic means. These persistent discharges greatly augmented lassitude already resulting from the general malarious influence, and contributed to weaken the most robust.

The soldiers considered themselves fortunate ". . . if they had only a little diarrhoea" (47). A rough idea of the size of the problem is found in the action of one medical director (48): When he found that large doses of the sulphate of magnesia were helpful in treatment, he ordered 150 barrels for his division. Note that the alleged efficacy of this therapy does not harmonize with Brinton's statement on etiology just cited.

The spectrum of diseases increased to include typhoid fever, malaria (47, 48, 49, 50), scurvy (47, 50), and others (36, 46). Medical Director Brinton wrote of this period (36):

> The type of disease, at this time prevailing, was chiefly a camp fever, assuming a more or less typhoid form, and attended with great fatality. The violence of this affection arose from several causes, the chief of which were the insalubrity of the camp sites, the impure water, and the scant supply of fresh meat and vegetables. The ground, too, on which the army was encamped was the field of battle. On this, and in its close vicinity, thousands of men and animals had been buried, and in certain portions of the plain the effluvia were most disagreeably perceptible to the passer by. As the result of these combined causes, the sick list of every regiment was rapidly increasing; and it unfortunately happened, that the regimental hospitals were not those in which the invalid could best be cared for.

A brigade surgeon at the general field hospital of the Army of the Ohio, on the basis of 1,700 patients, thought all presented the same disease, called variously ". . . Febris Typhoides, Diarrhoea, Dysentery, Scorbutus, and Debilitas" (47). He though the official classifications artificial as the diagnosis in a subject was changed with a change in his symptoms. This view probably reflects merely the problem in differential diagnosis in the absence of any objective tests when several diseases exist concurrently. This surgeon stated that necropsies on some cases revealed an absence of typhoidal ulcerations.

The Army of the Tennessee had also two pest hospitals for smallpox, each with about thirty cases (46). Vaccination of most of the troops limited the threat from this disease.

The experience of the Fifteenth Iowa, a new regiment, was typical for this situation (38). They arrived on April 6th from camp at Keokuk, where they had gone through measles. By April 13th, in one company only 35 men were able for duty because of weakness from diarrhea. By the 18th, there was scarcely a well man in the company: "The climate, water, and food has about finished us up." As the rains continued almost daily, the earth was washed from some of the buried men and horses. They were obliged to drink the seepage from the battlefield. In one camp the men had to place brush on the ground to hold their blankets above the surface water. By May 19th they had only 25 men in line:

> The mumps are raging in the Army and every other disease known to human beings. I have the jaundice and am as yellow as a Yankee pumpkin and so billious I cannot keep anything down that I eat and oh how sick I am.

On May 23rd they were down to sixteen for duty but all having diarrhea.

> The *dead march* can be heard at all times from sun up until sun down in the camps around us. . . . Not even a coffin is provided.

On May 25th three members of the company died, two of them from typhoid fever. One wonders how such regiments could retain an organization and any military value, yet most of them did.

The experience of Surgeon N. R. Derby at the general field hospital at Monterey is of interest (51). Before his 400 tents were pitched and equipped on May 14th, a stream of sick poured in. At the middle of June he had 1,792 patients, but few nurses and little food. Food could not be foraged locally as the army had taken it. In one group of forty soldiers detailed to him as nurses, twenty-five had to be admitted as patients. The mortality in this hospital was 9.76 per cent. This high rate probably resulted chiefly from typhoid fever, the most lethal of the prevalent diseases. It was ordered closed on June 16th.

As the army moved forward the anticipated wounds failed to materialize because of the method of advance, but disease remained a big problem (41):

> Now came the reign of Halleck—the reign of a book soldier—the reign of picks and spades, the reign of tedious camp life and camp diarrhea—the latter the worst scourge and deadliest enemy of every soldier. To the tortures of Tautalus it had an added physical suffering and wasting which nothing at our command seemed capable of staying. More fatal than bullets, its poisonous effects upon the blood continued with many long after the smoke of battle had cleared away, producing other diseases which made life a burden.

As the situation worsened, even the usual amenities were discontinued. In one division in which four-fifths were sick, the deaths averaged one a day per regiment (52). "For a while the dead were buried with the customary honors of war; finally the sound of the three volleys became so depressing to the sick that it was by order discontinued."

The opinions on the nature and causes of the prevailing army diarrhea were numerous. Professor E. A. Andrews thought that the diarrhea was only a small part of the picture, and that the disease was basically a "portal congestion" (37). The causes mentioned included (12, 32, 36, 38, 39, 40, 45, 49, 50, 52) the hot weather, cold rains, miry camps, poisonous air from the exhalations of the thousands of sinks, cesspools, and graves of men and animals, a full diet, a restricted monotonous diet, low organic acids in the food, fresh meat, salt meat, scarcity of vegetables, inactive life, rapid marching in the sun, poor ventilation of tents, exposure, confinement, and many others. Many blamed the dirty water without specifying the mechanism or agents, but one thought it was the wiggletails (32). The indifferent attitude that many took toward drinking water is illustrated by General Lew Wallace (53), who sent aides in advance along the line of march to require the citizens to place tubs and barrels of raw water in front of their homes.

It is impossible to determine from Halleck's reports the number taken up on the sick list during the three-month period or even the number sick at any one time. However, from the field returns of his three armies on May 31st, it is certain that the problem was large (54). Those present for duty numbered 80,568, the aggregate present was 97,315, and the aggregate present and absent was 173,315. Thus, nearly half of those carried on the rolls were not with the army. The difference between the first two figures (16,747) includes those present but not carrying muskets because they were detailed to other duty or were sick in the regimental hospitals. The difference between the second and third figures (76,460) represents those on leave for sickness or other reasons, the sick in the general hospitals, the deserters, those detailed to other duty, and other small categories. It is probable that the great majority were away because of physical disability. This represents an enormous reduction in the strength of the army. If these men had been present and able for duty, Halleck's force would have been large enough to besiege Corinth—something it never did and was incapable of doing in view of the disproportion between the relative size of the two armies and the encirclement required.

Some precise data for one division can be extrapolated to most or all of Halleck's fifteen divisions. On May 12th, Sherman's aggregate present and absent numbered 10,452, the present for duty 5,289, the absent sick 2,557, the absent wounded 855, and the sick in camp 600 (55). Thus 4,012 (about 40 per cent) were physically disabled.

The types of diseases in Halleck's armies were chiefly infectious. Their quantities are not accurately known, but a fair estimation is provided by the figures for the Department of the Tennessee (56). In addition to the Army of the Tennessee certain unidentified small garrisons and camps in the department are included as well as the Army of the Mississippi for the months of April, May, and June, 1862. The Army of the Ohio is not included. Therefore the figures that follow include only about two-thirds of the sick in Halleck's force, but they still have a certain value if this is understood. The total recorded diseases of all types were 70,338 and the deaths 1,336. The number of cases dropped each month, and the deaths fell from 804 in April to 215 in June. To a certain extent this represents the supplantation of typhoid fever by malaria. The doctors must have been busy.

The most common recorded disease was acute and chronic dysentery and diarrhea, 27,136 cases being reported in the three months (56). This figure must exclude many of the mild cases. The mortality was low—only 100 cases—but many others probably died at home then or later. It is not difficult to visualize how campsites all become fecally contaminated from such an outpouring, especially when there was flooding, flies were numerous, water for washing was scarce, and policing was lax, its rationale being unknown. From this vast experience came the opinion that the sulphate of magnesis was good for beginning the treatment ". . . to wash out the contents of the bowels" (48). Armies did not become immune by their exposure to such an abundant live "vaccine," and the disease persisted on a large scale through the war. While some were self-limited, other cases became chronic, so boys in blue and gray were living with and dying from this condition through the end of the nineteenth century, and it was a big problem for the pension bureau as the delayed sequels were uncertain.

The term *cholera morbus,* used for sharp severe attacks of vomiting and diarrhea, occurred in 476 soldiers. Only two died. This was a disease chiefly of warm weather, when the bacteria could flourish.

Because all diagnosis was purely clinical and without any confirmatory laboratory tests (except occasional autopsies), because many patients simultaneously had two or three diseases when all were so highly prevalent, and because the "fevers" could not accurately be separated, therapy was chaotic. The measures used for diarrhea were numerous. Some increased while others decreased intestinal motility; some tried to stop the diarrheas, others to flush it out. One brigade surgeon though that because all diarrhea and dysentery was under "malarious influences," it was necessary to administer quinine and whiskey freely (43). His other remedies were sulphate of magnesia and castor oil, followed by nitric acid and tincture gentian, quinine, Fowler's solution, sub-nitrate of bismuth, or opiates, as circumstances indicated. He thought raw onions almost a specific. Quinine was used not only as an antiperiodic and antipyretic but also as a tonic and even as a sedative (47). It would be beneficial when, unknown to them, the patient had also a malarial infection.

The second most common disease was malaria, with 12,000 cases. The intermittent fevers (quotidian, tertian, quartan, and congestive types) numbered 7,832 and the remittent fevers added 4,168 subjects. Significantly, only 69 were fatal, mostly in the congestive type. Some of the remittent fevers resisted antiperiodic therapy, suggesting that they were typhoids or some other disease. At that time, only a post-mortem examination could accurately differentiate a typhoid fever, typhus fever, and a few other diseases from falciparum and atypical malarias. The months of April, May, and June were intermediate in malarial frequency between the cold winter and September and October, the annual peak period. Many of these cases, no doubt, were relapses, some of them antedating enlistment.

The next largest group was the acute respiratory tract infections, with 3,069 examples. This figure is exclusive of the category of "Inflammation of the Lungs" (pneumonias) and others. Except in the pneumonias, the mortality was small. In the outdoor tent life in warm weather, these infections would not be expected to reach epidemic proportions.

The fourth largest category was typhoid fever, with 2,718 patients. To these should be added an unknown proportion of the 4,168 so-called remittent fevers. Of typhus fever only 41 examples were reported. Although Gerhard had described clinical differential features, they were not always evident. The rose spots of the abdomen were inconstantly present in typhoid. In the unquestioned typhoids, 286 were fatal.

Measles had done its harm and declined by now in most regiments. In this vast army, only 288 cases were reported in the three months. Most of the regiments had been recruited in 1861. In comparison, 648 soldiers had mumps, and 130 suffered from smallpox, although the regulations called for early and universal vaccination. In connection with the communicable diseases, it is of interest that no case of diphtheria was reported and only seven of scarlet fever. In view of the troubles with streptococci in later wars, this claim seems incredible. Actually, erysipelas was reported 221 times. This diagnosis included not only the "primary" disease but also some of the cellulitis that spread out a short distance from wounds. Consumption was reported in 172 and scrofula in 34 soldiers. Jaundice was noted in 1,112 men. These were probably chiefly examples of catarrhal (infectious) hepatitis as there were only six deaths and other diagnostic categories were available for the other forms of clinical jaundice. Syphilis (125 cases) and gonorrhea (287 cases) were sizeable problems that diminished in the field.

Among the related categories rheumatism was one of the largest. The 2,250 examples included 1,301 of the acute and 949 of the chronic forms. This diagnosis included rheumatic fever and other diseases. Chronic rheumatism was a favorite term for the malingerers at sick call. Of debility there were 1,566 cases and of nostalgia seventy. Nostalgia was sometimes given as the cause of death. It might produce debility, but this condition resulted oftener from chronic dysentery and other diseases.

General Beauregard claimed that scurvy appeared in his army, and it was unquestionably present in Union soldiers. It was reported eighty-seven times in the Armies of the Tennessee and the Mississippi alone. As a component of the clinical picture of hyponutrition plus multi-vitamin deficiency, often secondary to chronic dysentery and other diseases, it must have been far more common than that. Such examples passed under the terms "scorbutus" or "scorbutic tendency" and were not separately reported. The soldiers of both armies at Corinth had been on inadequate diets, continuously or intermittently, for some months and some of them for nearly a year. To this was added the factor of almost universal diarrhea. Foraging in the vicinity was not productive. Many of the commissary officers, instead of being experts in nutrition, were utterly ignorant, and some seem to have been dangerously inert to improvement even when prodded. To Beauregard's complaint about the inadequacy of the ration, Commissary General L. B. Northrop thundered that (57) "There is but one specific for scurvy, that is potash or its neutral salts. The lemon and potato owe their specific qualities solely to this alkali." Such ignorance in the man in his position was dangerous. He had practiced medicine in Charleston for about twenty years before the war.

Both scurvy and some of the chronic diarrheas improved in June, when a few local fresh vegetables and fruit became available. They provided variety, palatability, vitamins, and calories. The article most commonly mentioned as beneficial was wild blackberries (4, 24, 38, 50). It was claimed many times they were almost specific for old diarrhea cases. Onions were prized only slightly less (40). One surgeon claimed that "So universal was the improvement of diarrhoea on the free use of raw onions, that it seemed only to require a sufficiency of them to cure the entire army" (43). Even field corn in the milk, which became available a little later, was thought beneficial although the surgeons had warned it would be harmful.

No doubt the diet was often deficient. The ration most commonly issued in the field consisted of salt meat (bacon, "sow-belly"), hard bread ("hard-tack"), coffee, sugar, and occasionally beans. The Tenth Missouri had nothing else from April 22nd to June 8th, when fresh beef was issued for the first time (40). Many hospital patients developed decubitus ulcers, and suppurative parotitis as a complication of the serious fevers was not unusual (47). These and other facts suggest that malnutrition was not rare. Chronic diarrhea often improved when the patient was sent home, north or south, showing that the effective factor was not climate, as some alleged, but home-cooking.

Insects as possible disease vectors were abundant in number and types. In addition to the lice that infested nearly all regiments, flies abounded everywhere. They are not mentioned unless they became unusually pestiferous. A young Illinois colonel suffering from dysentery wrote in June that he had never seen house flies quite so thick (58). An Ohio officer had a horse stung to death by flies, and a nearby officer nearly lost his horse (59); these flies attacked the genitalia. Jiggers and spiders abounded in June (40). The shrubbery was already green along the Tennessee River in March (60), and mosquitoes made their appearance early in April (59); a little farther south, at Vicksburg, they were seen already in the first half of March. Fruit trees bloomed at Shiloh in March. A colonel from Ohio complained in May of wood ticks and infinite numbers of insects and worms (61). An idea of the temperature is also deductable from the amount of sunstroke: This disease jumped from three cases in April to thirty-five in May and thirty in June.

From the combined effects of many diseases some men still with the army were in bad condition early in June. On observer encamped near a field hospital noted the patients (62) ". . . moving about camp, living skeletons, around whose emaciated forms the coarse army clothing hung and flapped like animated scare-crows, hunting for something. Those were trying days for our troops. Generals saw divisions melt into brigades; brigades to regiments and regiments to battalions."

In the vast array of recorded information only one claim has been found for good regimental health (59). However, "good" was not defined, and one supposes its value expressed a relative judgment, high by the then current standards but low today.

## New Diseases

Several new and undiagnosed diseases were recorded during this time. In the Tenth Missouri many men had "abscesses" under the arm. They developed slowly, were intensely painful, and healed slowly (40). This seems to be a lay account of a suppurative or granulomatous lymphadenitis or bubo. Snakes, reptiles, and insects abounded in June. The author mentioned big spiders, lice, and jiggers that were almost invisible but left an inflamed spot. Could these lesions have been the peripheral component related to the "abscesses"? Perhaps this disease was a tick-borne tularemia or some related infection.

Another new disease was noted by a surgeon after Pope's army fell back to Camp Big Springs near Corinth (49). This was considered a good camp in woods with abundant water, full rations, and enough sanitary stores. The patients complained of a low feeling varying from fatigue to utter prostration. The pulse was never over 90, skin cool, tongue normal, urine and feces regular; no chill or fever; appetite increased. After some days restlessness and a tendency to delirium set in; a desire to walk was irresistible, and they could not be kept in bed. They rapidly lost flesh, became languid and feeble, but had no abnormal or increased secretions. After 12 to 20 days they became more quiet; or they might walk a great distance, return to bed, say they felt better, lie down, and die within five minutes. The Fourteenth Michigan lost eighteen cases of this type. Other regiments also had fatal cases, but most were sent to the general hospital, some dying on the way. The surgeon did not know what to treat: Quinine, alteratives, stimulants, purgatives, and counterirritants were without benefit. Postmortems revealed no abnormality. It was called "typhoid fever," but it was recognized as different. The local physicians named it the "walking fever," peculiar to this part of Mississippi.

## Sickness in the General Officers

The generals, who ultimately bore the responsibility for the health of their commands and supposedly knew the methods, could not keep themselves well either. No less than twelve of the twenty-nine Federal generals and six of the thirty-eight Confederates present were sick during the campaign, and two of them died. The figure for both, but especially for the Southerners, is probably far below the reality, the documentation being incomplete. In addition, a number of colonels who were acting as brigadiers by leading brigades were also sick. Unless it be assumed that these officers were careless or ignorant, these figures show the impossibility of avoiding the infections in the field with the knowledge then available. The same point could be made by studying the sickness in the medical officers.

General Henry Halleck was sick for a few days in June (63). Two weeks after the evacuation of Corinth he was confined to his tent by what he called the "Evacuation of Corinth," the most common disease in his army. If this was a microbial diarrhea, his food or water had probably been fecally contaminated like that of his lowest private despite his elaborate headquarters living accommodations.

One of Halleck's three army commanders, John Pope, was ill for a few days in June (64). Two of Pope's three divisional leaders also were sick: General E. A. Paine went home at the end of the campaign (65), and Schuyler Hamilton suffered from a severe illness during most of the time (66). A grandson of Alexander Hamilton and a brother-in-law of Halleck, he had survived a bullet in the abdomen and a lance thrust through the lung in Mexico. Now he contracted malaria, for which he went on sick leave, and he resigned in February, 1863. In this army two brigade leaders also were sick. General John Palmer experienced a typical attack of lobar pneumonia, which kept him off duty about eleven weeks from the end of May (67). Joseph B. Plummer survived a long sickness in Mexico and a wound at the Battle of Wilson's Creek in 1861, only to become sick in May, the result of "exposure in camp" (68), from which he died in August, 1862. This nonspecific expression most commonly meant dysentery.

In the Army of the Tennessee, Brigadier General Thomas A. Davies, leading a division, went north early in June on sick leave (69). General W. T. Sherman, another divisional commander, suffered from malaria early in June a few days after leaving Corinth, where he had probably been infected if the incubation period was average (2, 70). He was engaged in salvage operations around wrecked railroad cars at the time, and his understanding of the etiology was colorful but inexact:

> The weather was hot, and the swamp fairly stunk with the putrid flour and fermenting sugar and molasses; I was so much exposed there in the hot sun, pushing forward the work, that I got a touch of malarial fever, which hung on me for a month, and forced me to ride two days in an ambulance, the only time I ever did such a thing during the whole war.

The relationship to a mosquito bite two or three weeks earlier went unrecognized. Sherman had had malaria earlier in life. General John A. Logan also was sick for about three weeks in April and May (71). He had survived a bullet wound of the shoulder and a severe attack of diarrhea at Fort Donelson in February and had only recently returned to duty (7). It is possible that his disease at Corinth was a relapse.

In the Army of the Ohio, General Thomas L. Crittenden was sick when the campaign began and could not join his division until May 3rd (73). General W. B. Hazen had to leave his brigade in May because of an attack of malaria, which kept him out until July (74). Brigadier General James A. Garfield experienced a typical enteritis: He was well when he wrote home on April 9th, but on the 21st he was recovering from a severe, acute, painful, bloody diarrhea, which subsided by May 8th (75). He later had recurrences and lost much weight.

Among the Confederates, General Beauregard in June went off to a spa to recuperate from an attack of jaundice and a respiratory condition that began some months before. Although he remained within his military department, his departure was used as a pretext for relieving him from command. General John C. Breckinridge was ill in April after Shiloh while covering the retreat with his reserves (76). General J. M. Withers had a leave at about the same time (77). B. R. Johnson was sick in his quarters in May (78),

and General Thomas Jordan, Beauregard's chief of staff, had a sick
leave in June (79). Brigadier General J. L. Hogg died in his tent of
an acute dysentery on May 16th and was buried nearby.

Probably many more general officers were sick during this period.
The records of disease in officers of high rank are fragmentary, and
most of those mentioned here became recorded incidental to lost
time, or in home letters. The amount and type of infectious disease
was nearly the same as in the enlisted men. There is no evidence
that disease in these generals materially influenced the course or outcome of the campaign. At the end of June, however, General Bragg
complained that so many general officers were absent, sick or wounded,
that it was difficult to keep up any organization (80).

## Autopsy on the Corinth Campaign

The question arises whether the epidemics of enteritis, typhoid, and
malaria could have been prevented. Were either Beauregard or Halleck delinquent in supporting sanitation, hygiene, and preventive
medicine? Both questions must be answered in the negative. Other
leaders occupying the same positions would have had the same result.
The knowledge in medicine and field sanitation by which to prevent
these camp diseases did not exist. Their transmission chains can be
interrupted today at severel points, but this was not possible in 1862.
The disease-producing potential of water poorly paralleled its appearance or potability and that of food was not related to its palatability,
with rare exceptions. But potability, palatability and gross appearance
were the only criteria available by which to judge in 1862.

With the knowledge then available, however, the amount of disease
might sometimes have been reduced in several indirect ways. A campaign earlier in the season or after the fall frosts would have eliminated most of the malaria. The enteric diseases and the malaria
could have been reduced by a shorter campaign, and sometimes by
better camp police, *i.e.* by enforcing even the current standards. The
drainage of campsites for comfort and efficiency would have reduced
the mosquito population and the dissemination of fecal pollution after
flooding. The daily addition of several inches of soil to the sinks, with
or without lime, would have reduced the fly breeding. This was sometimes done, but to reduce odors and not to check the flies, whose role

in spreading infection was unknown. The careful disposal of all sewage, garbage, slaughter-house offal, and the ordure from the stables could also have reduced the fly population. Halleck waited a month for the roads to improve, prolonging the period of risk to disease. He could, at least, have moved his camps periodically to escape the stench. If he had been left in the command, Grant might have started sooner but otherwise camp conditions would have been no better. He later wrote that Corinth could have been taken immediately after Shiloh (9), but he was judging from hindsight.

Beauregard's problem was more difficult. The area within his line of defense available for camps was limited and crowded. It was described as filthy when the Federal army took over. Although commanders knew that motion improved army health, they rarely deliberately acted on this knowledge. Water was scarce in some places, and the sources must have become polluted.

In front of Corinth, Halleck reported his command as improving daily in health (11). The numerous complaints about having to camp on the Shiloh battlefield can be downgraded in this connection. The chief complaint was at the stench. This might have been unpleasant but it, in itself, was not unhealthy. Decomposing animals might be unsightly neighbors but they were dangerous chiefly by increasing the fly population, and not by directly contributing pathogens. The unburied human corpses had the same significance but, in addition, those that harbored the organisms of typhoid fever and dysentery might be sources of infections as these agents may survive for some days or more. The chief hazard from the Shiloh field came from the water supplies they had themselves polluted and from their own sinks. The soldier knew no regulations on protecting his food and mess gear from the flies coming from the latrines.

Sherman's orders on sanitation of April 30th to his division were of the best but they fell short of microbiological needs, and there is no evidence that his command was healthier than others (81):

> Immediately on reaching camp each colonel or commander of a regiment will select his spring or place of water, put a guard, and, if necessary, a chain of sentinels to it; and immediately on a halt for camp each captain, under the direction of the colonel, will cause a sink to be prepared for his company.

These orders meet less than half the problem.

General Halleck knew that armies were healthier when moving, and that Mississippi would be unhealthy for northern boys in the summer, and it is certain that this knowledge played an important part in the breaking up of his army group. An immediate change in position seemed desirable in April when he found enormous sick lists. However, he did not leave the Tennessee River then because of poor roads (82). Later he decided against following Beauregard because his army would, he feared, be disabled by disease in the "swamps of Mississippi." He apparently consulted medical officers about the health prospects, and was quite pessimistic (82) :

> I have no doubt that with all possible care in adopting every sanitary precaution our troops will suffer considerably from illness. In this climate it will be unavoidable. But under the advise of Dr. McDougall and his medical officers I think we can prevent the mortality from being greater than it was last winter in Missouri, Kentucky, and Tennessee.

It is true that measles, mumps, and some of the typhoid fever was now behind them. Also Surgeon McDougall had had success in the suppression of clinical malaria with quinine. In July, however, Admiral Farragut and General Thomas Williams found much disease at Vicksburg, and in 1863 Grant's campaign there was also impaired.

Other data pertinent to the wisdom of Halleck's decision not to pursue Beauregard deep into Mississippi in June and July are available. Thus, a comparison of malarial infection (intermittent and remittent fevers) in the Confederate and Federal Armies of the Tennessee shows the rates per 1,000 strength in June and July, 1862 to have been (83) : Confederate, 141 and 179 cases per 1,000 versus 62 and 62 cases in the Federals. Judged by this standard, the Confederate position was unhealthier than the Federal site.

It seems that the medical officers treated the sick but, with rare exceptions, had little part in the strategic decisions although they knew much about the mass behavior of diseases. There was even a residual tendency by some line officers to regard sickness as a manifestation of defective willpower and the sick as lacking discipline and patriotism. As an example, at a time in April when his division had many fever subjects, Sherman insisted on drills and reviews on the 15th, 17th, and 23rd. Then on the 26th he required the attendance of every man, sick or well; the sick were hauled to the drillfield in wagons or ambulances, where those unable to stand were carried in cots. One sick man died before returning to camp (4). This was drastic treatment for typhoid subjects in order to trap a few shirkers and malingerers. Such viewpoints toward sickness were not rare.

The war could not end until one of these armies, and the corresponding one in the East, were destroyed. By the dispersion of the components in June and July to form new combinations and threats elsewhere, that day was now postponed. The army of Halleck, one of the largest of the war, could have taken Vicksburg, Mobile, and Atlanta. Instead, its components took territory, which they then had to garrison—a self-exsanguinating process and inconclusive as long as the Confederate force remained in being. Only by becoming a Sherman and destroying industrial potential for arms and armaments, transportation, and food while sapping the will of the people for war but avoiding police operations could this depletion have been avoided. But Halleck was no Sherman, and the war dragged on nearly three years longer. The Sherman of 1862 lacked the vision and the authority of the man of 1864.

At Corinth the South lost a campaign because of uncontrollable disease, but it gained a strategic victory of sorts from the aftermath through the same agent, now an ally. Halleck, while at Corinth and for some time after going to the war department in July, was influential in if not responsible for the strategic planning for this area. In Washington, his experience with disease at Corinth seems to have been an important factor in his decision to withdraw McClellan's army from the Peninsula (Chapter 5). Disease, by influencing these two major decisions made by Halleck in the summer of 1862, greatly influenced the subsequent course of the war.

## References

1. *O.R., 10*: Parts 1 and 2; *17*: Parts 1 and 2; and *52*.
2. SHERMAN, W. T.: *Memoirs of Gen. W. T. Sherman.* New York, Charles L. Webster and Co., 4th ed., 1892, 2 vols. in one.
3. VAN HORNE, T. B.: *History of the Army of the Cumberland.* Cincinnati, Robert Clarke and Co., 1875, Vol. 1, 126-129.
4. WRIGHT, H. H.: *A History of the Sixth Iowa Cavalry.* Iowa City, State Hist. Soc. of Iowa, 1923, 539 p.
5. SNEAD, T. L.: With Price East of the Mississippi. In *Battles and Leaders of the Civil War.* New York, Century Co., 1887, Vol. 2, 717-734.

6. HORN, S. F.: *The Army of Tennessee*. Indianapolis, Bobbs-Merrill Co., 1941, Chapter IX.

7. ROMAN, A.: *The Military Operations of General Beauregard*. New York, Harper and Bros., 1884, Vol. 1, Chapters 24, 25.

8. MAURY, D. H.: *Recollections of a Virginian*. New York, Charles Scribner's Sons, 1894.

9. GRANT, U. S.: *Personal Memoirs of U. S. Grant*. New York, Charles L. Webster & Co., 1894, 2 vols. in one.

10. SCOTT, W.: *O.R., 51*: Part 1, 369-370.

11. HALLECK, H.: *O.R., 10*: Part 1, 666-667.

12. THOMPSON, S. D.: *Recollections of the Third Iowa Regiment*. Cincinnati, Published by the author, 1864, 396 p.

13. *O.R., 10*: Part 1, 680-683.

14. *O.R., 17*: Part 2, 42, 56, 61.

15. *O.R., 10*: Part 1, 668, 669, 671.

16. *O.R., 16*: Part 2, 62-63.

17. BEAUREGARD, G. T.: *O.R., 10*: part 1, 672-779.

18. *O.R., 10*: Part 1, 780.

19. *O.R., 10*: Part 1, 791-792.

20. WYETH, J. A.: *Life of Lieutenant-General Nathan Bedford Forrest*. New York and London, Harper & Bros., 1908, 667 p.

21. *O.R., 10*: Part 1, 781-784.

22. *O.R., 10*: Part 1, 784.

23. *O.R., 10*: Part 2, 262-263.

24. LAW, J. C.: Diary of a Confederate Soldier. *Southern Hist. Soc. Papers,* 12:22-28, 1884.

25. BEVIER, R. S.: *History of the 1st and 2nd Missouri Confederate Brigades*. St. Louis, Brand & Co., 1879, 480 p.

26. GAMMAGE, W. L.: *The Camp, the Bivouac, the Battlefield*. Little Rock, Arkansas Southern Press, 1958, 150 p.

27. GEORGE, H.: *History of the 3d, 7th, 8th and 12th Kentucky, C.S.A.*, Louisville, C. T. Dearing, 1911, 193 p.

28. LITTLE, G., and MAXWELL, J. R.: *A History of Lumsden's Battery, C.S.A.* Tuskaloosa, Ala., R. E. Rodes' Chapter, United Daughters of the Confederacy, 1905, 74 p.

29. TUNNARD, W. R.: *History of the Third Regiment Louisiana Infantry*. Baton Rouge, Published by the author, 1866, 393 p.

30. VAUGHAN, A. J.: *Personal Record of the Thirteenth Regiment, Tennessee Infantry*. Memphis, S. C. Toof, 1897, 95 p.

31. WEST, J. D.: The Thirteenth Tennessee Regiment, Confederate States of America. *Tenn. Hist. Mag.,* 7:180-193, 1921.

32. WARSHAM, J. W.: *The Old Nineteenth Tennessee Regiment, C.S.A.* Knoxville, Paragon Printing Co., 1902, 235 p.

33. CUMMING, K.: *A Journal of Hospital Life in the Confederate Army of Tennessee.* Louisville, John P. Morton & Co., 1866, 200 p.

34. PALMER, E.: Mrs. Ella Palmer. Reminiscences of her service in hospitals. Confed. Vet., *18*:72-74, 1910.

35. EDWARDS, J. N.: *Shelby and His Men.* Cincinnati, Miami Printing & Publishing Co., 1867, 551 p.

36. BRINTON, J. H.: *Med. and Surg. Hist.,* Vol. I, Part I, Appendix, 24-33.

37. ANDREWS, E. A.: Prof. Andrews' letter to the Medical Examiner. *Chicago Medical Examiner, 3*:342-346, 1862.

38. BOYD, C. F.: The Civil War Diary of C. F. Boyd, Fifteenth Iowa Infantry. *Iowa Jour. Hist., 50*:48-82, 155-184, 1952.

39. BRIANT, C. C.: *History of the Sixth Regiment Indiana Volunteer Infantry.* Indianapolis, Wm. B. Burford, 1891, 423 p.

40. FROST, M. O.: *Regimental History of the Tenth Missouri Volunteer Infantry.* Topeka, Kansas, M. O. Frost Printing Co., (n.d.), 317 p.

41. BELKNAP, W. H.: *History of the Fifteenth Regiment, Iowa Veteran Volunteer Infantry.* Keokuk, R. B. Ogden & Son, 1887, 644 p.

42. HAPPERSETT, J. C. G.: *Med. and Surg. Hist.,* Vol. I, Part I, Appendix, 250.

43. HATCHITT, J. G.: *Med. and Surg. Hist.,* Vol. I, Part I, Appendix, 250-251.

44. HOUGH, A. L.: *Soldier in the West.* Edited by R. G. Athearn, Philadelphia, Univ. of Pennsylvania Press, 1957, 250 p.

45. HUBBARD, G. H.: *Med. and Surg. Hist.,* Vol. I, Part I, Appendix, 42.

46. McDOUGALL, C.: *Med. and Surg. Hist.,* Vol. I, Part I, Appendix, 40.

47. PHELPS, A. J.: Camp Disease. Observations in the field near Corinth, Mississippi. *Amer. Med. Monthly, 18*:94-97, 1862.

48. WALKER, T. H.: Camp diarrhoea. *Chicago Med. Jour., 5*:478-480, 1862.

49. BATWELL, E.: Note on the fever that prevailed amongst the troops in Camp Big Springs Near Corinth, Miss., in June, 1862. *Med. and Surg. Reporter 13*:364-365, 1865.

50. HUBBARD, J. C.: Army Reports: Army of the Ohio, Camp Near Athens, Alabama. *Cincinnati Lancet and Observer, 5*:524-531, 1862.

51. DERBY, N. R.: *Med. and Surg. Hist.,* Vol. I, Part I, Appendix, 41.

52. BROWN, A. L.: *History of the Fourth Regiment of Minnesota Infantry Volunteers.* St. Paul, Pioneer Press Co., 1892, 594 p.

53. WALLACE, L.: *Lew Wallace: An Autobiography.* New York & London, Harper & Bros., 1906, 2 vols.

54. *O.R., 10*: Part 2, 235.

55. THORNDIKE, R. S., Ed.: *The Sherman Letters.* London, Sampson Low, Marston, & Co., 1894, 398 p.

56. *Med. and Surg. Hist.,* Vol. I, Part I, 90-95.

57. *O.R., 10*: Part 2, 571-572.

58. CAMM, W.: Diary of Colonel William Camm, 1861 to 1865. *Jour. Ill. State Hist. Soc., 18*:793-967, 1926.

59. GILBERT, A. W.: *Colonel A. W. Gilbert, Citizen-Soldier of Cincinnati.* Cincinnati, Hist. and Philosoph. Soc. of Ohio, 1934, 122 p.

60. WILSON, P.: Peter Wilson in the Civil War. *Iowa Jour. of Hist. and Politics, 40*:261-320, 1942.
61. SMITH, G. W.: *Life and Letters of Thomas Kilby Smith.* New York, G. P. Putnam's Sons, 1898, 487 p.
62. THATCHER, M. P.: *A Hundred Battles in the West.* Detroit, Published by the author, 1884, 416 p.
63. HALLECK, H.: *O.R., 17:* Part 2, 9.
64. FORCE, M. F.: *From Fort Henry to Corinth.* New York, Charles Scribner's Sons, 1882, 204 p.
65. *O.R., 10:* Part 1, 713.
66. *O.R., 10:* Part 1, 723-725.
67. PALMER, J.: *Personal Recollections of John M. Palmer.* Cincinnati, Robert Clarke Co., 1901, 631 p.
68. *O.R., 10:* Part 1, 805-806.
69. CHAMBERLIN, W. H.: *History of the Eighty-first Regiment Ohio Volunteer Infantry.* Cincinnati, Gazette Press, 1865, 198 p.
70. *O.R., 17:* Part 2, 11-13.
71. *O.R., 10:* Part 1, 755, 758-762.
72. TROWBRIDGE, S. T.: *Autobiography of Silas Thompson Trowbridge, M.D.* Vera Cruz, No publisher, 1872, 288 p.
73. *O.R., 10:* Part 1, 700.
74. HAZEN, W. B.: *A Narrative of Military Service.* Boston, Ticknor and Co., 1885, 450 p.
75. WILLIAMS, F. D.: *The Wild Life of the Army.* Michigan State Univ. Press, 1964, 325 p.
76. *O.R., 10:* Part 2, 403, 496.
77. *O.R., 10:* Part 2, 416.
78. *O.R., 10:* Part 2, 537.
79. *O.R., 10:* Part 2, 602.
80. *O.R., 17:* Part 2, 627-628.
81. *O.R., 10:* Part 2, 145.
82. *O.R., 16:* Part 2, 62-63.
83. *Med. and Surg. Hist.,* Vol. I, Part III, 104.

# VII

## The First Attack on Vicksburg

THE FIRST UNION attempt to take Vicksburg, reopen the Mississippi River, and divide the Confederacy was made early in the second year of the war. A joint army and navy enterprise coming up from below, it lasted just over two months. The naval bombardment failed to silence the defenses and epidemic disease reduced the regiments below the numbers needed for an assault. Consequently, the operation ended in a repulse without a pitched battle, and the river remained closed for another year. The question whether there was blundering or whether this result was then not preventable is a subject of this study. As we shall find, disease could hardly have been militarily more effective even if it had been deliberately used as a weapon.

### The Bold Advance to Vicksburg

The campaign took place during ten weeks in May to July, 1862, as two operations. Major General Benjamin F. Butler on May 1st had occupied New Orleans, which had surrendered without opposition to Admiral David Farragut a few days before (1, 2). The outlying places were also quickly taken by Federal troops. Farragut pushed up to Baton Rouge by May 8th, and the town was occupied by Brigadier General Thomas Williams with two regiments a few days later. The Navy Department urged Farragut to go up to Vicksburg, the most defensible site on the river. The Confederates, hearing of the passage into the river, sent Brigadier General M. L. Smith to organize the Vicksburg defenses (3). When the fleet and General Williams arrived on May 18th and demanded its surrender, Smith already had six batteries on the river and some thousands of troops guarding the land side, so the mayor was able to refuse.

Vicksburg lay about four-hundred miles above New Orleans by the very crooked river and the same distance below Memphis. The town was located on a high bluff on the east bank, the country in its rear cut by bayous. Most parts of the adjacent country were low and often flooded during high water. The town lay beyond the apex of a long U-shaped bend in the river, both arms dominated by the guns on the bluff. The peninsula and adjacent areas had been called the "DeSota Swamp." The weather was hot and dry during most of the campaign, but there was much green-scummed standing water in the area left when the flood stage had only recently subsided. Some desultory shelling took place on May 26th (3), but because the defenses appeared too strong General Williams returned to Baton Rouge by the 29th and Admiral Farragut to New Orleans, leaving only a few vessels in observation at Vicksburg.

The navy deemed the reopening of the river important enough to stop Farragut's designs on Mobile and order him back to Vicksburg with General Williams, now greatly reinforced. Butler ordered Williams". . . to take the town or have it burned at all hazards" (4). When they arrived for the second time, on June 25th, the situation had changed for the worse. Ten batteries now guarded the river approaches, Major General John C. Breckinridge with his corps from Corinth and other troops gave about 10,000 soldiers to the defense, and Major General Earl Van Dorn was in the overall command. General Williams had about 3,500 men in four northern regiments, and Farragut had been reinforced by a mortar fleet under Captain David Porter. In addition, on June 26th Flag Officer Charles H. Davis, having defeated the Confederates at Columbus and Memphis, arrived from upstream with his flotilla of gunboats and mortars. Farragut had about 106 guns and 13 mortars and Davis nearly as many more, but in a heavy bombardment on June 28th, they were unable to silence Van Dorn's guns, although a part of Farragut's ships passed above the town. The newly completed Confederate ram *Arkansas* steamed from the Yazoo River to the protection of the Vicksburg guns on July 15th, causing some damage in transit. During the sixty-seven days the fleet lay before the town, it periodically shelled the defending batteries without causing appreciable harm. General Smith reported his final losses as only seven killed and fifteen wounded. Not a single gun had been dismounted. The Federal combat losses also were light.

The casualties in the town were few, as there was no heavy

shelling. The civilians had been advised to leave. Some went to the country, others took to their cellars and a few to caves. As time went on, business was resumed, and a favorite walk of the people was around the courthouse cupola, from which to view the Yankee fleet and the army on the opposing peninsula (5). Although General Van Dorn reported the town "besieged" when he arrived (6), at no time was its communication cut off from Jackson and other points to the east.

It was soon realized that the city could be taken only from the land side, and that this would require additional troops. To Admiral Farragut's request for soldiers, Halleck replied from Corinth, where he had concentrated three sizeable and idle armies, that he had none to spare. General Williams, on Butler's orders, dug a ditch about a mile long across the base of the peninsula, expecting that the river, when admitted, would wash itself a new channel, which would by-pass Vicksburg (7). However, the plan failed because the river fell faster than the cut could be deepened (8). Butler belatedly realized he was conducting this, his main operation, within Halleck's department.

## Disease, Defeat, and Retreat

A new factor now entered the equation. The small combat casualties did not influence the campaign but the losses from disease—proportionately more Union than Confederate—soon prevented any prospect of victory. Doctor J. W. Thompson, the senior surgeon of Preston's Brigade of Confederates, found that these Kentuckians, contrary to expectations, suffered no more from the "malarious atmosphere" than Mississippi troops. They lost only one-third of their strength in a month, declining from 1,822 men on June 28th to 1,252 on July 27th (9). Another brigade of Kentuckians slept most of the time in bivouac with their clothes on despite the heat and did not have much sickness (5). A new regiment of Louisianians did not fare so well. Because of camp measles, malaria, and other diseases, they were reduced from about 900 men in May to 197 for duty by June 13th (10). They were then moved to a camp eighteen miles east of Vicksburg where, by July 23rd, 330 men were on duty and by October 3rd their strength was back to 773. A new battalion of

Mississippi boys rapidly melted away; one company originally about a hundred had only three able for duty by July 22nd (11). According to one account, nearly half the Vicksburg defenders were on the sick list by the third week of July suffering principally from malaria (12).

The health of the Union soldiers was bad already during the first upriver operation in May but it rapidly worsened during July. On May 29th, General Williams wrote (8) of his command:

> . . . the men have suffered from insufficiency of transportation, cramped and crowded more like live stock than men, without the means of exercise on board or room to form for inspection. Filth and dirt, with all the authority and supervision I could exert, abounded on vessels and men to a disgusting and of course most unwholesome degree. . . . the flooded country afforded no dry ground to land on . . .

Williams was the senior army officer present, and these conditions were his responsibility.

By the second expedition the flood had abated. Three of the regiments lived aboard their small, crowded river transports while the fourth plus Nims' battery bivouacked on the adjacent low-lying Louisiana peninsula that had only recently emerged from the water. They had departed Baton Rouge with no camp equipage except a few cooking utensils. The Seventh Vermont had only ten day's rations and a week's supply of quinine (13). They drank the muddy Mississippi River water. This river was the sewer for the persons upstream, afloat and ashore. Their food for many weeks had been salt pork and hardtack, well known to be a scorbutigenic diet (14). When the week's supply of quinine was exhausted, requisitions sent down to New Orleans were not honored by the medical director because of "irregularity" (14).

Sickness, chiefly malaria, increased rapidly in July. In the Ninth Connecticut almost the whole regiment was on the sick list at one time and eventually 153 died (14). There were not enough well men to spare a funeral escort. Nevertheless, General Williams exacted the most rigid discipline, ordering a brigade parade of the well men in the hot sun every day. The Seventh Vermont arrived on June 25th with nearly 800 men. By the middle of July fewer than a hundred were able for duty, and they too had to bury their companions without ceremony (13). Swamp fever, ague, dysentery, dengue, and general debility had played havoc. Assistant Surgeon Blanchard himself had malaria, and there were no medicines. Nims' battery of Massachusetts men had only twenty-one out of 140 members present for duty on July 31st (7). The Thirtieth Massachusetts arrived in June with 817 picked men (15). They worked on the ditch, slept in a swamp in which they built platforms of poles on which to lie, drilled five hours a day, and developed depression and scurvy on the salt meat and hard bread diet. When they departed in July more than half were sick chiefly with malaria, and during the six-month period, July to December, they buried 202 men— twenty per cent!

By July 17th General Williams would admit to Butler (8):

> The health of the troops has been much impaired by the absence of proper shelter. The quarters on board the transports are hot and crowded and those on shore are no protection against rain. Tents and boards are indispensable for shelter for the well and the sick—a rapidly increasing list.

Finally, on July 24th, Williams conceded defeat by disease (16):

> I will not attempt to disguise that I regret to leave this exceedingly . . . but with an increasing sick list, which must soon, if it has not already, reduce me below the ability for effective service, I have no alternative but to go.

On the following day Flag Officer C. H. Davis of the upper fleet explained the defeat to Secretary of the Navy Welles (17):

> Flag-Officer Farragut and Brigadier-General Williams went down the river yesterday. When I urged the latter to stay to keep open the communication above and below Vicksburg, he replied that of the 3,200 men brought here by him, only 800 were fit for duty; the other three-fourths of his command had died, or were in the hospital with fever. Sometimes, as many as ten died in a day.

Being afloat had not protected the navy from the same disaster although they had the facilities Williams lacked and blamed for his troubles. Flag Officer Davis had foreseen the end in a letter to Farragut on July 20th (17):

> . . . at this very moment there is not a vessel in my squadron which is

not rendered inefficient by sickness and vacancies, while of the fourteen vessels of which the squadron is composed seven only are here. . . . I have 129 mortar men and 1 army officer here. Of this number of 130, 100 are sick. . . . It will be with difficulty that I shall hold my own in the approaching sickly season.

Did he require a morbidity of one hundred per cent to concede defeat? Assistant Surgeon H. Beauchamp on the flagship *Benton* warned Davis on July 25th that the situation was deteriorating (18):

I apprehend that the character of our maladies will take on a more serious turn, changing from the ordinary intermittent to the remittent congestive and typhoid fevers of this climate.

Commodore Davis finally conceded defeat and advised a future course on July 31st (19):

Sickness had made sudden and terrible havoc with my people. It came, as it were, all at once. . . . But it seems to me that the only course now to be pursued is to yield to the climate and postpone any further action at Vicksburg till the fever season is over.

Lieutenant Colonel Alfred W. Ellet, commanding the ram fleet of the army, wrote *finis* on August 1st from Helena, Arkansas (20):

We were compelled to move north, owing to the crippled condition of our fleet from so large a proportion of our crews being disabled by sickness.

General Butler at New Orleans tried to put a better face on a bad situation while simultaneously coining absurd misinformation on the etiology of malaria. He conceded that his troops at Vicksburg had experienced much sickness, which had greatly weakened them. He reported on August 10th (21):

The overflow of the river and the number of dead animals in the swamps made a fearful malaria; but while it caused illness in almost the entire command it did not produce a large mortality.

The latter statement is false by almost any definition of "large" provided some of the delayed deaths are included. Men infected here were still dying when he wrote and long thereafter.

## A Dissection of the Repulse

It is clear that a severe epidemic of malaria made it impossible for the Union army to land and attack from the rear at Vicksburg even if it wished, and that the sickness was the immediate reason for the decision to abandon the campaign. The two fleets were also rendered ineffective by sickness. Whether Williams would have attacked after the naval bombardment, alone or with reinforcements, if the disease had not occurred is a different question which today cannot be answered. In any event, here is an example in which disease played a critical role in a campaign of considerable strategic importance, interrupting its course and terminating it without a battle.

Could this epidemic have been avoided by the knowledge then available? Yes, not by the means claimed effective by General Williams, but only by making the expedition during the cold months after a frost, as advised by General Scott in his anaconda plan (22). It was known that cold weather put an end to new cases of yellow fever, dengue, and malaria although occasional cases and recurrences of malaria after suppressive treatment might present themselves at any time. The explanation for these two sets of facts was a mystery. The plasmodium, its various species, its life cycle, and its transmission were not known. Even the gross pathological changes were not helpful and the micropathology, which held the clue, was not studied. Every one in the expedition, even the sailors in the middle of the river, were within the flight range of anophelene mosquitoes.

The original decision to send the expedition up the river was made in Washington, but we do not know by whom or on precisely what grounds, except that it was pushed by Secretary Welles. The decision to go in May was political and military, but with important medical overtones and factors, because of the reputation of that country. In early May, 1862, when the decision was made, there was no prominent military figure in Washington and Surgeon General Hammond was appointed only later that month. The decision to go then may have been a calculated risk, but whether the army or navy medical departments were consulted is uncertain. Once the military decision to proceed had been made, no medical facts then known could have prevented the epidemic, but its effects could have been mitigated if quinine had been provided in adequate quantities.

In this instance, disease struck one side harder than the other, and thus its effects were exceptionally important. Why did this happen? There seem to have been five main factors: (a) These were Northerners who had grown up with little malaria and not much dysentery. The regiments were the Third Wisconsin, Seventh Vermont, Ninth Connecticut, and the Thirtieth Massachusetts plus two batteries. (b) These troops had undergone physical deterioration from a bad environment and exposure for some months on the Gulf and in lower Louisiana. Their diet had been unpalatable and scorbutigenic, the water unpotable and probably bacteria-laden, and their quarters on ship were overcrowded and poorly ventilated. Much was learned about these effects in World War II, in the Pacific. These soldiers had lived for some time on Ship Island in the Gulf where disease conditions had been bad (23). (c) The terrain at Vicksburg was low and wet. Mosquito breeding places were probably far more numerous than around the higher camps across the river occupied by the Confederates. The Southerners had less dysentery probably due to the use of water from wells. (d) Quinine was in short supply. In his last two weeks at Vicksburg, Surgeon S. K. Towle of the Thirtieth Massachusetts had no quinine, and he was driven to substitute capsicum and nitric acid, both probably ineffective. (e) Last, and probably most important in explaining the explosive nature of the epidemic, were the 1,200 Negro refugees from the local Louisiana plantations used by Williams as laborers on the canal. They had, presumably, lived long in the worst parts of this malarial delta country and many of them were probably carriers of the parasite. If this conjecture is correct, the usual long, slow buildup from a few carriers to a massive epidemic would have been greatly accelerated. The Southern troops, mostly several miles away from this concentrated focus of infection and beyond the usual flight-range of the mosquitoes, would have been spared the full effects for a time, as they were. There was, however, soon a rapid increase in the infection rate in the Confederates, probably from indigenous sources, and at Baton Rouge, two weeks later, they too were decimated many times over by a sharp epidemic.

Two pertinent documents bearing on the Vicksburg area as malarious country have been found. In 1861, the whites and Negroes on nearby plantations had suffered unusually severely from the disease and many had died (24). On one plantation with a large white family and 150 Negroes, an entry in a diary on November 27th said that everybody on the place had been sick off and on all summer, and they were eagerly awaiting the frost. Then, in 1863, Assistant Surgeon Junius N. Bragg spent about ten days in July with an Arkansas regiment in the plantation country west of Vicksburg and he wrote that "This is certainly the most unhealthy place I have seen" (25). He described the prevailing bilious fever as being easily controllable with quinine. As late as 1881, Vicksburg had the second highest mortality rate from malaria among twenty-three Southern cities (26). Its rate of 318 deaths per 100,000 population per year was exceeded by Shreveport (428), but the rates at New Orleans (150), Memphis (107), Charleston (40), Richmond (31), and Atlanta (24) show that they were healthier at that time. From Corinth, Mississippi General Halleck wrote on June 25, 1862, "If we follow the enemy into the swamps of Mississippi there can be no doubt that our army will be disabled by disease" (27).

The Federal regiments at Vicksburg were all new. They had not been battle-tested but they had survived camp measles and mumps. They had sailed down the east coast to an unknown destination with high hopes. Now they experienced disabling, demoralizing casualties although they had not yet fired a gun in action. The Confederate regiments from Louisiana and Mississippi also were unblooded, but most of the Kentucky men, brought here by Breckinridge, had been at Shiloh and some at Mill Springs also. They were unhappy at being in Mississippi because it was unhealthy country, but even more, later on, because they missed the only major battle of the war on their native soil—at Perryville.

From the medical viewpoint one can inquire whether the preventive measures and treatment were in accord with the best knowledge of the time. The most glaring shortage was in quinine, essential for that time and place. Surgeon Charles H. Rawson had earlier emphasized the great importance to the medical officers in the western theater of quinine and opium in the management of malaria and diarrhea (28):

> Disease thus far has been easily controlled, although the consumption

of quinine and opium I fear would frighten the faculty east; but with us the daily demand and consumption, though large, only shows that without it our regiments would be but skeletons in form, and soon cease to exist. Give the western surgeon quinine and opium, and he is prepared to meet most of the ills of life . . .

This injunction could not be followed at Vicksburg because of the shortage. Less intelligent but common views of malaria and its management were those attributed to officers of a Connecticut regiment stationed near New Orleans at this time (29). The assistant surgeon kept them drilling every day in the broiling sun saying ". . . if we don't exercise and perspire abundantly we shall get poisoned with malaria and die." Much drinking was permitted by General John W. Phelps, an old army regular, on the basis that ". . . the men must have whiskey or die of country fever; even quinine won't save them without whiskey."

The general supplies of the drug were still adequate, North and South, in the first half of 1862. The failure at Vicksburg, on the Union side at least, seems to have been in procurement. The exact bottleneck cannot be located but blame seems due at some point. The matter was one of the inadequate usage of the available knowledge rather than of ignorance, and in a failure of distribution more than in the science of therapeutics.

The medical planning and preparation for the upriver expedition appear to have been slight. The medical supplies and drugs were quickly exhausted, although it was known that the command was harboring some acute enteritis since the Ship Island weeks in the Gulf and that they were entering malarious country in season. General Williams was known as a stern disciplinarian, who insisted on drill and parades despite the greatest heat and even mild sickness. The pathological effects of neither malaria nor dysentery microorganisms are mitigated by exercise or by will-power, self or imposed, and they cannot successfully be ignored.

Although dysentery, typhoid and other diseases were present among these troops (30, 31), the principal epidemic was almost certainly malaria. At first it seems to have been chiefly of the benign intermittent type. Considering the poor physical condition of the men and the inadequate treatment, the mortality was comparatively low.

Later it presented as a malignant form of remittent fever with a strong tendency to take on the congestive type (15, 32). Malnutrition, superinfection by other strains of malaria, and concurrent dysentery may account for the changed picture. Eventually the mortality was quite high, as has been cited, and the question arises whether falciparum malaria was present.

There are claims that dengue fever also was present (13, 33), but it was probably not a major cause of disability. No major outbreak of dengue was reported in Louisiana or Mississippi that year.

Although great medical problems were crucial military factors in this campaign, not a single army, brigade, or regimental surgeon is mentioned in the published official records. According to the number and size of the army units concerned, the quota of medical officers in William's force should have been nine and with the Confederates two or three times that number. There is even no assurance that General Williams had a surgeon on his staff, and nothing in his record shows him qualified himself to make the needed decisions in medicine, sanitation, and epidemiology.

The medical services, pay, and fate of the 1,200 to 1,500 Negro laborers, "gathered" from the nearby plantations (7), also are not mentioned in the records. Surely their services were not voluntarily donated by their planter-owners. At an average of something over $1,000 apiece, they represented an investment not readily relinquished. If they were escapees who volunteered their help, how did they live during the subsequent five months that elapsed before Grant occupied nearby Young's Point? The policy of the Confederate government on the Negro problem was still prewar, while that in Washington had wavered and it did not become firm until the announcement of emancipation in September. General Williams explained neither how he obtained these laborers nor whether he provided for them. An assistant surgeon was detailed to them from the Thirtieth Massachusetts (15), but his medical stores were scanty.

Brigadier General Thomas Williams seems to have been in the Union command by chance. The war found him, aged forty-six, a captain in the Fourth Artillery twenty-four years after graduation at the Military Academy. He had been Butler's acting inspector general at Fortress Monroe in the summer of 1861, and this led to his selection for the New Orleans expedition in 1862. As Butler's senior lieutenant, he was the logical choice to be sent up river with the navy. Although their number would have warranted a divisional structure, his force was organized as a brigade. Consequently he was the only general officer with the expedition, and his subsequent death at Baton Rouge left it without an experienced officer of any grade.

General Williams' reaction to his catastrophe was rather typically fatalistic and stoical of the time. Already on July 21st, in a letter home, he was steeling himself for the inevitable (34):

> The sick report receives its customary addition, and I'm preparing to send all the sick down to Baton Rouge, some 1100! But I'm not discouraged; I know these things to be the accustomed accompaniment of war. The troops do not, and therefore despond more or less.

When he died ten days after departing Vicksburg, General Williams had not yet written his postaction report and had submitted no return. In the interim his adjutant and aide were both incapacitated by malaria, and he had trouble at Baton Rouge from the continuing illness, as well as from colonels who disagreed with his discipline and his management of the Negro refugees. In his available official correspondence he had not stressed the disease but to home and his colleagues he had conceded the bad situation, which seems to have been ignored by most historians. There is no doubt that intercurrent disease caused an enormous morbidity which finally disabled him for exerting effective strength against the Vicksburg defenses. He was outnumbered on land but had much naval firepower in support. Even with a much larger command he would not have been able to win the town after the epidemic appeared and took control from him.

## Medical-Military Lessons

This is a prime example of the outcome of an important military action being determined by intercurrent disease. General Scott's wise advice to wait until November to open the river was ignored. A campaign in November of 1861 would have been impractical because of lack of trained soldiers and armed river ships, and Grant's campaign, beginning in November, 1862, met heavy opposition in the elements and Confederate defenders. It too experienced heavy losses from sickness that winter—typhoid and dysentery rather than the malaria and dysentery of William's men. However, malaria later struck Grant's forces too, but chiefly after the surrender.

This campaign attracted little national attention. Apparently no reporters were present on either side. Moreover, the eyes of the country were being directed to the large army groups of Halleck and Beauregard at Corinth, to McClellan's struggle on the Yorktown peninsula for Richmond, and to Pope's new Army of Virginia before Washington. A part of the opponents at Vicksburg met at Baton Rouge in August, which resulted in a Union victory, but it too passed almost unnoticed. On the river, however, sickness was recognized already in 1862 as the cause of the repulse (35).

Despite the crucial role of disease in this campaign, the military seemed to learn no lesson from it. Up to the time of his death, William's effort at Baton Rouge had been managed no better than the one up stream. Quinine was still in short supply. No medical or military commission or board on either side investigated either disaster, and no lessons were learned for the use of Grant and Banks and of Pemberton and Gardner in this same area in 1863, or for Steele, Price, and E. Kirby Smith in 1864.

The leaders at Vicksburg dispersed, General Williams to die in battle ten days later, General Van Dorn to meet death in nine months by the pistol of Doctor Peters over an affair of personal honor, Admiral Farragut to damn the torpedoes in Mobile Bay two years later and win a prominent place in history, and General Breckinridge, the former vice president and presidential candidate, to revert to politics, his proper medium, to become the last Confederate secretary of war. General Butler did not have another chance to reopen the big river, losing his command in a few months over cotton, household silver, and other touchy articles and practices. Grant, at the end of his best campaign, would accept Pemberton's surrender of Vicksburg on the Fourth of July of the following year, his success coming, finally, by a land approach from the rear. Malaria was still highly prevalent in the area and dysentery and typhoid were added, but his large army was far better organized, supplied, and led, and the losses from sickness, although very large, did not become crucial.

## References

1. IRWIN, R. B.: Military operations in Louisiana in 1862. R. U. Johnson and C. C. Buel, Eds. *Battles and Leaders of the Civil War*, 3:582-584, 1884.

2. GREENE, F. V.: *Campaigns of the Civil War.* VIII. The Mississippi. New York, Charles Scribner's Sons, 1882, 276 p.
3. SMITH, M. L.: *O.R., 15:*6-12.
4. BUTLER, B. F.: *Private and Official Correspondence of Gen. Benjamin F. Butler.* No city, Privately issued, 1917, Vol. 1, 562.
5. GEORGE, H.: *History of the 3d, 7th, 8th and 12th Kentucky, C.S.A.* Louisville, C. T. Dearing Printing Co., 1911, 193 p.
6. VAN DORN, E.: *O.R., 15:*14-19.
7. WHITCOMB, C. E.: *History of the Second Massachusetts Battery.* Concord, N.H., Rumford Press, 1912, 111 p.
8. WILLIAMS, T.: *O.R., 15:*22-35.
9. THOMPSON, E. P.: *History of the First Kentucky Brigade.* Cincinnati, Caxton Publ. House, 1868, 119, 158.
10. HALL, W.: *The Story of the 26th Louisiana Infantry.* No city, No publisher, 1890?, 228 p.
11. CHAMBERS, W. P.: My journal. *Publ. Miss. Hist. Soc. (N.S.) 5:*221-386, 1925.
12. PIRTLE, J. B.: Defense of Vicksburg in 1862. *So. Hist. Soc. Papers, 8:* 324-332, 1880.
13. HOLBROOK, W. C.: *A Narrative of the Service of the Officers and Enlisted Men of the 7th Regiment of Vermont Volunteers.* New York, Amer. Bank Note Co., 1882, 219 p.
14. MURRAY, T. H.: *History of the Ninth Regiment, Connecticut Volunteer Infantry.* New Haven, Conn., Price, Lee & Adkins Co., 1903, 446 p.
15. TOWLE, S. K.: Letter from Surgeon Towle to Surgeon-General Dale. *Boston Med. and Surg. Jour., 67:*119-124, 1862.
16. WILLIAMS, T.: *O.R.* (Naval), Ser. I, *23:*239.
17. DAVIS, C. H.: *O.R.* (Naval) Ser. I, *23:*237-238, 240.
18. BEAUCHAMP, H.: *O.R.* (Naval), Ser. I, *23:*240-241.
19. DAVIS, C. H.: *O.R.* (Naval), Ser. I, *23:*271-272.
20. ELLET, A. W.: *O.R.* (Naval), Ser. I.
21. BUTLER, B. F.: *O.R., 15:*39-46.
32. SCOTT, W.: *O.R., 51:*369-370.
23. SOULE, H.: From the Gulf to Vicksburg. In *War Papers,* pp. 51-71. Michigan Commandery, Military Order of the Loyal Legion. Detroit, James H. Stone & Co., 1898, 325 p.
24. ANDERSON, J. Q., Ed.: *Brockenburn: The Journal of Kate Stone, 1861-1868.* Baton Rouge, Louisiana State Univ. Press, 1955, 400 p.
25. GAUGHAN, T. J.: *Letters from a Confederate Surgeon, 1861-65.* Camden, Ark., Hurley Co., 1960, 276 p.
26. *Med. and Surg. Hist.,* Vol. I, Part III, 87.
27. HALLECK, H.: *O.R., 16:* Part 2, 62.
28. RAWSON, C. H.: Health of troops in Missouri. *Amer. Med. Times, 3:*300, 1861.

29. DeForest, J. W.: *A Volunteer's Adventures*. Edited by J. H. Croushore. New Haven, Yale Univ. Press, 1946, 237 p.

30. Anonymous surgeon: Letters from a Surgeon of the Mississippi Squadron. *Boston Med. and Surg. Jour.*, 67:38-39, 1862.

31. Anonymous surgeon: Letter to editor. *Boston Med. and Surg. Jour.*, 66: 280, 1862.

32. Towle, S. K.: *Med. and Surg. Hist.*, Vol. I, Part III, 153-154.

33. Green, J. W., Edited by A. D. Kirwan: *Johnny Green of the Orphan Brigade*. Univ. of Kentucky Press, 1956, 217 p.

34. Williams, G. M.: The First Vicksburg Expedition. In *War Papers*, 52-69 of Vol. 2. Wisconsin Commandery, Military Order of the Loyal Legion. Milwaukee, Burdick, Armitage and Allen, 1896, 455 p.

35. Wilcox, C. E., Edited by E. L. Erickson: Hunting for cotton in Dixie. *Jour. Southern Hist.*, 4:493-513, 1938.

# VIII

## The Battle of Baton Rouge

THE BATTLE OF Baton Rouge, in August, 1862, resulted from a Confederate attempt to recapture this strategic town consequent to the Federal repulse at Vicksburg two weeks earlier. The Union defenders retained control despite the absence, in hospitals, of half their troops, but only because the Southerners had unexpectedly, while *en route,* lost nearly two-thirds of theirs. The organizational structure (essentially that of an army corps or small army) for the 2,500 attacking troops of Major General John C. Breckinridge looks ridiculous, but this appearance resulted from depletion by acute epidemic disease and not faulty military organization. This small force comprised the remnants of two divisions with about eighteen regiments. The military decision to proceed with the planned offensive in the face of such a medical catastrophe can be criticized. The operation was begun during the incubation period of the epidemic, a bit of bad luck that proved just as harmful as if the infection had been deliberately planned by the enemy.

### The Strategic Considerations

Baton Rouge, about 130 miles by water above New Orleans, had originally been occupied in May, 1862, by the Federal troops of Brigadier General Thomas Williams sent up by General Ben Butler (1, 2, 3, 4). Williams had here based his attempts in May and June to take Vicksburg, and to it he had returned on July 26th after abandoning that campaign (5). This place was chosen because it seemed healthier than New Orleans for his sick men (5, 6, 7). Baton Rouge was a town of about 7,000 people. It was proud of the state capitol, the former Federal arsenal and barracks, an orphan's home, insane asylum, churches, commercial buildings, homes, and a race track. Most of these structures became involved in the military operations as hospitals, barracks, storehouses and other uses.

Also on July 26th, Confederate Major General Earl Van Dorn instructed General Breckinridge to proceed with 6,000 troops selected from the Vicksburg defenses by railroad to Camp Moore in northeastern Louisiana (8). Here he should pick up Brigadier General Daniel Ruggles with about 1,000 men and, moving overland eighty miles, take Baton Rouge from the rear. The stated strategic objectives were to gain a base from which to exploit the Red River and to mount a campaign on New Orleans (8). The Red River country could provide communications with Texas as well as provisions and supplies for Vicksburg and points east. No difficulty was expected as the Confederates outnumbered the enemy, were familiar with the country, had more combat experience, and would be fighting for their home soil.

## The Battle of August 5th

After a long night march, the Confederates advanced at dawn in a heavy fog in a single line half-a-mile long. One regiment and a piece of artillery was in reserve behind each division (9). General Breckinridge hoped to enjoy the music of his band in the State House by nine o'clock. In a predawn crossfire, precipitated by some partisan rangers, the horse of Brigadier General Ben Helm, a brother-in-law of President Lincoln, was shot and he was badly injured in the fall (10). The attack was expected, General Williams having had strong scouting parties out; the horses of one battery had been standing in harness for three days and nights (11). Williams had not intrenched but he had selected three lines east of the town for successive defense. One regiment held in reserve was not committed and another one on the end of the line found little work (12). The Twenty-first Indiana fortunately held the center. It was the largest Union regiment, having 585 men on the field (13), and it was the only one equipped with breech-loaders (3). Three Union batteries were handled efficiently. Four Union gunboats stood by to lend their fire but they were able to give little support. The rebel ram *Arkansas* had come down from Vicksburg to help but developed mechanical trouble, ran aground, and had to be destroyed on the following day.

The battle raged for about five hours. The Union line was driven back to the suburbs. By 10:00 A.M. both sides were exhausted and in the heat the rebels were thirsty, having had no water since crossing the Comite River at 11:00 P.M. the previous night, except for what they could find in cisterns (9). After destroying the Union camps they had overrun, the Confederates withdrew. Some regiments had become mixed because of the woods, bayous, fog and smoke, and had shot into each other. Some confusion also resulted from the heavy losses in senior officers. Four Southern brigade and one divisional commander were wounded (10). General Williams, leading the Twenty-first Indiana in a charge in person because all its field grade officers had been wounded, was shot through the heart by a musket ball (14). Because his seven regiments were still organized only as a brigade, no general officer was present to succeed him. He had previously sent his most senior and competent colonel to New Orleans in arrest. No experienced officer remained, and General Butler had to send up his engineering officer, the twenty-six-year-old Lieutenant Godfrey Weitzel, to obtain an evaluation. The Union casualties were 383, of which 84 were dead, and General Breckinridge reported a loss of 446 (10).

## The Medical Situation at Baton Rouge and Camp Moore

Of the Confederate troops taken to Baton Rouge by General Breckinridge, the major Vicksburg contingent had suffered in the malaria epidemic at that place, described in the preceding chapter. Breckinridge selected healthy-appearing men on July 27th, but before the battle of August 5th many were down, showing that they had been in a remission or in the incubation period. The troops joining at Camp Moore were in little if any better condition, so that by the morning of the attack the command had been reduced from 6,000 to about 2,500 effectives (1, 2, 8, 10). They were all that remained able for duty in eighteen or nineteen regiments plus some bodies of local partisans; the well averaged only about 140 per regiment. The Kentucky Brigade had dropped from 1,822 men at Vicksburg to 584 at Camp Moore on August 11th (15). The brigade then had only two field officers, both indisposed, and less than two officers per company. Quinine was still in short supply. An enlisted man who had been left behind sick at Vicksburg wrote on August 2nd (16): "We skin willow and dogwood trees, boil the bark and drink the tea. I am having fever again every day."

The Confederate depletion by disease continued large right up to the hour of the attack. General Breckinridge had 3,400 men when he left Camp Moore on July 30th. By the evening of August 4th, only ten miles from his destination, he wrote (10):

> The sickness had been appalling. The morning report of the 4th showing but 3000 effectives, and deducting those taken sick during the day and the number that fell out from weakness on the night march I did not carry into action more than 2,600 men.

A southern officer left a candid description (17): He thought Breckinridge departed Camp Moore on July 30th in hot weather with about 4,000. About one-third had no shoes and some were "almost naked." No water was provided between the streams, ten to fifteen miles apart, except for some green-scummed ponds. "Men sickened and fell out of the ranks every mile we marched . . ." The General, an eloquent speaker, gave them a stirring address just before they marched to the attack.

The Federal defenses consisted of three batteries and seven regiments, four of which had arrived with Williams from Vicksburg about July 26th in bad condition from malaria. They had not improved much by the day of battle. The other three regiments were little better off on the morning of the 5th. Of a paper strength of around 5,000, about 2,500 were in the fight, some of them leaving the regimental hospitals to carry a musket. It is said of these soldiers that not 1,200 could have marched five miles in pursuit because of malaria and chronic dysentery (4). In Nim's battery, only twenty-one of its 140 members were present for inspection on July 31st (11). On August 1st, few of the seven regiments had over 200 men able for full duty and the Fourth Wisconsin had only sixty (18). Several were dying every day. The Seventh Vermont had 520 sick on the morning of battle and only 250 for duty (19). The sick list of the Thirtieth Massachusetts was over 400 (20).

On August 2nd, General Williams notified Butler that he expected an attack soon, and he added (21):

> I hope the rebels have as many sick as I have. Perhaps (let us hope at least) that a battle may to our sick exert all the effects of the best tonic in the pharmacopoeia.

He would find the tonic of battle a poor substitute for quinine. The fact that some sick men left hospitals to bear muskets shows that morale was good, but only the mildly ill could respond.

## The Aftermath

Inasmuch as the Southern offensive failed to achieve either of its objectives, the battle must be counted a Federal victory. However the fruits of victory were lost. General Breckinridge soon occupied and fortified the bluff at Port Hudson, thirty miles above Baton Rouge, obtaining there the base he desired below the mouth of the Red River. This stronghold cost the Union a large and bloody effort by General Banks a year later, in which many of these same regiments lost heavily. Then, on August 20th, General Butler evacuated Baton Rouge as having no military value. It was reoccupied by the Confederates for a while but retaken by Federal forces without a fight in December, 1862 and retained thereafter.

A surgeon from another regiment described these troops shortly afterward (22):

On their return to New Orleans these regiments were a sight to behold. The scenes on board the boats which brought the sick beggar description —the dead and living locked in one embrace. Reduced to shadows by diarrhea and fever, a single paroxysm sufficed to snap the cord. Men put on board at Baton Rouge for simply debility were enveloped in their winding sheets before they reached New Orleans: I counted seven dead bodies on one boat. These remittents or intermittents had but one paroxysm; seldom would there by any febrile reaction. The collapse was almost as perfect as in cholera—features shrunken, skin cold and livid, voice husky, pulse small and quick, stomach irritable and mind torpid.

This seems to be the picture of cerebral malaria in highly debilitated, malnourished men.

Nothing was wrong with the patriotism, bravery, and heroism of these soldiers, Union or Confederate. The seven Northern regiments, easier traced than the Southern, at the end of the war left a remarkable record of endurance and valor, and of soldiering under conditions of extreme hardship. The Sixth Michigan eventually had 582 deaths, 504 of them by disease (23); the Seventh Vermont lost 407 from disease out of a total of 420 deaths; the Sixth Wisconsin dead numbered 127 in battle and 314 from disease. The mortality in the

other four regiments was in the same high range. These units
eventually, through later accessions, had around 1,500 men on the
rolls, but only a few of them were present at risk at any one time.
One surviving colonel complained of the swampy Gulf area that
to bury their dead "The plain board coffins must be held under
water in the shallow, swampy graves, while the clammy earth is
thrown in" (24). After nearly two more years in the Department
of the Gulf, some of these regiments were shipped to the Army of
the James with the Nineteenth Corps in 1864, and some of them
were in line at Appomattox. Some of the Confederate regiments
came into Bragg's Army of Tennessee. Others were surrendered a
year later by Pemberton at Vicksburg or by General Frank Gardner
at Port Hudson a few days later.

## Retrospective View

This is another example of a battle lost because of the depleting
effects of an intercurrent epidemic disease. The Confederate morbidity
was disproportionately larger than that in the Union force. Because
they were on the offensive, they could not tolerate such disproportion.
The disease responsible was principally malaria, although both sides
also suffered from acute and chronic dysentery and diarrhea. The
Confederate army, originally the larger, by the day of battle no longer
had any numerical advantage, and because it was on the offensive,
thirsty and exhausted, it could not win. The help of a small amount
of the strength lost since their departure from Vicksburg could have
reversed the result.

The important role of disease in the outcome of this battle
escaped attention, diagnosis, and remedial action. No military or
medical investigation was made by either side. In their postaction
reports the responsible senior surviving officers conceded the disease
factor and then ignored it to confine their writing to straight military
matters. Thus, General Van Dorn wrote only that the enterprise
failed because "I could not anticipate the sudden illness of 3,000
picked men" (8). Although disease was important and wounds
numerous, the surgeons are mentioned in only one Federal and three
Confederate reports. Assistant Surgeon Alfred F. Holt of the Thirtieth
Massachusetts was cited ". . . for humane courage, taking on his

back, under hot fire, the wounded soldiers as they fell," and not for treating the great number of ill (25). The postaction report of General Butler cited eighty-one officers and men by name, but this number included only one medical officer (7). In the nearly four-hundred pages of reports of medical officers published in the official *Medical and Surgical History,* about one inch is devoted to this campaign. This is the report of Surgeon Ezra Read of the Twenty-first Indiana, the regiment that fought the hardest (13).

No medical lesson was learned from this campaign. The senior commanders soon left the area and a year later, at Port Hudson forty miles away, the mistakes were repeated but on a far larger and costlier scale. Entire regiments were there ruined by the same two diseases plus typhoid fever. There is nothing in the record to suggest that a straight and full presentation of the facts at Baton Rouge ever reached Washington or Richmond. The major reports, by Generals Ben Butler and Van Dorn, neither of whom was present, are not in conformity with others and they are misleading. The statement of General Butler that the malaria had a low mortality ignores the facts. Surgeon Towle of the Thirtieth Massachusetts said that eighteen men died in the swamp at Vicksburg, 114 more in the months of July, August and September, and a total of 202 (20 per cent of the regiment) in six months (26). He characterized the malaria as a malignant form of remittent fever with a strong tendency to assume the congestive (*i.e.* cerebral) type. Scurvy was also present in the command, as they had been exclusively on a salt pork and hardtack diet for over six months.

What lessons could have been learned? The foremost "mistake" made was medical-military. It was General Van Dorn's decision to begin the campaign at that time rather than to wait for frost or the control of the epidemic with quinine. Whether he consulted the Confederate medical department is not a matter of record. This enterprise was a direct continuation of the Vicksburg campaign and fully two-thirds of the troops of both sides came from there. The epidemic that had stopped that campaign had not yet run its course, and among the Confederates it had probably not yet reached its peak. The medical director on General Van Dorn's staff (if there was one), by requiring daily or frequent reports of the regimental surgeons, could have determined the status of his epidemic and roughly predicted its course. The concurrence of two epidemics, malaria and dysentery, would have complicated but not invalidated his forecast.

Secondly and equally important was the probability that, given adequate quantities of quinine, the Confederate surgeons could have brought the malarial component of this epidemic under control within a few weeks. This would have greatly increased Breckinridge's chances of success. At the same time the ration should have been improved to eliminate all scorbutic tendency or "taint," as it was called.

A third mistake also was medical-military. It was the decision of Breckinridge to proceed from Camp Moore in the face of a continuing large daily shrinkage in his ranks. He believed the Union defending force to be far larger than his own. In retrospect it looks foolhardy for him to have ignored the disease factor and to have proceeded at that time. His Thirty-first Alabama went into action with only ninety-five rank and file (27). Where were the other 900 men of this regiment? The Nineteenth, Twentieth, Twenty-eighth, and Forty-fifth Tennessee regiments had been depleted so greatly that they fought this battle consolidated as a battalion (10)! Regardless of his original orders, Breckinridge faced a different situation on August 4th from that prevailing when he departed Vicksburg, or even Camp Moore, and a new look was indicated.

Moreover, for the Confederates this was a shoestring operation for which prior planning seems to have been inadequate. General Breckinridge conceded that he had little transportation, indifferent food, and no shelter. Half his men had no coats and hundreds had no shoes or socks. Nevertheless, they were audacious and gallant (10). Gallantry, however, cannot prevail over scurvy, chills and fever, severe malaise, weakness, profound perspiration, headaches, vomiting, and frequent compulsive and exhausting bloody evacuations of the bowels.

At this late date there was still much misuse of medical talent, many physicians serving in combatant positions as privates or in the line. As in this instance, they were sometimes detailed to serve as surgeons during battle. Doctor I. F. Delony, a private in the Thirty-fifth Alabama, was detailed an assistant surgeon (28)

... and deserves particular mention, he being up with the regiment at all times, caring for the wounded and encouraging the men. I respectfully ask that Dr. Delony be discharged, that I may contract with him as assistant surgeon.

One would think that Doctor Delony could have been far more usefully employed during the preceding few weeks by the Confederacy than as a musketeer. Sent to Mobile, Montgomery, or some other city for quinine and administering it on his return, he might have reversed the outcome of this battle.

On the Union side the failure of General Williams to get along well with his officers influenced this battle by depriving him of able leaders. He had to go into battle without two of his regimental commanders (one of them his senior colonel) and a number of other officers, all recently ordered in arrest to New Orleans. He had issued an order to expel all Negro refugees from camp. Colonel Halbert E. Paine of the Fourth Wisconsin (later a major general by brevet) refused and he was arrested. General Butler sent him back on August 6th to take the command as the surviving senior (12). Colonel F. W. Curtenius of the Sixth Michigan and all of its officers down to the third ranking captain had also been sent to New Orleans in arrest for refusing to move the regiment from a campsite in town to a bivouac without tents because half their men were sick and they were burying one a day (24). Hearing of the impending battle, they had requested permission to serve with the regiment, but they were not released from arrest by Williams until "The cause of all difficulty had been removed"—by his death. One of these officers thought that General Williams ". . . is stuffed full of the small things of the regulations. He appears determined to wage war by means of inspections; . . a mind twenty years pickled in alcohol . . ." (24). Some of this criticism seems to reflect the inevitable hardships of this combat theater and poor subordination more than on the competence of Williams. It was said that cotton bought in Baton Rouge for three cents a pound could be sold in New York for a dollar but that General Williams refused to have anything to do with such traffic (3).

On both sides the subordinate officers and the enlisted men for the most part stoically or passively accepted the bad situation. Only the officers of the Sixth Michigan objected to an order they considered harmful to their men, and they carried the point nearly to mutiny. From arrest in New Orleans, they wrote letters to Governor Austin Blair, Senator Zachariah Chandler and to the Detroit *Advertiser* (24). At the time of their vigorous protest it was said that ". . . the surgeon's command outnumbers that of the general . . ."

Apart from the disease component, the Confederate force appears to have had sizeable military advantages in numbers, experience, and leadership. Its organizational structure of about eighteen regiments in four brigades divided between two divisions gave it many senior officers in comparison with the Union single brigade of seven regiments. Inasmuch as the number of opposing soldiers on the field was about even, the prior Confederate losses had been far greater. It is true that this loss had not all been recent or from illness. It included casualties in combat at Mill Springs, at Shiloh, and in the first Corinth campaign. As such it also represented combat experience for the officers and men not equalled by the Federals. General Williams had been in no real battle. In contrast, General Breckinridge had directed a corps at Shiloh, and Generals Ruggles, Clark, Smith, and Allen had there led sizeable commands. Generals Ruggles and Helm were graduates at West Point and Colonel T. B. Smith at the Nashville Military Institute. The Confederate failure at Baton Rouge resulted not from a lack of combat-experienced leadership but from inadequate medical direction and knowledge on the part of that leadership.

The full statistical story on disease is not known. Baton Rouge lay within the Department of the Gulf, and the Union data were included in the reports of that department. In twenty Federal military departments, the prevalence of diarrhea and dysentery, expressed in cases per 1,000 mean strength for each year, stood highest in the Department of the Gulf. The figure for the year ending June 30, 1862 was 1,637 cases, and for the following year it was 1,473. Thus each man, on the average, had reported sick with this disease nearly twice. The corresponding figure for the Department of the East (New England states, New York, New Jersey, and Pennsylvania) was only 296 (29). In malaria the Department of the Gulf, with a figure of 930 cases, ranked third, coming after the Department of Arkansas (1,287) and the Department of North Carolina, 1,035 cases (30). Thus each man in this department had on the average one attack of malaria during the year. Baton Rouge, itself, in 1881 stood fifth among twenty-three Southern cities in deaths from malaria (31). Its rate per 100,000 population was 171 deaths. Shreveport, with a rate of 429 stood highest but New Orleans with 150, Nashville with 41, Charleston with 40, and Atlanta with 24 were far healthier.

Surgeon S. K. Towle of the Thirtieth Massachusetts wrote to the *Boston Medical and Surgical Journal,* in 1863, from his hospital located in the Louisiana Blind and Mute Asylum in Baton Rouge that he hoped soon to return to his practice in New England (32):

> . . . where malaria is not inhaled at every breath, where nature is not always antagonistic to the physician, and where a vigorous, rapid, and complete convalescence is not an impossibility.

## References

1. GREENE, F. V.: *The Mississippi.* New York, Charles Scribner's Sons, 1882, 276 p.
2. IRWIN, R. B.: Military operations in Louisiana in 1862. In *Battles and Leaders of the Civil War,* Edited by R. U. Johnson and C. C. Buel. New York, The Century Co., Vol. 3, 1888.
3. HOFFMAN, W.: *Camp, Court and Siege.* New York, Harper & Bros., 1877, 285 p.
4. WILLIAMS, G. M.: The First Vicksburg Expedition, and the Battle of Baton Rouge, 1862. In *War Papers,* Commandery State of Wisconsin, Military Order of the Loyal Legion. Milwaukee, Burdick, Armitage & Allen, Vol. 2, 1896.
5. WILLIAMS, T.: *O.R., 15*:22-24.
6. BUTLER, B. F.: *Butler's Book.* Boston, A. M. Thayer & Co., 1892.
7. BUTLER, B. F.: *O.R., 15*:39-46.
8. VAN DORN, E.: *O.R., 15*:14-19.
9. EVANS, C. A., Ed.: *Confederate Military History.* Atlanta, Confederate Publishing Co., Vol. 10, 1899.
10. BRECKINRIDGE, J. C.: *O. R., 15*:76-82.
11. WHITCOMB, C. E.: *History of the Second Massachusetts Battery.* Concord, N.H., Rumford Press, 1912, 111 p.
12. GARDNER, I. B.: Personal experiences with the Fourteenth Main Volunteers from 1861-1865. In *War Papers,* Maine Commandery, Military Order of the Loyal Legion. Portland, Lefavor-Tower Co., Vol. 4, 1915.
13. READ, E.: *Med. and Surg. Hist.,* Vol. I, Part I, Appendix p. 335.
14. *O.R., 15*:55-58.

15. *O.R., 15*:1125-1126.
16. CHAMBERS, W. P.: My journal. *Publ. Miss. Hist. Soc.* (New series), *5*: 221-386, 1925.
17. PIRTLE, J. B.: Defence of Vicksburg in 1862—The Battle of Baton Rouge. *So. Hist. Soc. Papers, 8*:324-332, 1880.
18. MURRAY, T. H.: *History of the Ninth Regiment, Connecticut Volunteer Infantry.* New Haven, Conn., Prince, Lee & Adkins Co., 1903, 446 p.
19. *O.R., 15*:49.
20. TOWLE, S. K.: Letter of Surgeon S. K. Towle. *Boston Med.* and *Surg. Jour., 67*:119-125, 1862.
21. *O.R., 15*:34.
22. SANGER, E. F.: On the fevers that prevailed in New Orleans and its vicinity in 1862. *Med. and Surg. Hist.,* Vol. I, Part III, 331.
23. FOX, W. F.: *Regimental Losses in the American Civil War.* Albany, Albany Publ. Co., 1889, 595 p.
24. BACON, E.: *Among the Cotton Thieves.* Detroit, Free Press Steam Book and Job Printing House, 1867, 299 p.
25. *O.R., 15*:42.
26. TOWLE, S. K.: *Med. and Surg. Hist.,* Vol. I, Part III, 153-154.
27. *O.R.,15*:84-85.
28. *O.R., 15*:96.
29. *Med. and Surg. Hist.,* Vol. I, Part II, 17-18.
30. *Med. and Surg. Hist.,* Vol. I, Part III, 77, 79, 97.
31. *Med. and Surg. Hist.,* Vol. I, Part III, 87.
32. TOWLE, S. K.: *Boston Med. and Surg. Jour., 70*:49-60, 1864.

# IX

## The Department of Arkansas in 1863-1865

THE DEPARTMENT OF ARKANSAS ranked high among the most unhealthy Union commands in the latter part of the war, and it was one of the least efficient. Large numbers of troops were fed seriatim into the area, yet a few months later not enough were present to interrupt the raiding columns of Generals J. O. Shelby and Sterling Price. From one-half to two-thirds of the soldiers carried on the rolls were absent from duty most of the time, chiefly because of disease. The Confederates also suffered from much sickness. The half-life of regiments was often less than a year (the usual figure) from disease alone. The Federal column sent into Arkansas achieved its original goal, but it was not able to proceed farther because of insufficient numbers due to a high morbidity from disease. The Confederate counter-efforts were handicapped by the same cause. The result was essentially an eighteen-month stalemate, punctuated by guerilla activity.

The area provides an opportunity to study the impact of disease on two large, fairly stable, previously "conditioned" military populations (Federal and Confederate); the picture, moreover, is not complicated by heavy combat casualties; furthermore, military medicine had developed about as far as it would go during the war. The period under study is long enough to reveal any seasonal variations, an important feature in some "natural" bacterial warfare effects. Some of the regiments were never in a major battle, yet they ended the war about as small as many that had fought at Gettysburg and in other big name battles. There seem to have been few deterrents to the exertion of their maximal effects by the disease-producing microbes.

The period to be studied is from July 1, 1863 to June 30, 1865. During most of this time the Federal Department of Arkansas and the Confederate Division of Arkansas comprise the area under study. Because of better documentation the Union health problem is emphasized.

## The Military Operations

The operations of interest here began in August, 1863, from the joint planning of Generals John Schofield at St. Louis and Grant at Vicksburg (1). The Department of Arkansas, consisting of that state plus the Indian Territory on the frontier to the west, was not organized until several months later, but the medical data from the entire period are studied. To the north was the harried Department of the Missouri and to the south the cotton-minded Department of the Gulf. The fall of Vicksburg and Port Hudson in July had bisected the Confederacy, and patrolling Union gunboats maintained a hiatus. Soldiers, livestock, foodstuffs, cotton, sugar, salt and other produce could no longer be sent east in quantity. West of the big river the Confederate authority was represented chiefly by the Trans-Mississippi Department commanded first by General Th. H. Holmes and, after the spring of 1863, by General E. Kirby Smith at Shreveport (2). The main source of those supplies not produced in the area was by importation through Mexico by way of Texas. General Smith would surrender the last large Confederate army in Texas on May 26, 1865 to end the war. This late date represents less Confederate power than Union inertia of long standing. Because of the poor communications with Richmond, this had long been virtually a semi-independent empire. Its District of Arkansas included most of the area of our present interest. Here the commanders during this time were successively Generals Th. H. Holmes, Sterling Price and John Magruder.

The mission of the Federal offensive was to drive the Confederates away from the Mississippi and to destroy or neutralize their sizeable army, thus protecting Missouri and St. Louis. An objective not verbalized was to help collect cotton for Northern mills. To achieve these objectives Grant assigned classmate Major General Frederick Steele. He was a former frontier infantry captain, quiet, unimaginative, fairly competent, and, so some thought, soft on rebels. As it turned out he lacked drive and initiative. No other Union departmental commander was more content comfortably to settle down like a police precinct captain.

The column of General Steele that left the Mississippi in August, 1863 for Little Rock was called the Army of Arkansas, but it was essentially an army corps, and it was eventually designed the Seventh Corps (3). Apart from Steele there were at first only two general officers for the three divisions and eight brigades. Its approximately thirty-three regiments had been raised in the so-called western states (Ohio and beyond) in 1861 and 1862. All of them had been in service for at least eight months, most of it in the field. Because the aggregate was only about 12,000 for duty, the regiments had already lost about two-thirds of their original strength, although most of them had not been in a major battle. They had campaigned variously in Missouri, northern Arkansas (at Pea Ridge and Prairie Grove), Tennessee, and Mississippi. The majority had recently been with Grant at Vicksburg or in garrison at Helena or elsewhere. They had been in service long enough to be through their measles, mumps, and whooping cough, and they were now experiencing the usual camp diseases—dysentery, typhoid fever, and malaria. Steele reported much malaria in the two brigades coming to him from the Yazoo River, and a large proportion of the Helena garrison on the levees was sick (4). This was a bad omen.

Their Confederate opponents had fought variously in the same operations or at Wilson's Creek, at Iuka and Corinth, at Arkansas Post, or recently at Helena. Morale, however, was bad. The soldiers from Missouri and northern Arkansas were unhappy at having to abandon their homes. General Holmes reported to Davis in March, 1863 that only 6,000 effectives out of 12,000 with him in North Arkansas that winter had arrived back at Little Rock. The remainder in about equal parts had deserted, had been left behind sick, or had died (5): He added that "All the medical officers agree that it was owing to the diet and exposure, poor beef and corn-bread being the only diet. . ." On assigning General E. Kirby Smith to this department, Secretary Seddon warned him that General Holmes had lost the confidence and attachment of all, that General T. C. Hindman had by acts of violence and tyranny rendered himself odious, and that the army had dwindled by desertion, sickness, and death from 40,000 or 50,000 to 15,000 or 18,000 (6).

On July 4th, Holmes had attacked the Union works at Helena in a belated attempt to help Pemberton, besieged at Vicksburg. The effort had been handily repulsed, and Holmes had returned to Little Rock after a loss of 1,636 men (2).

When Steele advanced from Helena the objective was Little Rock near the center of the state, over a hundred miles west on the Arkansas River. The route crossed rivers, bayous, some swampy country, and a prairie (7). The town fell without a major action on September 10, 1863, and it was made the departmental headquarters. The main Confederate force, unable to subsist so far from a base, withdrew southward to Arkadelphia and Camden.

General Steele also occupied Fort Smith, upriver near the Indian Territory, and many other points north of the Arkansas River, including Devall's Bluff, Pine Bluff, and the mouth of White River. From his main base at Helena his supply line ran precariously across country or up White River to Devall's Bluff and from there by a railroad to Little Rock, the Arkansas River not being navigable most months of the year. At these various places troops in brigade strength were stationed. Because of marauding by raiders and guerillas Steele also occupied many smaller places, at least intermittently. Although patrolling was active, resistance was never quenched, but it became possible to install a provisional state government in January, 1864. Nevertheless, the people of Arkansas suffered greatly from plundering and civil warfare.

Early in March, 1864, Steele was ordered to support the Red River campaign of General N. P. Banks against Shreveport. Steele was to advance the Federal front from the Arkansas to the Red River line (8). Because of slow communications, problems in supply, inertia, and a faulty situation analysis (9), he started only at the end of March. Near Camden he was repulsed by Generals Smith and Price. Learning that Banks had been defeated at the Sabine Cross Roads and Pleasant Hill on April 9th and 10th, he started back for Little Rock. A severe rear guard action developed at Jenkins' Ferry on the swollen Saline River on April 30th in which he lost about 2,500 men but saved his army. This was his only sizeable action in Arkansas.

In June, 1864, General J. O. Shelby crossed the Arkansas River for the second time to recruit and raid in the northern part of the state. In August General Sterling Price joined him with three divisions for a move against St. Louis (10). This raid had to be timed for the ripening corn, suitable for men and stock. They returned through Arkansas several months later, again meeting no resistance. Although Price achieved no permanent gains (11), there was dissatisfaction in Washington at Steele's poor performance. Shelby's command had passed undeterred through his line at least four times and Price twice, and there were irregularities in his administration (12, 13). His dispersed forces lacked mobility, secure communications, safe supply, and mutual supportability. Steele was replaced in the departmental command by General J. J. Reynolds (14), and in 1865 he took part in the Mobile expedition of General E. S. R. Canby. From the summer of 1864 Canby commanded all of the trans-Mississippi country south of Missouri. From September of 1863 till the end of the war, the Department of Arkansas was engaged essentially in policing a state, which it was never quite able to pacify. The steady erosion by disease permitted only a small part of its theoretical strength to be exerted at any time.

## Disease in Arkansas

The medical problem by size and type is described by various data compiled after the war. The total Federal casualties during the two years under study were phenomenal considering the small size of the population at risk. The load carried by the relatively few medical officers, many of whom became sick, is also spectacular. The figures for the Negro soldiers are not available but the total white casualties severe enough to be placed on the sick report numbered 182,662 (15). This figure includes 178,194 diseases and only 4,457 examples of wounds, accidents, and injuries combined. The deaths in the two groups were 2,348 and 166 respectively. The mortality figures for disease are misleading as many additional deaths occurred in soldiers sent home or to hospitals in the north. The mean monthly strength on the rolls (including some Negro regiments) was 28,462, but the actual strength in the units in the field was usually about half that figure, which represents essentially the population undergoing exposure. This was smaller than a modern infantry division, and the number of sick is startling by contrast.

The most important communicable diseases in the Union army are shown in Table XVII. Malaria led the list. Its prevalence rate for each year per 1,000 strength was 1,287 (16). According to this figure every soldier on the average had an attack of malaria every year and some had two. Among fourteen Federal military departments reporting, this department stood highest. In contrast, the lowest rate, 144 cases, was reported by the Department of the East, composed of the northeastern states. The second highest rate was found in the Department of North Carolina (1,035), and the third by the Department of the Gulf (930). These figures for "total malarial fever" include the intermittent, remittent, and typho-malarial fevers. The departments ranking high had long warm seasons and much water. The examples of intermittent fever numbered 62,999 and of remittent fever 9,442 (Table XVII). The mortality was low and occurred chiefly in the so-called "congestive" type of intermittent fever. The quotidian, tertian, and quartan types were all represented. Falciparum malaria has not been recognized in the available clinical descriptions, and the low mortality suggests it was rare or nonexistent here.

A member of the Thirty-third Iowa described the malaria and dysentery ("universal") at Clarendon in August. He thought the air was thick with the "Clarendon shake" (17). A bugler blowing morning "quinine and whiskey" sick call had a sudden shaking ague before finishing. Two successors had the same experience, so it was decided there was ague in the bugle.

It was unusual for malaria to be more common than enteritis in that war. The reasons for this reversal in Arkansas are uncertain. The eastern part of the state contained some low-lying rich cotton land and numerous streams and bayous. Most of the Union soldiers had spent at least one summer in the south, and there were many slaves in the area, so there were probably many carriers of the malaria plasmodium as source and ample breeding sites for mosquitoes as vectors.

Except for some sporadic suppressive medication with inadequate doses of quinine, no measures were taken against malarial infection. One soldier mentioned that he had draped his bunk with a mosquito

TABLE XVII

Principal Communicable Disease in the Department of
Arkansas (Union) from July 1863 through June, 1865*

|  | | Number cases | Number deaths |
|---|---|---|---|
| 1. | Intermittent fevers (malaria) | 62,999 | 266 |
| 1a. | Remittent fever (malaria?) | 9,442 | 111 |
| 2. | Dysentery and diarrhea | 42,761 | 809 |
| 2a. | Cholera morbus | 497 | 5 |
| 3. | Bronchitis and epidemic catarrh | 8,017 | 12 |
| 4. | Purulent ophthalmia and conjunctivitis | 4,566 | 0 |
| 5. | Rheumatism, acute and chronic** | 4,342 | 13 |
| 6. | Boils | 2,906 | 0 |
| 7. | Gonorrhea (orchitis and stricture excluded) | 1,919 | 0 |
| 8. | Inflammation of lungs (pneumonia) | 1,800 | 227 |
| 9. | Typhoid and typho-malarial fevers | 1,751 | 362 |
| 10. | Jaundice | 1,493 | 9 |
| 11. | Measles | 1,161 | 71 |
| 12. | Syphilis (omits tertiary forms) | 1,119 | 2 |
| 13. | Erysipelas | 1,010 | 32 |
| 14. | Mumps | 805 | 1 |
| 15. | Smallpox and varioloid | 386 | 39 |
| 16. | Consumption | 180 | 35 |
| 17. | Diphtheria | 130 | 1 |
| 18. | Inflammation of brain and cord | 121 | 62 |
| 19. | Typhus fever | 50 | 6 |

*Compiled from *Medical and Surgical History*.
**Not communicable, but retained for comparison.

bar—an unusual measure but directed against them as pests; this
was at Devall's Bluff in 1864, where he was assigned to duty in an
ordnance storehouse (18). The health of the troops was bad at that
time. The mosquitoes came early in many parts of the state. Surgeon
Bragg, on April 9th, thought fishermen on the Arkansas River at
Little Rock caught more mosquito bites than anything else. Near
Vicksburg in July, he observed (19) ". . . the mosquitoes are the
largest, hungriest, and boldest of their kind, and they make their
attacks always at night." There was much sickness and within a
month his regiment (Grinstead's Arkansas), in service only about
a year, was reduced to 100 men for duty and almost every one had
chills. He, himself, was sick but ". . . the bare idea of going home
for chills and fever for me was simply ridiculous."

With respect to diarrhea and dysentry combined the Department
of Arkansas ranked fifth among sixteen Union army departments
(20). Its prevalence rate per 1,000 mean strength per year was 698
cases. Thus, on the average, seven soldiers out of every ten were
sick once each year with one or another of these enteric diseases. As

with malaria, the rate of infection tended to be lower in the northern latitudes. Thus, the departments adjoining Arkansas, namely, the Department of the Gulf to the south, the Department of the Tennessee to the east, and the Department of the Missouri to the north had rates respectively of 963, 764, and 323 cases. The highest rate (1,160) was reported by the Department of the South (South Carolina, Georgia, and Florida) and the lowest (323) by Missouri. Acute enteritis was probably underreported more than any other lesion because of the many mild, self-limited cases. Many "walking dysenterys" were not reported. From this area, as elsewhere, came reports of the sickness of entire regiments (17). The practice of messing in small groups rather than by regiments probably reduced the number of infections transmitted by food, eating utensils, and dish towels.

In the two-year period, 42,761 cases of dysentery and diarrhea appeared on the records in Arkansas. Of them, 809 died in the department. This figure does not represent the entire mortality as some died elsewhere during or after the war. The figures for cholera morbus were 497 cases and only five deaths.

Surgeon Charles H. Lothrop of the First Iowa Cavalry wrote of the terrible march through the swamps and fens of Arkansas (21) "where the very air was surcharged with deadly miasm. Many brave men fell victims to diarrhoea, malaria and typhus." The flies and mosquitoes were rarely mentioned by writers because they were common pests also in civilian life. In contrast, many complained at having to drink fetid water from the Mississippi, the White and other rivers and from the bayous and ponds, but because they disliked the bad taste rather than for fear of disease-producing agents. At Brownsville, in August and September, a member of the Thirty-second Iowa wrote that no men were able for duty, the sick were lying everywhere, men were not available as nurses or burying details, the surgeon was short of medicines, and the hard tack was full of "live things" (22).

Surgeon John L. Taylor of the Third Missouri Cavalry stationed at Little Rock described his experiences with these diseases up to June, 1864. Most cases exhibited a fluid fecal matter mixed with blood and mucus, which usually yielded readily to saline cathartics. For the obstinate cases he used an elaborate regime. As to causation, he wrote (23):

Four-fifths of the cases were attributable to exposure to wet and cold; the remaining fifth to malaria and the use of unwholesome food, such as fresh pork, green apples, etc. Five cases were attended with more or less fever, which was attributable, no doubt, to malarious poison. There cases I have denominated on the prescription book 'malarial dysenteric diarrhoea'.

Confused etiological concepts such as these were the rule. The mass of observational material could easily be misinterpreted. On this basis rational preventive and therapeutic measures were not possible. Some men probably had both dysentery and malaria simultaneously in this population in which the infection rate of one disease was over one hundred per cent each year and of the other disease only slightly less. With not a single diagnostic aid, except to look at the feces for blood or to make a therapeutic test with quinine, differential diagnosis was difficult if not impossible.

Whatever measures were taken in Arkansas against diarrhea and dysentery were not effective as the prevalence rate per 1,000 soldiers increased from 698 for the year ending June 30, 1864 to 804 in the following year (20).

Typhoid fever was recorded with the "continued fevers." This category included typhoid, typhus, the "common continued," and typho-malarial fevers. Probably the majority were true typhoids, judging by the relatively high mortality and the ulcerated Peyer's patches usually found on postmortem examination. The prevalence rate for the continued fevers in the Department of Arkansas was 33 cases per year for each 1,000 strength (24). In frequency this department ranked nineteenth among the twenty-three reporting. The highest rate (105) was experienced by the Department of Washington and the lowest (23) by the Department of the Pacific. The troops in the Department of Arkansas had been longer in service and they were more scattered than in most departments. No severe epidemic has been identified in any unit or in any month, but the disease made its appearance in each of the twenty-four months under study. Even assuming that some soldiers had acquired an immunity before the war or in 1861 and 1862 in the army, the relatively low rate is not fully explained.

In this department typhoid fever was reported in 715 Union soldiers and typho-malaria in 1,036. The mortality frequency was slightly higher in the typhoid group—190 versus 172—but it was relatively high in both. Some examples of paratyphoid were probably included in these figures. Typhus fever was reported in fifty soldiers, of whom six died. The terms typhus and typhoid were sometimes used interchangeably. If rose spots were absent, some doctors diagnosed typhus. Any distinction was based on the clinical findings, which were not reliable. The fifty cases were distributed throughout the twenty-four-month period, and there was no epidemic. It is probable that the majority were typhoid infections.

Rheumatism, the only noncommunicable disease in Table XVII, ranked fifth. Among 4,342 cases there were thirteen deaths. Probably some, and possibly many, examples of rheumatic fever were included in these figures because postmortem examinations in other departments sometimes disclosed gross pancarditis and cardiomegaly in rheumatics. However, only two examples of scarlet fever were reported during the two-year period, and of 130 reported as diphtheria only one died. It is possible that scarlet fever was underdiagnosed, and that examples of croupous pharyngitis of streptococcal etiology were misdiagnosed as diphtheria. The large figure for erysipelas (1,010 cases, 32 deaths) is misleading today as this diagnosis then included the examples of cellulitis that extended locally around wounds, nearly all of which were infected; only a small proportion represented a "primary" streptococcal type of erysipelas.

The importance of tuberculosis is greatly underemphasized by the figure of 180 cases of consumption and thirty-five deaths. Excluded are the examples diagnosed scrofula and hemorrhage from the lungs and the tuberculosis in nonpulmonic sites. The mortality was higher than is indicated because many died at home.

The occurrence of so much smallpox in the second half of the war despite the regulations requiring vaccination reflects both carelessness and resistance to the procedure. Also, recruits might be added to the regiments from time to time when vaccine was not at hand. Varioloid was diagnosed when the pustular disease was clinically mild. It is possible that some chicken pox was included, as there was no separate category for this type of eruption.

The sizeable jaundice group is of interest in connection with the numerous enteric infections. Such clinical descriptions as are available depict a mild, self-limited, sporadic or epidemic disease. The great majority were probably examples of catarrhal jaundice (hepatitis). The peak frequency occurred in August and September of 1864. Yellow fever did not extend up to this department during the war. Neither the boils nor the pink-eye were particularly seasonal. The frequency of both venereal diseases remained remarkably uniform except for one unexplained peak in syphilis. The figures include none of the tertiary syphilis or gonococcic epididymitis and strictures.

## Military Effects of Disease: Federal

Disease was always common throughout the department and it influenced many military operations. How many it actually prevented, there is no way of knowing. Before departing Helena, the sick unable to march were sent to a hospital established on August 9th to receive them (7). On August 18th, the sick numbered 1,111, and 200 additional men had been detailed to act as nurses (25), showing that the command was unhealthy when the campaign began. As the army moved across country to Little Rock, additional patients were dropped off in hospitals, newly established for the purpose, at Clarendon on August 17th, at Devall's Bluff on the 28th, at Brownsville on September 3rd, and at Little Rock on the 17th (7). Here the general hospital took over the one abandoned by the Confederates with some seriously sick patients and three medical officers. It occupied the brick building of St. John's College, some newly built wooden wings, and the old U. S. Government Arsenal. A great shortage of medical supplies could not be relieved until December 21st (7).

The loss in military efficiency was far greater than is implied by the size of the sick list. From Devall's Bluff already on August 23rd General Steele demanded reinforcements (eventually supplied him) to prevent a disaster: One thousand of those present were unfit for duty but, more important, half the command was absent (26). The principal diseases, he said, were fevers and, lately, chills and fever. Only his cavalry division, that had joined from Missouri, was in good condition (27). Then, from Little Rock, General Steele reported that he was unable to pursue Price, as he wished, because of his great losses (28). He thought that with 6,000 more infantry he could drive

Smith and Price into Mexico. Actually, he already had far more than that absent sick from his own army. If his statement is valid, disease seriously altered military events. With Smith out of the way in 1864, sizeable armies would have been released in two departments for immediate service at Mobile or elsewhere.

Steele's aggregate for duty dropped from about 12,000 at Helena (26) to 10,477 a month later at Little Rock (29). Actually his loss was far greater than that because a cavalry division had joined him. Disregarding this accession, the combat casualties numbered only 136 (eighteen of them killed). Because deserters and discharges were few during such a successful offensive operation, it is assumed that most of the reduction represents sickness. Some convalescent patients had been returned to duty during the month so that the prevalence of sickness was more than twelve per cent. The attrition continued so that recruits and regiments had to be sent to the department throughout 1864.

As far as is known, the health was bad at all stations in the department, and the available data reveal no local differences. Probably because of better documentation, most of the complaints emanated from Little Rock, Helena, and Devall's Bluff. When it became necessary on August 1, 1864 to send troops from Helena against raider Shelby, two relatively new regiments, the Sixth Minnesota and Thirty-fifth Missouri, could together muster only 400 men because of sickness (30).

An inspection of the military posts on the Mississippi River a few days later (August 12, 1864) found the health of the troops at Helena ". . . very bad indeed. This appears to be the most deadly place on the river" (31). In the Sixth Minnesota the inspector found an aggregate effective of only 325 out of an aggregate present of 937:

> The regiment left Cairo for this place two months ago with over 900 strong and hearty men for duty. They have been terribly afflicted at this unhealthy spot till the sick-list is now 598. It has increased in the last two days forty-five, and there are a number of deaths daily. The regiment is fast going to destruction under the scourge of sickness which has assailed it, and officers and men are disheartened. Not 100 men could march ten miles. To save this fine body of men and render them effective for the field they should be moved and kept in garrison where there are good hospitals till they are reinvigorated. I recommend

that they be immediately ordered into garrison at Vicksburg. They would there probably be effective with 600 men in October.

In the Forty-seventh Iowa, a 100-day regiment, the same inspector found an aggregate effective of only 537, bad sanitary conditions, a sick report of 310, ignorant officers, and a fear they would fall victims to the bad climate. Some were dying daily. As their term of enlistment would expire in four weeks, no recommendations were made. The Fifty-sixth Infantry (colored) also had bad sanitation, a large sick report, dirty arms, deficient equipment, and unsoldierlike appearance, the fault of the company officers. Several other regiments were also in bad condition.

It is significant that this inspection and these medical evaluations and recommendations were made not by a medical officer but by an old regular, Major General N. J. T. Dana. One can ask what the local commanders and the post, brigade, and regimental medical officers were doing while this tragedy was developing. The recommendation of the inspector was not carried out, and the sequel appears in the official records for September 30th (32). By then, more than 400 had been sent from the Sixth Minnesota to hospitals in St. Louis and Memphis, 175 more were on sick report, and only 79 were able for duty. Note that this took place in the last year of the war. The chief disease was malaria, which could not be prevented because its cause and method of transmission were unknown.

The reason for the failure to adopt the recommendation is not a matter of record. It might have been an oversight. On the other hand, the selection of Vicksburg as a recovery area from malaria does not seem very wise. Grant's army had suffered there very severely the previous summer and two divisions of the Ninth Corps had been nearly ruined before they were sent North.

Finally, in January, 1865, Halleck suggested that Helena be abandoned on account of its unhealthiness and unimportance (33). This advice also was not accepted.

At another major base, Devall's Bluff, Brigadier General C. C. Andrews commanding the post was criticized for not pursuing raider Shelby more vigorously. In self-defense he recounted the essential duties that had prevented, and added that "It is no small job either to dig the graves that are now required" (34). One small regiment had buried six of its men and another seven in twenty-four hours.

The heavy erosion by sickness continued through the summer of 1864. Of an aggregate of 15,667 present and absent in the cavalry division on August 20th, 2,568 were sick (35). It is of interest that their horses suffered also; on the same date, 6,387 were serviceable and 2,271 were unserviceable. Grant commented that Steele ought to dismiss his quartermaster for allowing animals to starve in Arkansas when the enemy could supply his beasts (36). From January 1 to September 1, 1864, 5,000 horses had died, nine-tenths of them from starvation. The soldiers were better fed but even they developed malnutrition. Of scurvy, 2,277 examples with fourteen deaths were reported. The disease made its appearance in every month, and it increased gradually.

Even the navy had trouble on the Mississippi. Admiral Farragut explained to General Canby on October 29th that "The sickness has cramped him (Commodore Palmer) a little by killing off our engineers. I hope the fever is over, however" (38).

Despite the assignment of many thousands of Union troops to the department in the latter part of 1863 and in 1864, the number present for duty was never large. The highest figure was reached in June, 1864, when 29,605 were reported (39). The large attrition is indicated by the figure on the same date for the aggregate present and absent, which was 49,169. As the sickly summer passed, the difference became greater, so that by October the corresponding figures were 17,618 and 44,506 (40). By now only slightly more than one-third of the men on the rolls were present bearing arms. Taking into account also those that had been medically discharged or died, present regimental effective strength averaged about one-fourth of the original enrollments.

## Military Effects of Disease: Confederate

In 1862, the Confederates had already found Arkansas unhealthy for military operations. Walker's Texas Division spent nearly three months in the area that autumn. They crossed the Red River on September 8th, arrived at Little Rock on the 23rd, and moved on to Devall's Bluff on White River in October. Here (41) . . .

> The fever and ague, having broken out amongst the troops, spread
> to an alarming extent; more than half the division was confined with

them, and amongst the members of several regiments there was not a sufficiency of men well enough to do guard duty.

Beginning late in October the division occupied a camp near Austin, Here ". . . dysentery and fevers" found many victims. The historian claims that fully 1,500 soldiers died in this camp, which they abandoned late in November.

The Confederates had many sick also in 1863, after attacking Helena in July. The District of Arkansas admitted having an aggregate of 31, 933 soldiers but only 14,508 were available for duty (42). In camp around Jacksonport, Shelby's brigade had much sickness but few deaths (43). Doctor Edward W. Cade, a graduate in 1858 of Jefferson Medical College, was serving as a cavalry lieutenant and shared this epidemic. He suffered from diarrhea and a slight fever, and in his company only fourteen men were able for duty (44).

Comments about the health of Confederate soldiers in a number of localities in Arkansas were made in the letters of Assistant Surgeon Junius N. Bragg. In addition to mumps and other diseases, he suffered from recurrences or new infections of malaria from 1862 to the end of the war. Of Arkansas Post he wrote in December, 1862 (19):

> This Ark. Post is a *vile* place. It is so unhealthy here in the summer season, that nothing can live except mosquitoes. I am credibly informed by the oldest 'inhabitant' that the *snakes* have *chills* here in the summer . . . So many soldiers here have Jaundice, that the command looks as if it were composed of Indians.

During the four years Doctor Bragg had duty in camp or hospital in more than a dozen different places in the central and southern parts of the state, and he found them all unhealthy. His regiment was in only one battle but at one time it had only a hundred men able for duty.

The return of General Holmes for the District of Arkansas for March, 1863 showed 20,687 present for duty but 41,305 present and absent (45). The corresponding figures for November of that year were only 11,371 and 25,623 (45). There had been no large combat losses during the eight months or sizeable transfers to other departments. Presumably, many had been lost to the service because of disease. Nearly half the effectives had melted away in eight summer months.

Several pertinent comments on health were written in a routine report on August 13, 1864, by the colonel commanding Marmaduke's brigade in General Price's raid into Missouri (46). The brigade had 819 men and 69 officers present for duty, but 120 were present sick and 443 were absent sick. Even so, the health of the brigade had improved materially since they had crossed the Arkansas River, but, "A great many of the men are barefooted."

On October 17th, Chief Surgeon W. B. Welch of Fagan's Division wrote from deep in Missouri that sickness had greatly increased in the division in the last fortnight, that the affections were chiefly catarrh, bronchitis, pneumonia, rheumatism, and glandular swellings, that the men were debilitated for want of sufficient food, that clothing and blankets were needed, and that the ration of one-half pound of flour was not enough (47). General Fagan indorsed that he was unable to supply bread and clothing. The pattern of disease had changed in this division while on the move in November.

An assistant surgeon twenty-four years old, who had already been at the surrenders of Island No. 10 and Arkansas Post, wrote with rare candor and prophetic eugenic vision from a Confederate hospital at Little Rock in March, 1863 (19):

A new generation when not disturbed by foreign causes, lasts thirty three years. Now the times upon us will melt a generation away in five years. If this war lasts three years longer, few indeed, of those who went forth at its beginning to dwell in huts, to sleep on the moist ground, to march weary miles through pelting storms, to shiver around a campfire, to have frostbitten feet as the reward of being a good sentinel, to be waited with scum and contempt by those whose rights and property they are defending, and to face the leaden hail of death, will ever return to their homes and friends.

When he wrote, the local Confederate cemetery already filled six acres.

## Medical-Military Comments

The general officers in Arkansas also experienced a full quota of disease. Although they were ultimately responsible for the health of their commands and had the authority to enforce any sanitary and hygienic standards they wished, many of them, Federal and Confederate, became sick. Two of the Union infantry generals were physicians who had practiced medicine before the war (48): Brigadier General Nathan Kimball, from Indiana, commanded a brigade or division at Little Rock for many months, and Brigadier General Cyrus Bussey, from Iowa, served at Fort Smith for an equal period. Their troops were no healthier than others, and Bussey became sick in Arkansas with malaria in 1862; in 1863 and again in 1864 he suffered from recurrences or reinfections of that disease, for which he had to take a leave in 1964 (49). A third physician, serving as an infantry general at Fort Smith although not assigned to the Department of Arkansas, was Major General James G. Blunt. He contracted a severe febrile illness which kept him in bed for weeks and is said eventually to have caused his death (48).

An incomplete list of other sick generals shows that C. C. Andrews suffered from malaria in 1863-1864 (50), N. B. Buford from an unnamed disease in 1864-1865 (51, 52), Powell Clayton from bilious fever in 1864 (53), and F. Salomon from an unidentified sickness in 1864 (54). Less is known about the health of the Southerners, but General Th. H. Holmes was sick in 1863 (55), John B. Magruder in 1864 (56), and John S. Marmaduke in 1864 (57). Both Holmes and Magruder, as the commanders of the District of Arkansas at the time of their illnesses, were responsible for the health in the area.

General Steele's career was nearly terminated, in part by the sickness in his department that helped to prevent effective measures against General Price, who twice passed through his department undeterred. On November 12th, General Halleck suggested he be replaced by a more active commander (58). At this time, his aggregate present and absent was 44,506 but only 17,618 were present for duty (59). Nearly two men out of three were absent, most of them because of sickness. The disparity between the two figures had been increasing steadily during the summer. Halleck was inclined to blame Steele, characterizing his command as unclean, demoralized, inactive, and inefficient (12). Actually Steele could have prevented no diseases except smallpox and scurvy, but he might have more assiduously provided quinine. His defects were not medical but military—low degrees of vigor, ambition, and alertness.

Inasmuch as the major communicable diseases could not be prevented by any camp lore, the large amount of sickness cannot be blamed on the inadequacies of the volunteer commanders, as is often done. Generals Holmes and Magruder who were responsible for the District of Arkansas, Steele their Northern counterpart, and Buford at Helena were all old regular army officers. They were not more effective in the control of disease than any one else.

The civilians in Arkansas also suffered severely. On April 16, 1865, the commander at Fort Smith, Brigadier General Cyrus Bussey, a physician now an infantry general, wrote (60):

> An army cannot get through Arkansas now. There are no supplies in the country; the people who are left are in a starving condition. . . . I am confident the enemy will not again cross the Arkansas river in force.

There seem to have been more political than medical repercussions from the large amount of sickness in Arkansas. For example, Governor Stephen Miller of Minnesota, on April 4, 1865, requested of the new departmental commander that the Third Minnesota be transferred to active fighting so that they might have an opportunity to die at the post of honor. In eighteen months of working on the fortifications at Devall's Bluff, 150 had died of the fever incident to that terrible climate, and the survivors now made this request (61).

Military operations must have been difficult in this department in which regiments rapidly lost strength, where one-half to two-thirds of the men on the rosters were ineffective, where the malaria prevalence rate was 1,287 cases per year per 1,000 strength and other infections were also common, where 178,194 medical casualties occurred in two years in a military population averaging only about 15,000 men under exposure, and where malaria could reduce a regiment of 937 strong men to 79 within a few weeks. One base was ordered abandoned although it was only slightly more unhealthy than some others. The total number of troops fed into this department in less than two years was well over 50,000, of which only Mower's force from the Sixteenth Corps escaped with its health (in the autumn of 1864). The total number of soldiers killed and permanently rendered medically unfit by disease is not known but it was very large. In retrospect, it is possible to question whether the Arkansas operation was justified. Certainly it was not essential.

However, it is hard to evaluate the influence of this burden of disease on military events. One big but immeasurable effect was simple military inertia. There was a great tendency to settle down and try to be comfortable. After the initial campaign, in nearly eighteen months General Steele took the offensive in force only once, and that was under direct orders. The objective was not won, but the failure was Steele's only in part. In the records he did not blame disease for the departmental lethargy directly, but only by requesting more men. However, if sizeable numbers of his sick men had been returned to duty he would have had to use them or send them to a more active department.

From hindsight it is clear that this department contributed little to the Union victory. After July, 1863, it became evident that the war would end when the two main Confederate armies—the Army of Tennessee and the Army of Northern Virginia—were made ineffective. The nearly 50,000 troops in Arkansas could have hastened that end if they had been added to the main Union armies. Their departure from Arkansas would have thrown a greater load on the Departments of the Gulf, of the Missouri, and of Kansas, but these three departments were not being maximally used either. That the Confederate soldiers from Missouri and Arkansas in the Division of Arkansas would have been sent east of the Mississippi after Steele had departed is unlikely because of their unhappy experiences there in 1862 and because of their current low morale; their friends in Walker's Texas Division practically refused to be transferred east early in 1864.

In the Department of Arkansas, pathogenic microbes of a number of kinds had an opportunity to show their capabilities with little or no deterrence. Except against smallpox, no effective countermeasures were deliberately taken. The chains of transmission of malaria, dysentery, typhoid fever, and other diseases in Table XVII were unbroken, except sometimes by chance. One fortuitous favorable factor was the dispersal of the soldiers in many scattered units. An unfavorable factor was the necessity of maintaining the large units near the large streams.

A comparison of the control of disease in 1863-1865, as exemplified by this department, reveals no improvement over that in 1861-1862 as described in the seven preceding chapters. No new improved method of prevention, diagnosis, or treatment had been discovered.

Because the Union disease cases outnumbered the casualties in combat and camp accidents combined about 40:1, the microbes proved themselves highly effective as weapons.

# References

1. *O.R., 22*: Part 1, 18-24.
2. SNEAD, T. L.: The conquest of Arkansas. In *Battles and Leaders of the Civil War*. Edited by R. U. Johnson and C. C. Buel, New York, Century Co., Vol. 3, 1888.
3. *O.R., 34*: Part 2, 41-42.
4. *O.R., 22*: Part 1, 474-477.
5. *O.R., 22*: Part 2, 796-797.
6. *O.R., 22*: Part 2, 802-803.
7. SMITH, J. R.: Extracts from the Sanitary Reports of the Department of Arkansas for 1863, 1864, and 1865. *Med. and Surg. Hist.* Vol. I, Part I, Appendix p. 343-346.
8. *O.R., 34*: Part 3, 27, 56, 76-77.
9. *O.R., 34*: Part 2, 516, 522.
10. *O.R., 41*: Part 2, 1023, 1040.
11. *O.R., 41*: Part 3, 1068, 1076-1077.
12. *O.R., 41*: Part 3, 434-435, 468-469.
13. *O.R., 41*: Part 4, 24-25.
14. *O.R., 41*: Part 4, 711.
15. *Med. and Surg. Hist.*, Vol. I, Part I, 419, 571.
16. *Med. and Surg. Hist.*, Vol. I, Part III, 97.
17. SPERRY, A. F.: *History of the 33d Iowa Infantry Volunteer Regiment*. Des Moines, Mills & Co., 1866, 237 p.
18. GILLET, O.: Diary of Lieutenant Orville Gillet, U.S.A., 1864-1865. Edited by T. R. Worley. *Ark. Hist. Quart.*, *17*:164-204, 1958.
19. BRAGG, J. N.: *Letters of a Confederate Surgeon, 1861-1865*. Edited by T. J. Gaughin. Camden, Ark., Hurley & Co., Inc., 1960, 276 p.
20. *Med. and Surg. Hist.*, Vol. I, Part II, 17-18.
21. LOTHROP, C. D.: *A History of the First Regiment Iowa Cavalry Veteran Volunteers*. Lyons, Iowa, Beers and Eaton, 1890, 422 p.
22. SCOTT, J.: *Story of the Thirty-second Iowa Infantry Volunteers*. Nevada, Iowa: J. Scott, 1896, 526 p.
23. TAYLOR, J. L.: *Med. and Surg. Hist.*, Vol. I, Part II, 86-87.
24. *Med. and Surg. Hist.*, Vol. I, Part III, 203.
25. *O.R., 22*: Part 2, 459.
26. *O.R., 22*: Part 1, 472, 473, 474-477.
27. *O.R., 22*: Part 2, 438.
28. *O.R., 22*: Part 1, 480.
29. *O.R., 22*: Part 2, 523.
30. *O.R., 41*: Part 1, 190-191.

31. *O.R., 41*: Part 2, 711, 714-716.
32. *O.R., 41*: Part 3, 502.
33. *O.R., 48*: Part 1, 649.
34. *O.R., 41*: Part 2, 220.
35. *O.R., 41*: Part 3, 504.
36. *O.R., 41*: Part 3, 468-469, and Part 4, 569-571.
37. *O.R., 41*: Part 4, 569-572.
38. *O.R., 41*: Part 4, 307.
39. *O.R., 34*: Part 4, 606.
40. *O.R., 41*: Part 4, 341.
41. By a Private Soldier (J. P. BLESSINGTON): *The Campaigns of Walker's Texas Division.* New York, Lange, Little & Co., 1875, 314 p.
42. *O.R., 22*: Part 1, 439-440.
43. EDWARDS, J. N.: *Shelby and His Men.* Cincinnati, Miami Printing & Publ. Co., 1867, 551 p.
44. ANDREWS, J. Q., Ed.: *A Texas Surgeon in the C.S.A.* Tuscaloosa, Ala., Confed. Publ. Co., 1957, 123 p.
45. *O.R., 22*: Part 2, 810, 1084.
46. *O.R., 41*: Part 2, 1065.
47. *O.R., 41*: Part 4, 1003-1004.
48. STEINER, P. E.: *Physician-Generals in the Civil War.* Springfield, Ill., Charles C Thomas, Publisher, 1966, 194 p.
49. *O.R., 44*: Part 3, 116, 149, 174.
50. ANDREWS, C. C.: *Christopher C. Andrews . . Recollections: 1829-1922.* Cleveland, Arthur H. Clark Co., 1929, 327.
51. *O.R., 41*: Part 1, 190 and Part 3, 502.
52. *O.R., 48*: Part 1, 856-857.
53. *O.R., 41*: Part 3, 213, 632-633.
54. *O.R., 41*: Part 2, 384.
55. *O.R., 22*: 520.
56. *O.R., 41*: Part 4, 1029-1030.
57. *O.R., 41*: Part 2, 1041.
58. *O.R., 41*: Part 4, 529.
59. *O.R., 41*: Part 4, 341.
60. *O.R., 48*: Part 2, 107.
61. *O.R., 48*: Part 2, 31-32.

# Index